I0094173

RURAL LAND OWNERS

OF

BARBOUR COUNTY, ALABAMA

1851

by

MARIE H. GODFREY
EUFAULA, ALABAMA

Southern Historical Press, Inc.
Greenville, South Carolina

Copyright 1990
By: Southern Historical Press, Inc.

All rights reserved. No part of this publication may be reproduced,
stored in a retrieval system, transmitted in any form, posted
on to the web in any form or by any means without the
prior written permission of the publisher.

Please direct all correspondence and orders to:

www.southernhistoricalpress.com
or
SOUTHERN HISTORICAL PRESS, Inc.
PO BOX 1267
375 West Broad Street
Greenville, SC 29601
southernhistoricalpress@gmail.com

ISBN #0-89308-670-3

Printed in the United States of America

INTRODUCTION

In 1851, A. B. Herbert, Register, made maps of every township of Barbour Co., Ala. showing ownership of each parcel
of rural land. These maps were marked "Correct up to March
1st, 1851". Names of the land owners were abstracted from
the maps with a description of the land by Section, Township and Range.

The primary purpose of this book is to make available to
the researcher as much documented information as possible
concerning these land owners - namely dates and places of
birth and death, names of spouses, names of parents and
former places of residence. In the absence of documented
proof, speculation is occasionally included. Approximate
dates and places of birth as well as year of arrival in
Alabama are from the 1850 Census of Barbour Co. unless a
different reference is given. The spelling of both given
names and surnames varies according to the reference used.

It is the hope of the author that this book will help the
readers trace their family lines prior to their arrival
in Barbour Co., Ala..

REFERENCES

All records are Barbour Co., Ala. unless specified.
Land descriptions give Section, Township and Range, thus
    4-10-26 would be Section 4, Township 10, Range 26.
About 1866, parts of Barbour Co. were cut into Russell and
    Bullock Cos.. This land is shown by (R) for Russell
    Co. and (B) for Bullock Co. following the description.

KEY TO ABBREVIATIONS

CR - Conveyance Record (deeds)
OR - Orphans' Record (estates)
Mar. - Marriage Record
Vol. I -"Early Settlers of Barbour Co., Ala.", Vol. I,
        by Marie H. Godfrey
Vol. II - "Early Settlers of Barbour Co., Ala.", Vol. II,
        by Marie H. Godfrey
MRA -"Memorial Record of Alabama"
DAB - "Dictionary of Alabama Biography"

Abney, N., Nathan. 1 & 30-12-28. Nathaniel Abney, b. ca 1821 S. C., to Ala. by Feb. 1847 (CR G, p. 417). Martha ----- (wife?), b. ca 1831 S. C..

Abney, W.. 7,10,20 & 29-10-29. William Abney, b. 21 Nov. 1802 Edgefield Dist., S. C., d. 12 June 1879 ("The Times & News", July 1, 1879), to Fla. by 1830, to S. C. by 1836 & to Ala. by 1839. Elizabeth ----- (wife)', b. 13 Feb. 1808 S. C., d. 16 Jan. 1870 ("The Bluff City Times", Feb. 3, 1870). Both buried Fairview Cem., Eufaula, Ala..

Adams, A.. 17-10-28. Jesse Allen Adams, b. 1791 Wilkes Co., N. C., d. 1866, son of Jesse Allen Adams, grandson of John Adams (from County Cavan, Ireland to Wilkes Co., N. C. in mid-1700's). (Mr. Cleveland Adams, Auburn, Ala.). Elizabeth Bryant (1st wife), d. before 1850 (ibid). Mary ----- (2nd wife), b. ca 1792 N. C..

Adams, H.. 12-8-23. Harmon Adams, b. ca 1811 Ga., d. ca 1887 Henry Co., Ala. (OR 26, p. 298), to Fla. by 1840, to Ala. by 1845, son of Thomas Adams of Thomas Co., Ga. (CR H, p. 572). Martha Everett (wife - m. 8 Jan. 1835 Thomas Co., Ga.), b. ca 1811 Ga., granddaughter of Jesse Slater who died by 1841 Thomas Co., Ga. (CR H, p. 573/6).

Adams, T. T.. 6 & 7-12-26(B). Thompson Thornton Adams, b. 17 Dec.1809 Ga., d. 1 Feb. 1881 (Adams Bible), to Ala. by 1839. Frances Ann Porch (wife - m. 28 Sept. 1837), b. 8 May 1818 Ga., d. 21 Dec. 1906 (Adams Bible). Also in the household in 1860 were Samuel Adams (b. ca 1784 Va.) and Martha Adams,(b. ca 1798 Ky.).

Adcock, Joseph. 26-13-26. Joseph Adcock died by Sept. 1856 (OR 7, p. 546), probably never lived in Barbour Co.. Lucy ----- (wife - CR G, p. 133/4).

Alexander, E.. 7,8,9,15,16 & 18-9-29. Ezekiel Alexander, b. 3 March 1803 Hancock Co., Ga., d. 6 Dec. 1879 ("The Times & News", Dec. 9, 1879). buried White Oak Methodist Church Cem., son of Asa Castello Alexander (Rev. Soldier), b. 21 July 1760 Wilkes Co., Ga., d. 1834 Dale Co., Ala., m. 1784 Faithy Wooten (a cousin), b. 1767 Ga., d. 1808 (daughter of Thomas & Sarah Rabun Pope Wooten), grandson of Capt. Samuel Alexander, b. 1733 Mecklenburg Co., N. C., d. 1823 Twiggs Co., Ga., m. (1) 1752 Olivia Wooten (2) Susannah Whitfield Bush, great-grandson of Rev. John Alexander, b. 1703, m. Bertha Castello (daughter of James Castello and Sarah Williams), both buried Camden Co., Ga. ("Alexander Family"from files of Mrs. H. M. Newell). Ezekiel Alexander m. (1) Edeline Dawson (or Davidson) 15 July 1824 in Jones Co., Ga., b. ca 1800, d. 19 April 1850, buried White Oak Methodist Church Cem., (2) Mrs. Sarah Tucker 21 July 1853 (3) (Mrs.?) Catherine Doughtie 21 Oct. 1872, b. ca 1821, d. 9 April

1881 ("The Eufaula Weekly Bulletin", April 16, 1881).

Allen, A.. 12-11-28. Albert Allen, b. ca 1811 Va. (1860 Census) - about 1851, he was of Muscogee Co., Ga. (CR J, p. 341).

Allen, B.. 28-10-28. Benjamin Allen, b. ca 1794 Ga., in Ala. by 1830, to Ga. by 1835, to Ala. by 1838. Anna ----- (wife?), b. ca 1804 N. C..

Alley, John. 29-13-26(B). John Alley, b. ca 1820 Pa., in Ala. by 1843. Rebecca ----- (wife?), b. ca 1823 Pa. (1850 Census - 1860 Census says b. ca 1826 Ala.).

Allison, R.. 10,11,13 & 14-13-25(B). Reubin Allison, b. ca 1807 Ga., to Ala. by 1839. Louisianna King (wife - m. 7 July 1836 Greene Co., Ga.?).

Alston, John. 30-12-28. John J. Alston, b. ca 1830 Ga.. In 1850, he was living with Martin Bolivar (b. ca 1778 N. C.), Elizabeth Bolivar (b. ca 1801 Ga.) and Elizabeth Alston (b. ca 1839 Ga.).

Anderson, M. W.. 33 & 34-9-28. M. W. Anderson, b. 5 Jan. 1802 S. C. (1850 Census Henry Co., Ala.), d. 6 Feb. 1877. Caroline E. ----- (wife), b. 1 Aug. 1827 S. C., d. 28 May 1905 ("Eufaula Times & News", June 8, 1905), both buried in the Anderson family cemetery near the Henry Co. line.

Anderson, R.. 12-9-25, 3-13-25(B), 12-11-27, 20-10-28 & 30-11-28. In 1838, Reubin Anderson was of Montgomery Co., Ala. (CR B, p. 426).

Andrews, C. J. M.. 13-12-28. Cornelius J. M. Andrews, b. 4 April 1821 Lincoln Co., Ga., d. 29 Feb. 1872 (buried Fairview Cem., Eufaula, Ala.), in Ala. by 1841, heir (son?) of Mrs. Rhoda Andrews who was heir (sister?) of Archibald C. Slack (OR 6, p. 260/2). Catharine Johnson (wife), b. ca 1823 Fla., daughter of Isham & Elizabeth Johnson (Vol. I, p. 99).

Andrews, Rhoda. 32-12-29. Rhoda Andrews (widow), b. ca 1788 Ga., d. by 1854, heir (sister?) of Archibald C. Slack (OR 6, p. 260/2).

Andrews, Wm. A.. 5-11-29 & 5 & 31-12-29. William A. Andrews (Dr.), b. ca 1819 Ga., d. Aug. 1881, buried Spring Hill Cem. ("The Eufaula Weekly Bulletin", Aug. 13, 1881), heir (son?) of Mrs. Rhoda Andrews. Martha Daniel (1st wife), b. ca 1824 Ga., d. by 1860, daughter of James L. Daniel (OR 4, p. 82). Laura E. Wilson (2nd wife - m. 21 Sept. 1859), b. ca 1839 S. C., d. 8 March 1905 ("Eufaula Times & News", March 9, 1905) daughter of Levi Russell Wilson & Margaret ----- (Foy Bible).

Anglin, F.. 7,8,17 & 18-10-26. Franklin Anglin, b. ca 1804
Ga., d. 25 Dec. 1859 (OR 11, p. 207), in Ala. by 1839. His
first wife may have been Rebecca, daughter of Thomas Warren.
Nancy Warren (2nd wife), b. ca 1824, d. by Jan. 1856 (OR 6,
p. 573/7), daughter of Thomas Warren and Rebecca -----, granddaughter of Thomas Warren who died by 1821 Edgefield Dist.,
S. C. (Vol. I, p. 167). Ioma ----- (3rd wife), b. ca 1843.

Angling, John. 1-11-24. John Anglin is not in the 1850 or
1860 Census of Barbour Co.. On 26 Dec. 1850, William Anglin
& wife Lavinia sold him the above land (CR J, p. 117). He
may have been the John Anglin who married Sarah Cope 26 Nov.
1848 in Pike Co., Ala..

Anglin, Wm. 1 & 36-11-24. William Anglin, b. ca 1798 Ga.,
probably died by 1870, in Ala. by 1832. He served in the
War of 1812. Lovey Maddox (wife - m. 3 Dec. 1812 Putnam Co.,
Ga.), b. ca 1803 Ga., probably died by 1870.

Appling, Thos. K.. 13 & 24-12-29. Thomas K. Appling, b. ca
1825 Ga.. Sarah J. Flake (wife - m. 4 Jan. 1849), b. ca 1832
Fla., daughter of Dr. William Flake ("Independent American",
Troy, Ala., Nov. 14, 1855).

Arrington, A. N.. 4-8-26. Amos Arrington, b. ca 1832 Ga.,
(1860 Census), son of William Arrington (OR 5, p. 395).
Sarah C. Cole (wife - m. 22 May 1851), b. ca 1832 Ga. (1860
Census).

Arrington, F. M.. 13-11-24. Francis Marion Arrington, b. ca
1828 Ga., son of William Arrington (OR 5, p. 395). Sarah E.
Stephens (wife - m. 14 June 1854).

Arrington, Wm.. 11, 12, 13, 14 & 19-11-24. William Arrington,
b. ca 1778 N. C., d. by Feb. 1852 (OR 4, p. 409/10), in Ga. by
1828, to Ala. by 1850. Elizabeth ----- (wife), b. ca 1780
N. C., d. by Jan. 1853 (OR 5, p. 90).

Ashley, James. 36-11-24. James Ashley, b. ca 1808 N. C., in
Ga. by 1835, to Ala. by 1839. Sarah ----- (wife?), b. ca 1812
N. C..

Atwell, G.. 35-12-25. George W. Atwell, b. ca 1826 N. C.,
son of James Atwell (CR B, p. 909). Mary Jane Peterson (1st
wife - m. 11 Dec. 1848). Sarah Peterson (2nd wife - m. 7 Feb.
1850).

Avrett, E. D.. 14-13-29(R). Early D. Averett, son of David
and Elizabeth Averett who moved to Jernigan (now Russell Co.)
from Stewart Co., Ga.. (Averett Family from files of Mrs. H.
M. Dixon). Ann Eliza Averett (wife - m. 24 Oct. 1844), dau.
of Matthew Averett (ibid). In 1850, they were living in La.
(Russell Co., Ala. Settlement Record 1856 - 1859).

Averett, J.. 17-11-29. John Averett, heir of Elizabeth Averett who died by May 1856 (Russell Co., Ala. Settlement Record 1856 - 1859).

Averett, M., Matthew. 13, 14 & 24-13-29 & 18-12-30. Matthew Averett, b. ca 1785 Ga., d. 1 July 1857, buried in the family cemetery near Jernigan (Russell Co., Ala.), to Jernigan from Stewart Co., Ga. after 1839. Keziah Miller (1st wife), daughter of James Miller who died by 1822 Hancock Co., Ga. (Mrs. Louise C. Martin, Eufaula, Ala.). Sarah A. Quarles (2nd wife - m. 4 Nov. 1852 Russell Co., Ala.), widow of Samuel Quarles of Stewart Co., Ga.(Ibid).

Avrett, W.. 18-12-30(R). William Averett, b. ca 1805 Ga., son of Matthew Averett & Keziah Miller (Averett Family from Mrs. H. M. Dixon). Susan ----- (wife), b. ca 1815 Ga.

Avritt, Wilson B.. 14-13-29(R). Wilson B. Averett, son of David & Elizabeth Averett (Averett Family from Mrs. H. M. Dixon). Sarah McLendon (wife - m. 19 Sept. 1844 where?), b. 16 June 1829, d. 23 Aug. 1912 Mars Hill, Ark., daughter of John McLendon and Mary Averett, granddaughter of Matthew Averett & Keziah Miller (ibid).

Ayres, S., Samuel. 26-9-27. Samuel Ayres, b. ca 1811 S. C., in Ala. by 1839. Nancy ----- (wife?), b. ca 1813 S. C..

Bailey, H., Hosea. 30 & 31-11-27. Hosea Bailey, b. 29 July 1808 Ga., d. 24 Aug. 1888, buried Clayton Cem.. Mary Willaford (2nd wife - m. 10 July 1855), b. 7 July 1821 Ga., d. 3 July 1895, buried Clayton Cem..

Bailey, James. 8-9-26 & 32-10-27. James Bailey, b. ca 1808 Ga., to Ala. by 1846. Martha ----- (wife?), b. ca 1811 Ga. (1860 Census says N. C., 1870 & 1880 say S. C.).

Baker, E.. 22-10-27. R. Ellison Baker, b. 18 March 1823 S. C. (1860 Census), d. 1898, buried Louisville Cem.. Mary Cooper (wife - m. 27 Sept. 1849), b. 1 Jan. 1827 Ala. (1860 Census), d. 12 Dec. 1909, buried Louisville Cem., daughter of Archibald Cooper who died by April 1860 (OR 10, p. 686).

Baker, E. H.. 11,12 & 13-9-27. Enos H. Baker, b. ca 1828 S. C., son of James Baker, Jr. who died by 1850, grandson of James Baker, Sr. who died by 1847. In 1855, Enos H. Baker was living in Texas (Original Papers, Box 10).

Baker, F. E.. 25-12-24, 6 & 32-11-25 & 19 & 32-12-25. Franklin E. Baker, b. ca 1822, son of Jeremiah Baker who died by 1848 (OR 3, p. 579/81). Elizabeth ----- (wife?), b. ca 1822 Ga.. A Franklin E. Baker m. Eliza Ann Chapman 22 Oct. 1839 Muscogee Co., Ga..

Baker, James J.. 19 & 20-10-27. James J. Baker, b. ca 1818
S. C., d. by Jan. 1865.(OR 14, p. 461/2). Nancy Williamson
(wife - m. 8 Sept. 1849), b. 1830 Ala., d. 1914, buried Rocky
Mount Cem..

Baker, Jeremiah. 28 & 29-12-25(B). Jeremiah Baker died by
1848 (OR 3, p. 245). He was of Pike Co., Ala. in 1822 (Monroe
Co., Ga. Deed Book A, p. 38). Elizabeth ----- (wife - OR 3,
p. 574/5).

Baker, Larkin. 11-9-25. Larkin Baker, b. 5 Oct. 1807 S. C.,
d. 20 April 1874, son of Thomas Baker who died by 1826 Edgefield Dist., S. C. (Edgefield Dist., S. C., Pkg. 283). Ellen
McDaniel (wife - Winefred Horne, Clayton Ala.), b. 22 Aug. 1811
S. C., d. 10 Oct. 1902. Both buried Bethlehem Cem..

Baker, Lydia. 10 & 11-9-27. James Baker, Jr., d. by 1853
(Original Papers, Box 10), son of James Baker who died by 1847
(OR 3, p. 54) and his wife, Patience, who died by 1853 (Original
Papers, Box 10). Lydia ----- (wife), b. ca 1810 S. C..

Baker, Robert. 20-10-27. Robert Baker, b. ca 1790 S. C., son
of James Baker who died by 1847 (OR 3,p. 54). No wife living
in 1850.

Banks, R. P.. 22-9-24. Robert P. Banks, b. ca 1811 S. C., to
Ala. by 1838. Mary Ellen ----- (wife), b. ca 1816 S. C..

Barber, J. P.. 34-11-35 & 34 & 36-12-25. Jared P. Barber, b.
ca 1808 Ga., possibly living in Butler Co., Ala. in 1865 (OR 15,
p. 105/7). Mary Morris (1st wife - m. 16 Feb. 1837 Thomas Co.,
Ga.), b. ca 1815 N. C.. Nancy ----- (2nd wife?). In Dec. 1846,
Jared P. Barber gave a slave to Laura Morris (daughter of Daniel
Morris?) (CR G, p. 540/1). In Nov. 1865, Nancy, wife of J. P.
Barber of Butler Co., Ala. was an heir of James Morris, Sr.
(OR15, p. 105/7).

Barefield, W. P.. 26 & 27-10-28. In 1844, William P. Barefield, son of Miles Barefield, was of Dale Co., Ala. (CR G,
p. 4/5). In 1859, Miles Barefield (wife Faitha) and William
P. Barefield sold land in Henry Co., Ala. (Henry Co., Ala.
CR H, p. 438/9).

Barham, J. W.. 12-13-25(B). No further record.

Barham, W., Wm. A.. 11 & 12-13-25(B). William A. Barham, b.
ca 1819 N. C., d. by Jan. 1859 (OR 9, p. 583). Mrs. Nancy
Turman (1st wife - m. 15 Oct. 1847), b. ca 1812 Ga., widow of
Samuel Turman who died by March 1837 Harris Co., Ga. (OR 2,
p. 82). Rebecca (Kennedy?) (2nd wife - m. ca 1850/1 - CR L,
p. 243), b. ca 1822 N. C..

Barker, G. W.. 5 & 36-11-24. George W. Barker, Methodist
Minister, b. 15 June 1812 N. C. (1860 Census), d. 18 April
1899, son of Alex & Mary Barker of Rockingham Co., N. C.
(MRA, Vol. II, p. 817/8). Tamer E. Lynch (wife), d. 4 June
1899, age 81 years, 11 months, 4 days, daughter of Sirach
Lynch (d. Va.) & Sally Moseley (d. Muscogee Co., Ga.) (ibid).
Both are buried in Clay Hill Church Cem., Pike Co., Ala..

Barnes, A. M. (?). 27-13-25(B) - no further record.

Barnes, Milton. 34-13-29(R). Milton Barnes, b. ca 1824 Ga..
Polly Holleman (wife - m. 24 Aug. 1852).

Barnett, A.. 1 & 11-11-28. Dr. Augustus William Barnett, b.
24 Aug. 1825 Washington Co., Ga., d. 29 March 1898, buried
Fairview Cem., Eufaula, Ala. ("Eufaula Times & News", March
31, 1898), son of Samuel Barnett & Elizabeth Worsham of Wash-
ington Co., Ga., grandson of Capt. William Barnett and Jean
Jack of N. C. and of Lt. Richard Worsham & Mary Wingfield of
Washington Co., Ga., great-grandson of John Barnett (b. 1717
Ireland, d. 1804 N. C.) & Ann Spratt (DAB, Vol. III, p. 102).
Celeste B. Truetlin (1st wife - m. 18 Dec. 1849), b. 12 Aug.
1833 S. C., d. 8 Aug. 1871, buried Fairview Cem., Eufaula,
Ala.., daughter of Gabriel Truetlin & Anna Comm, granddaughter
of John A. T. Truetlin & Margaret Miller and of George Comm &
Anna Woolfork, great-granddaughter of Gov. John Adam Truetlin
(DAB, Vol. III, p. 102). Adele Conner (2nd wife - m. 30 Mar.
1875) of Cokesbury, S. C. ("Eufaula Times & News",Mar. 31,·189

Barnett, A. S.. 20-13-26(B). Alexander Barnett bought land i
12-13-28 on 17 June 1843 (CR F, p. 129) - no further record.

Barnett, T. J.. 30-11-29. Thomas J. Barnett, b. Sept. 1812
Del., d. 13 April 1852, buried Fairview Cem., Eufaula, Ala..
He was a master carpenter and built many of the oldest build-
ings in Eufaula. Mary A. (Martin?) (wife), b. ca 1821 Ga.,
d. ca April 1896 Mongtomery, Ala., buried Eufaula. (The
Clayton Courier, April 4, 1896).

Barron, A. J.. 5 & 6-13-25 (B). A. J. Barron, b. ca 1818 Ga.
to Ala. by 1845. Sarah ----- (wife?), b. ca 1824 Ga.. An
Andrew J. Barron m. Sarah Ann Eliza Stanton 13 Jan. 1840 in
Upson Co., Ga..

Barry, G. L.. 29-12-26. George L. Barry, b. ca 1813 Md.,
to Ga. by 1836, to Ala. by 1838. Margaret ----- (wife), b.
ca 1823 Md..

Barry, W. J. G.. 9-9-26. William J. G. Barry is not in any
early census of Barbour Co.. He married Selety Carroll 17
March 1845.

Bass, A., Allen. 24 & 25 -9-25 & 19 & 30-9-26. Allen Bass, b. ca 1798 N. C., d. by May 1854 (OR 6, p. 9/10, in Ga. by 1835, to Ala. by 1846. Allen, Josiah and John Bass owned land near each other, which is a good indication that they were related. Frances ----- (wife), b. ca 1804 N. C..

Bass, John. 11-9-25. John Bass, b. ca 1788 N. C.. Isabel ----- (wife?), b. ca 1815 Ga..

Bass, Josiah. 23 & 24-9-25. Josiah Bass, Sr., b. 8 July -1802 Sampson Co., N. C. ("The Clayton Courier", June 7, 1890), d. 6 May 1890, in Ga. by 1835, to Ala. by 1837. Mary ----- (wife), b. 18 Sept. 1812 N. C., d. 15 Oct. 1901. Both are buried in the family cemetery.
OR
Josiah Bass, Jr., b. ca 1829 N. C.. Ailcy Hutson (wife - m. 7 April 1850), b. ca 1835 Ala., d. by 1854.

Bates, G. M.. 11-11-27. George M. Bates, b. ca 1806 S. C., d. 15 Dec. 1882 ("The Eufaula Weekly Bulletin", Dec. 20, 1882). His estate names, among others, John and Thomas Bates of Batesburg, Lexington Co., S. C.. Rosanna M. ----- (wife), b. ca 1816 S. C., d. 20 Oct. 1884 ("Eufaula Weekly Times & News", Oct. 21, 1884).

Bates, W. M.. 1-11-27 & 15,16,22 & 23-12-27. Wilson Michael Bates, b. 3 July 1815 S. C., d. 7 Sept. 1875, probably at Griffin, Ga. ("Eufaula News", Jan. 9, 1875). Nancy ----- (wife), b. ca 1812 S. C., d. 12 Oct. 1850 ("Southern Christian Advocate", 29 Nov. 1850). Sarah Elizabeth Shorter (3rd wife) m. 3 Feb. 1867, widow of James Lingard Hunter (see S. E. Hunter)

Battle, C.,Cullen. 15,22,23,26 & 27-13-27 & 21-11-29. Cullen Battle (Dr.), b. 11 March 1785 Edgecombe Co., N. C., d. 4 June 1879 ("The Times & News", June 5, 1879), lived in Hancock Co., Ga. before coming to Ala. by 1838 (CR B, p. 435), probably a son of Dempsey Battle who died by 1815 in Edgecombe Co., N. C.. Jane A. Lamon (wife), b. Feb. 1799, d. 7 July 1883 Tuskeegee, Ala. ("Eufaula Times & News", July 24, 1883). She was an heir (daughter?) of John Lamon of Nash Co., N. C. (Edgecombe Co., N. C. Deed Book 17, p. 291). They are buried in Shorter Cem., Eufaula, Ala..

Battle, J. E.. 13-11-27. James Edward Battle probably did not live in Barbour Co.. Sarah Lusana Smith (wife), daughter of Sion Smith (CR G, p. 193/4).

Batts, J., Jesse. 21,22,26,27,28, 33 & 34-12-26. Jesse Batts, b. ca 1818 Ga..He may have married (1) Olive Newsome 28 April 1840 Washington Co., Ga.. He m. (2) Mary Ann Jordan 6 June 1843 Washington Co., Ga., b. ca1824 Ga..

Baxter, Jas. S.. 19 & 20-9-25. James S. Baxter, b. 19 May
1823 S. C., d. 2 May 1892, buried Pea River Presbyterian
Church Cem., son of James Baxter (from Charleston, S. C.
area) who died 22 Oct. 1827 Lowndes Co., Ala. and Sarah
Patience Briton (John Johnston, Brundidge, Ala.,) who was
born 8 Jan. 1796 Williams Dist., S. C., died 6 May 1879,
buried Pea River Presbyterian Church Cem.. Sarah Currie
(1st wife), b. 6 Feb. 1816 Richmond Co., N. C., d. 16 April
1856, daughter of Angus Currie, Sr., b. 1775 Scotland, d.
24 Aug. 1840 and Catharine (McLean?), b. 1775 Scotland, d.
5 Nov. 1842 (Pea River Presbyterian Church Records). Margaret G. Cameron (2nd wife - m. 5 March 1857), b. 13 April
1833 N. C. (1860 Census), d. 7 May 1910. They are all buried
in Pea River Presbyterian Church Cem..

Baxter, J. E.. 11,12 & 13-9-24. No further record.

Baxter, Thos. R. (should be F.). 20-9-25. Thomas F. Baxter,
b. 16 June 1827 Ala., d. 26 Feb. 1908, brother of James S.
Baxter (John Johnston, Brundidge, Ala.). Mary Ann McLean
(wife - m. 6 Dec. 1846), b. 6 June 1828 Ala., d. 11 Feb. 1900.
Both are buried in East Side Cemetery, Headland, Ala.. There
are also markers for Thomas F. & Mary A. Baxter in Pea River
Presbyterian Church Cem..

Beasley, J. G.. 24 & 25-10-25. John G. Beasley, b. 11 May
1792 (Anson Co., N. C.?), d. 24 July 1883, in Ala. by 1828
(Vol. II, p. 2). Martha Allums (wife - m. 9 March 1820 in
Baldwin Co., Ga.), b. 4 Jan. 1802 Washington Co., Ga., d.
11 Aug. 1880. Both are buried in the Beasley family cemetery
(Vol. II, p. 2).

Beasley, Wm.. 25-10-25. William M. Beasley, b. 17 Nov. 1801
N. C., d. 7 March 1877, in Ala. by 1833. Elizabeth Allums
(wife), b. 29 March 1814 Ga., d. 6 Sept. 1902. Both are
buried in Louisville Cem.. (Vol. II, p. 7).

Beauchamp, A. H.. 8-11-27. Andrew Hammell Beauchamp, b. ca
1827 Ala., d. by 1883, son of William Beauchamp & Nancy Perkins, grandson of Littleton Beauchamp (Rev. Soldier), b. 25
May 1759 Somerset Co., Md. and Nancy -----, to Baldwin Co., Ga
after 1780, d. Henry Co., Ala. 1822. His widow, Nancy, may
have married J. C. Weaver of Randolph Co., Ga. 5 Feb. 1846
("Southern Christian Advocate", 27 Feb. 1846), great-grandson
of Edmund Beauchamp, Jr. & Elizabeth -----, great-great-grandson of Edmund Beauchamp, Sr. (from London to Somerset Co., Md.
by 1665) & Sarah (daughter of Ambrose Dixon), great-great-
great-grandson of John Beauchamp of London, England (Beauchamp family folder, Ala. Dept. of Archives & History, Montgomery, Ala.). Sarah A. Lowman (1st wife - m. 28 May 1845),
b. 19 Dec. 1829, d. 2 May 1852, buried Wyecott Cem., daughter
of John J. & Mary Lowman (Vol. I, p. 5). Margaret Euphemia

Allen (2nd wife - m. 21 Feb. 1854), b. 16 July 1836 Kilbarchon, Scotland, d. June 1886 Eufaula, Ala., daughter of Dr. George L. Allen & Janet Stewart (Vol. I, p. 5 & DAB, Vol. III, p.119).

Beauchamp, G .. 28,29,32,33 & 34-11-27 & 32-11-29. Green Beauchamp, b. ca 1801 Ga., d. 17 Dec. 1883, buried White Oak Station Cem., son of Littleton Beauchamp (Vol. I, p. 6). Caroline H. Kennon (wife), b. ca 1811 Ga., d. after 1884 (Vol. I, p. 6). Also in this household in 1850 was Jane Kennon, b. ca 1785 Ga..

Bedsole, John. 7-11-29. John Bedsole, b.ca 1802 N. C.. He was of Muscogee Co., Ga. in 1849 when he bought this land. Catherine ----- (wife?), b. ca 1809 N. C..

Bell, J., John. 24-10-25, 6-9-26 & 10,21,24,29,30 & 31-10-26. John Bell, b. 13 Jan. 1807 S. C., d. 21 Nov. 1890, to Ala. by 1837. Laney Hurst (wife - m. 1828 S. C.), b. 1803 (or 1808) S. C., d. 17 June 1873. Both are buried in the family cemetery (DAB, Vol. III, p. 126).

Bennett, Geo.. 28-11-26. George W. Bennett, b. ca 1831 Ala. (1860 Census), d. after 1880, son of Redmond Bennett (Vol. II, p. 10). Susannah (Coston?) (wife) b. ca 1825 S. C. (1860 Census).

Bennett, J. R.. 1-13-28(R). No further record.

Bennett, O., Orren. 27-11-26. Orren Bennett, b. ca 1824 Ala., probably never married, son of (Luke?) & Elizabeth Bennett (Vol. II, p. 10).

Bennett, Redmond. 22-11-26. Redmond Bennett, b. ca 1797 N. C., d. by June 1855, in Ala. by 1832, son of (Luke?) & Elizabeth Bennett (Vol. II, p. 10). Mariane E. Grant (2nd wife - m. 7 May 1843), b. ca 1815 S. C..

Bennett, Ryan. 1,6,7 & 12-10-26 & 28 & 29-11-26 & 1-10-27. Ryan Bennett, b. 1809 N. C., d. 12 Sept. 1883, buried Clayton Cem., son of (Luke?) & Elizabeth Bennett (Vol. II, p. 10). Emily Bishop (1st wife - m.23 Dec. 1835 Henry Co., Ala.), b. 8 Feb. 1816 Ga. (Bishop Bible), d. between 1850 & 1854, dau. of William & Nancy Bishop (Vol. II, p. 12). Margaret Daniel (2nd wife? - m. 7 Nov. 1854).

Bennett, T. B.. 29-13-26 (B). Thomas B. Bennett, b. ca 1811 S. C., d. after 1857, to Ala. from Ga. by 1838, son of James Bennett (d. by 1852, will written Macon Co., Ala.) (OR 4, p. 683/4). Elizabeth ----- (wife), b. ca 1821 Ga..

Benson, G., G. W., Geo. W.. 6 & 7-9-26 & 21-10-28. George W. Benson, b. ca 1806 N. C., in Ala. by 1843. Susannah Harrelson, b. ca 1808 S. C., daughter of Nancy Harrelson (CR B, p. 890). Nancy Harrelson was probably the wife of Moses Harrelson who died ca 1828 (Horry Co., S. C.?), who was a son of Josiah Harrelson who died by 1824 (Horry Co., S. C. Will Book A, page 9).

Bentley, John. 12-8-25. John Bentley, Sr., b. ca 1800 N. C., to Ala. by 1840. Fanny Thomas (2nd wife - m. 25 July 1849), b. ca 1816 N. C..

Benton, B.. 30-10-26. Bethel Benton, son of Samuel Benton who died by 1834 (Original Papers) - not in any early census. Martha ----- (wife, CR B, p. 537).

Benton, Henry. 34-9-27. Henry Benton, b. ca 1814 S. C., to Ala. from Ga. by 1849. Also in this household in 1850 was Mary Benton, b. ca 1770 S. C.. Luraney ----- (wife?), b. ca 1830 Ala..

Benton, Isaac. 11-9-25. Isaac Benton, b. 24 April 1818 S. C. d. 17 Oct. 1906, in Ala. by 1842. He is buried in Bethlehem Cem., son of Samuel Benton who died by 1834 (Original Papers), wife Sarah. In 1850, Sarah Benton, b. ca 1796 N. C., was in the Isaac Benton household. Letty ----- (wife), b. 15 May 1823 Ga., d. 5 April 1896, buried Bethlehem Cem..

Berry, J. W., John W.. 12-9-27, 12-12-27, 7-9-28. John W. Berry, b. ca 1815 Ga., to Ala. by 1842, had a military land grant in 12-9-27 on 13 Jan. 1852 (#28808). Palmyra ----- (1st wife?), b. ca 1818 Ga.. Lydia Ann E. Martin (2nd wife, m. 9 Aug. 1857), b. ca 1838 Ga..

Betts, Elish & W.. 34 & 35 - 12-28. This land was owned jointly by Elisha Betts and William Henry Betts (nephew of Elisha Betts - CR C, p. 226). William Henry Betts is in the 1840 Census, age 20/30, but not in any later census. Elisha Betts, b. ca 1788 Va.. Maria ----- (wife?), b. ca 1800 Ga..

Beverly, D. G.. 28-9-25. Daniel G. Beverly, b. ca 1816 N. C. Nancy Beasley (2nd wife - m. 25 Jan. 1849), b. ca 1830 Ala., d. by 1870 (Vol. II, p. 5), daughter of John G. Beasley and Martha Allums (Vol. II, p. 2).

Biggers, L. M.. 4 & 5-13-27. L. M. Biggers is not in any census of Barbour Co., but his son, Lorenzo J. Biggers, was a resident of Eufaula on 5 May 1875 when L. M. Biggers died in Muscogee Co., Ga. (OR 20, p. 491).

Bigham, J., Jas., James.. 4-10-28 & 32&33-11-28. James Bigham, b. ca 1803 Ga., Isabella ----- (wife?), b. ca 1810 Ga..

Bishop, J. B.. 25-11-26 & 6-12-27. James B. Bishop, b. ca
1815 S. C., d. by Feb. 1872 (OR 20, p. 200/2), son of William
Bishop and Nancy Pitts (OR 5, p. 19/21). Nancy Streater (wife -
m. 16 Feb. 1843), b. ca 1822 N. C., d. 8 Aug. 1904 (Eufaula
Times & News", Aug. 11, 1904), daughter of Shepperd M. Streater who died by March 1861 (OR 11, p. 807/12).

Bishop, N., Nancy. 4,14&24-11-26 & 7-11-27. William Bishop
d. 29 Sept. 1843 (Bishop Bible), in Twiggs Co., Ga. in 1819
(Vol. II, p. 36). Nancy Pitts (wife), b. ca 1794 S. C., d.
12 Oct. 1853 (Bishop Bible).

Bishop, W., Wesley. 2&12-11-26. Wesley Bishop, b. 20 Oct.
1819 Twiggs Co., Ga., d. 24 March 1884 (Vol. II, p. 36), son
of William Bishop & Nancy Pitts (Bishop Bible). Cynthia
Crews (1st wife - m. 24 Feb. 1848), b. 24 March 1829 Ala.,
d. 16 June 1851 (Vol. II, p. 36), daughter of Arthur Crews
and Mary V. King (ibid). Louisa M. M. Laura Weaver (2nd
wife - m. 11 Nov. 1862) (ibid).

Bizzell, B.. 13,14,23&26-8-23. Bennett Bizzell, b. ca 1775
N. C., d. by June 1851, may have been in Darlington Dist.,
S. C. in 1810 (Vol. II, p. 17). Mary ----- (wife), b. ca
1785 S. C., d. by June 1851 (ibid).

Bizzell, W., W. A.. 13-8-23 & 23-8-24. William A. Bizzell,
b. ca 1825 Ala., son of Bennett Bizzell (Vol. II, p. 20).
Jemima ----- (wife), b. ca 1829 Ga..

Blackstock, E.. 11-13-29(R). Jesse G. Blackstock, b. 22
June 1821 Ga., d. 14 Jan. 1851, buried Glenville Cem. (now
Russell Co., Ala.). Elizabeth S. ----- (wife), b. ca 1822
Ga.. A Jesse Blackstock m. Elizabeth Askew 23 Dec. 1841
Henry Co., Ga..

Blair, W., Wm.. 12&24-11-26 & 7&19-11-27. William Blair,
b. ca 1805 S. C., d. July 1886 ("The Eufaula Daily Times,
Aug. 1, 1886), in Ala. by 1832. Elizabeth Bishop (wife - m.
18 Dec. 1831 Henry Co., Ala.), b. 28 Dec.1811 S. C., d. 26
Oct. 1880 ("The Clayton Courier", Oct. 30, 1880), daughter
of William Bishop and Nancy Pitts (Bishop Bible).

Blakey, A.. 16-10-26. Asa Blakey, b. ca 1810 Jones Co., Ga.
(1906 CSA Census), heir (son?) of Jesse Blakey who died by
Nov. 1842 (OR 2, p. 48). Margaret C. Blakey (wife - m. 10
March 1852), b. ca 1819 Ga. (1860 Census).

Blakey, S. W.. 21&22-10-26. Silas W. Blakey, b. ca 1815 Ga.,
d. by 1876 (OR 21, p. 253), heir (son?) of Jesse Blakey who
died by Nov. 1842 (OR 2, p. 48). Sarah Blakey (wife - m. 7
Jan. 1840 Baldwin Co., Ga.), b. ca 1812 Ga..

Bludworth, T. F., Thos.. 3-11-35. Thomas F. Bludworth, b. ca 1801 N. C., d. by Feb. 1868 (OR 16, p. 656), in Ga. by 1829, to Ala. by 1850, son of John Bludworth, b. ca 1750/65 New Hanover Co., N. C., d. before 1830 Newton Co., Ga. and Ann DeVane, b. ca 1754/69 Bladen Co., N. C., grandson of Timothy Bludworth, b. 1736 New Hanover Co., N. C., d. 14 Aug. 1814 Washington City and Priscilla ----- (Mrs. Dorothy Hill, Laguna Hills, Ca.). Thursey Dawson (wife - m. 17 Jan. 1825 Jasper Co., Ga.), b. ca 1804 N. C., d. by Feb. 1868 (OR 16, p. 656).

Bobit, T., Thos.. 27-11-26. Thomas Bobit, b. ca 1792 S. C., in Ala. by 1833. Ann ----- (wife), b. ca 1812 Ga., heir of Joseph Duckworth who died in Jones Co., Ga. by 1835 (CR A, p. 86).

Bond, S. H.. 29-10-26 - no further record.

Borders, Stephen. 7-11-25. Stephen Borders bought land here in 1848, at which time he was of Harris Co., Ga. (CR H, p. 298). He died there by 1864 ("History of Harris Co., Ga." by Barfield, p. 101).

Borders, Wm. M.. 5-11-25. William M. Borders, b. ca 1815 Ga., owned land joining Stephen Borders - to Ala. from Ga. by 1846. Martha Alexander (wife - m. 7 Aug. 1837 Harris Co., Ga.), b. ca 1816 Ga..

Boswell, W. H., Wm.. 21-13-25(B) & 18&19-11-27. William H. Boswell, b. ca 1815 Ga.. In 1843, he was of Talbot Co., Ga. (CR E, p. 304). Elizabeth Lowman (wife), b. ca 1826 S. C., heir of John J. Lowman (CR 11, p. 307/9).

Bottoms, B.. 20-9-28. Burrell Bottoms, b. ca 1815 S. C. (1860 Census), d. Sept. 1872 (Original Papers, Box 32). Sarah ----- (wife?), b. ca 1818 Ga..

Boulware, F. C. (should be P.). 18-13-25(B). F. P. Boulware, b. ca 1824 S. C.. Mary ----- (wife?), b. ca 1826 S. C.. Also in this household in 1850 was William Reed, b. ca 1826 S. C..

Bowden, Jas.. 27-10-26. James Bowden, b. ca 1802 N. C., to Ala. by 1836. Elizabeth ----- (wife?), b. ca 1805 N. C..

Bowen, Levi. 9-11-28. Levi Bowen, b. ca 1805 N. C., to Ga. by 1833, to Ala. by 1842. Mary ----- (wife?), b. ca 1808 N. C..

Boyd, Francis M.. 33-11-24. Francis M. Boyd, b. 7 Sept. 1823 S. C., d. 30 June 1902 (UDC files), to Ala. from Ga. by 1846. Mary Frances Storey (?) (wife - m. 9 July 1843), b. 27 March 1822, d. 19 Jan. 1890 (UDC files).

Boykin, F., Francis. 3,10&11-12-28. Francis Boykin, b. ca
1826 Ga., d. 11 Aug. 1863. Louisa Anna Nuchols (wife), b.
ca 1831 Elbert Co., Ga., d. Aug. 1895 ("Eufaula Times and
News", Aug. 8, 1895). She m. (2) Hiram Hawkins 22 Sept. 1864.
He was born 9 Sept. 1826 Bath Co., Ky., son of Thomas Hawkins and Mary Dean. His first wife was Mary Workman of
Bath Co., Ky. (MRA, Vol. I, p. 430/9).

Boyleston, J. C.. 25-9-25 & 25-9-26. Joseph C. Boyleston,
b. ca 1801 S. C., d. 23 Nov. 1860 (OR 11, p. 426), son of
George Boyleston & Alice Hardin Cloud (David Robertson,
Jefferson, Texas). Leonora C.----- (2nd wife), b. ca 1820
S. C..

Bradberry, J. H., Jas. H.. 15&22-13-26. James H. Bradberry,
b. ca 1816 Ga., d. by Oct. 1856 (OR 7, p. 537). Part of
this land was patented by Joseph Bradberry in 1843 (Barbour
Co., Ala. Tract Book). Jane ----- (wife?), b. ca 1818 S. C..

Bradbery, Mary. 13-13-26. This land was patented by Joseph
Bradberry in 1843 (Barbour Co., Ala. Tract Book). He is not
in any early census, nor is Mary Bradberry. A Joseph Bradberry m. Polly Haynie 20 June 1813 Madison Co., Ga..

Bradley, Robert. 20&29-11-26. Robert Bradley, b. ca 1809
Edgefield Dist., S. C., d. June 1890 ("The Clayton Courier"
June 14, 1890), in Ala. by 1828 (Vol. I, p. 9), son of Hobbs
Bradley who died Edgefield Dist., S. C. (MRA, Vol. I, p.
403/4). Elizabeth Kemp (wife - ibid), b. ca 1809 S. C., d.
1873 (Vol. I, p. 9).

Bradley, S. C.. 17&18-12-27. Samuel C. Bradley, b. ca 1799
Ga., in Fla. 1832/8, to Ala. by 1850. Delilah ----- (wife?),
b. ca 1800 Ga..

Brantley, C. C.. 8-13-24(B). Charles C. Brantley, b. ca 1812
Ga., heir of James Brantley who died by 1842 (OR 1, p. 320).
Elvira Adams (wife - m. 12 Sept. 1841), b. ca1823 Ga., possibly
daughter of Mary Adams, b. ca 1796 N. C. (1850 Census).

Brantley, W., Wm.. 30-13-26(B). William Brantley, b. ca
1810 N. C. (1850 Census - 1860 Census says b. ca 1809 Va.).
Eliza ----- (wife?), b. ca 1823 Ga.. Also in this household
in 1850 was Eliza Worrell, b. ca 1790 Ga..

Britt, M., Matthew, M. Estate. 5-11-29 & 5&32-12-29. Matthew
Britt, b. 12 Aug. 1795 Va., d. 31 May 1852, possibly son of
Edward and Sarah Britt (d. 22 Feb. 1857, age 85, buried Fellowship Cem., Bullock Co., Ala.). Elizabeth (Sinquefield?) (wife),
b. ca 1824 Ga..

Broach, W. A.. 29-9-24. William A. Broach, b. ca 1820 S. C.
(1850 Census - 1860 Census says b. ca 1825 Ala.). In his

household in 1850 were Rhoda Eidson (b. ca 1790 S. C.),
Rachel A. Broach (b. ca 1825 S. C.) and Francis Eidson
(b. ca 1834 Ala.). Rhoda Eidson (b. ca 1787 S. C.) was
also enumerated in the household of James Eidson (b. ca
1788 S. C.). There were no Broach children in this household. William Broach m. Nancy Eidson 28 Jan. 1855. In
1850, she was in the household of James Eidson - she was
born ca 1830 Ga.. In 1860, Rhoda Eidson (b. ca 1798 N. C.)
was living with F. W. (Francis) Eidson - also in this household was Ann Broach (b. ca 1832 Ala.). James Eidson (b. ca
1790 S. C.) was head of a household - in it was Sally Eidson (b. ca 1826 Ga.).

Brooks, E.. 1-11-28. Esau B. Brooks, b. 23 Oct. 1807 Ga.,
d. 18 Jan. 1884 Dale Co., Ala., buried Old Daleville Cem.,
Dale Co., Ala.. In 1851, he was living in Coffee Co., Ala.
(CR J, p. 342). Martha P. McCoy (wife), b. 8 Oct. 1808
Ga., d. 24 June 1892, buried Old Daleville Cem., Dale Co.,
Ala., sister of David F. McCoy who died by Nov. 1846 (OR
2, p. 294).

Browder, I. C.. 12,23&26-12-27. Isham C. Browder, b. ca
1805 N. C., d. Oct. 1869, possibly son of Elizabeth Browder
who died by Feb. 1845 (OR 2, p. 156). Mary Ann Martha Hils-
man Tarver (wife - m. 14 Sept. 1841), b. ca 1825 Ala., dau.
of Benjamin H. Tarver who died by Jan. 1855 (OR 6, p. 305).

Browder, M. A.. 7,8,17&18-12-29 & 19&31-13-29(R). Milton
A. Browder, b. 17 Jan. 1802 N. C., d. 25 July 1859, buried
Mitchell family cemetery, Russell Co., Ala.. Mary M. Wilson
(wife), b. 28 Dec. 1815 Rockingham Co., N. C., d. 1 Dec. 1859,
buried Mitchell family cemetery, daughter of Jessie Wilson
(Cemetery inscription).

Brown, C. L.. 26&35-12-27. Charles L. Brown, b. ca 1824 Ga.,
in Ala. by 1846, possibly son of Reuben E. Brown, b. ca 1794
S. C.. Mary M. ----- (wife?), b. ca 1825 S. C..

Brown, D.. 30-11-29. John Brown, d. by Sept. 1841. Dorothy
----- (wife), b. ca 1796 S. C., d. Sept. 1871 Hamilton, Ga.
(Vol. I, p. 13).

Brown, Jesse. 4&5-10-24. Jesse Brown, b. ca 1798 Ga., in
Ala. by 1841. Elizabeth ----- (wife?), b. ca 1805 Ga.. A
Jesse Brown m. Elizabeth Pierce 19 Dec. 1826 Wilkinson Co.,
Ga..

Brown, John P.. 28-10-25. John P. Brown, b. ca 1809 Ga.,
in Fla. 1832/9, in Ga. 1841/5, to Ala. by 1848. Julia -----
(wife?), b. ca 1809 Ga..

Brown, J. W.. 10,11,12&13-12-25 & 12&13-13-28 (B). John W.

Brown, b. ca 1799 Ga.. Martha T. Hunter (wife - m. 8 Dec. 1825 Hancock Co., Ga.), b. ca 1809 Ga., d. 4 Dec. 1873, buried Glenville Cem., Russell Co., Ga..

Brown, J., Jonathan. 18-11-29. Jonathan Brown, b. ca 1785 S. C., to Ga. by 1838, to Ala. by 1840. Eliza ----- (wife?), b. ca 1800 N. C.. Also in this household in 1850 were Martha Kiels, b. ca 1833 Ga. and Joseph Kiels, b. ca 1835 Ga..

Brown, Thos. 3-11-26. In 1839, Thomas Brown was of Mont-gomery Co., Ala. (CR B, p. 609).

Browning, Jesse. 14-9-26. Jesse Browning, b. ca 1801 S. C., in Ala. by 1838. Jane ----- (wife?), b. ca 1797 S. C..

Brunson, C. J.. 13&14-11-27 & 17-11-28. Charles J. Brunson, b. ca 1827 Ga.. In 1856, Charles J. Brunson, Mary Jane Brun-son and Mary Hickman sold land in 13&14-11-27 (CR M, p. 540). Joel Brunson m. Mary Hickman 6 Jan. 1848 - consent of her mother, Polly Hickman (Mar. I, p. 308). Mary ----- (wife?), b. ca 1834 Ga..

Brunson, M. A.. 29&30-12-27. Marion A. Brunson, b. 1810 S. C., d. 17 April 1867. Catharine C. Mellard (wife - m. 12 May 1846 Pike Co., Ala.), b. 7 Jan. 1826 Charleston, S. C., d. 23 Feb. 1898, daughter of Rev. James H. Mellard (Southern Christian Advocate, 19 June 1846). Both are buried in Fair-view Cem., Eufaula, Ala..

Bryan, Annis. 6-10-28. Annis Bryan, b. ca 1796 Ga.. In 1850 she lived with her daughter and son-in-law, Lucinda & William Holland. In 1860, Joel Stokes signed a quit-claim deed to the above land (CR Q, p. 119/20).

Bryan, H. L.. 7-10-28. H. L. Bryan, b. ca 1820 N. C., to Ala. from Ga. by 1842. Mary ----- (wife?), b. ca 1824 Ga.. She may have been the Mary Bryan named in the estate of William Head who died by Feb. 1857 (OR 9, p. 311).

Bryan, Jas.. 31-12-27. James Bryan, son of John Bryan who died by Feb. 1847. In 1847, James Bryan was living in Fla.. (OR 2, p. 177).

Bryan, J. C.. 31-12-27 & 30&31-12-28. John C. Bryan, b. 1814 Ga., d. 1891 Rome Ga. (Vol. II, p. 105), son of John Bryan who died by Feb. 1847 (OR 2, p. 177). Janet McLeod (wife - Vol. II, p. 105), b. ca 1816 Ga..

Bryan, Needham, N.. 8-9-27 & 33-10-28. Needham Bryan, b. ca 1819 Ga., in Ala. by 1845. Elizabeth Echols (wife - m. 11 May 1843), b. ca 1819 Ga..

Bryan, Robert. 21-13-27. Robert Bryan, b. ca 1786 Ga..
Tabitha ----- (wife?), b. ca 1785 S. C.. Also in this
household in 1850 were Eliza Mims, b. ca 1833 Ga. and Benjamin Mims, b. ca 1835 Ga..

Bryan, Susan. 31-12-28. John Bryan died by Feb. 1847 (CR
G, p. 418/9). He was in Ga. by 1820 and in Ala. by 1837.
Susan ----- (wife), b. ca 1797 S. C., d. by Oct. 1854 (OR
6, p. 171). A John Bryan m. Susan Dykes 16 July 1818 Pulaski Co., Ga..

Bryan, Theophilus, T.. 5,6&32-12-29. Theophilus Bryan, b.
ca 1799 N. C., to Ala. from Ga. by 1848. Levina Weathers
(2nd wife? - m. 19 Jan. 1841 Muscogee Co., Ga.), b. ca 1820
Ga..

Bryan, Wm.. 28-9-28 & 5-12-29. In 1842, Wm. Bryan of Macon
Co., Ga. deeded land in 30-12-28 to John Bryan of Barbour Co.,
wife Harriet signed in Dooly Co., Ga. in 1844 (CR F, p. 84) -
(see Susan Bryan).

Bryan, W. M.. 35-11-37 & 12-12-27. William M. Bryan, b. ca
1816 Ga., in Rome, Ga. in 1891 (OR 26,p. 461/2), son of John
Bryan who died by Feb. 1847 (OR 2, p. 177). Epsey Head (wife
m. 30 Nov. 1841), b. ca 1824 Ga., daughter of William Head,
granddaughter of Richard Head, Sr. (Rev. Soldier).

Buford, J., Jeff. 17,19&21-9-24 & 26&27-9-28 (partly in Henry
Co., Ala.). Jefferson Buford, b. 17 Aug. 1807 Union Dist.,
S. C., d. 28 Aug. 1862, son of John Ragsdale Buford & Esther
Eaves (DAB, Vol. III, p. 251/2). Mary Ann Rebecca White (1st
wife), b. 24 June 1823 Whiteville, N. C., d. 16 July 1852,
daughter of John H. White (DAB, Vol. III, p. 251/2), b. 15
Feb. 1789 N. C., d. 4 July 1861 Macon Co., Ala. and Rebecca
-----, b. 24 June 1783 Bladen Co., N. C., d. March 1866 Macon
Co., Ala.. All of the above are buried in Fairview Cemetery,
Eufaula, Ala.. Mrs. Elizabeth H. McNeill (2nd wife - DAB,
Vol. III, p. 251/2), b. ca 1832 Pa..

Bullard, H., Henry. 5,10&32-11-25. Henry Bullard, b. ca 1819
N. C. (1860 Census) - children born Ga. 1832, 1838, 1842 and
1844, born Ala. 1840 and 1848. Emily Baker (wife - m. 15
March 1838 Stewart Co., Ga.), b. ca 1818 Ga. (1860 Census),
daughter of Jeremiah Baker who died by 1848 (OR 3, p. 579/81).

Burgess, D.. 24-9-25. Dempsey Burgess, b. ca 1798, in Ga.
from 1828 to 1833, in Ala. by 1850. Roxanna ----- (wife?),
b. ca 1792 N. C..

Burnet, Al.. 6-11-29. Alexander Burnet, b. ca 1802 Ga., to
Ala. after 1840. Martha ----- (wife?), b. ca 1798 S. C..

Burke, S. G.. 11&14-13-26. Solomon G. Burke bought the above land in March 1853 from Snow M. Boynton and wife Leander of Marion Co., Ga. (CR K, p. 406/7). He probably never lived in Barbour Co..

Burleson, S. J.. 18-12-26. Seaborn J. Burleson, b. ca 1813 Ga., to Ala. by 1842. In 1850, he was enumerated next to Aaron Burleson, b. ca 1785 Ga.. Malinda Welder (wife - m. 26 Dec. 1830 Henry Co., Ga.?).

Burleson, S. W.. 32&33-12-25. Simeon W. Burleson, b. ca 1810 Ga., in Ala. by 1830. Molsey ----- (wife?), b. ca 1813 Ga.

Burnham, James. 32-9-28. No further record.

Burnham, W.. 33-9-28. William Burnham, b. ca 1818 N. C., Sarah ----- (wife), b. ca 1829 Ala..

Burnley, J. B.. 36-11-28. Jeremiah B. Burnley, b. ca 1810 Ga., d. by Nov. 1873 (OR 19, p. 556/60), probably never married.

Burt, H. Z.. 5-13-27. When Hilliard Z. Burt bought the above land in 1844, he was of Talbot Co., Ga.(CR G, p. 25/6).

Bush, C., Council. 27-10-27. Council Vernon Bush, b. 4 May 1817 Laurens Co., Ga., d. 29 Dec. 1893, son of Moses E. Bush and Julia Ann Calhoun. Rebecca Bishop (wife - m. 20 Oct. 1843), b. 8 May 1823 Ala., d. 28 May 1855, daughter of William Bishop and Nancy Pitts (Vol. I, p. 19). Council and Rebecca Bush are buried in Clayton Cem..

Bush, D., D.A.. 36-11-26 & 5&8-10-27. David Allen Bush, b. 10 May 1819 Ga., d. 4 June 1875, son of Moses E. Bush and Julia Ann Calhoun. Julia Ann Flowers (wife), b. 1821 Ga., d. 29 May 1892, daughter of Abner and Rebecca Flowers. Both are buried in the family cemetery (Vol. I, p. 19/20).

Bush, E. and N., N. J., Nancy, Nancy J.. 23,26,27&34-10-27. Moses Eason Bush, b. 27 April 1797 Ga., d. 25 April 1847, son of John Council Bush, b. 1 April 1781 Johnston Co., N. C., d. after 1814, and Edy (Tison?) of Trent River, N. C. & Laurens Co., Ga. (Vol. I, p. 18). Julia Ann Calhoun (1st wife - m. 9 April 1815 Laurens Co., Ga.), b. 12 Oct. 1794 Laurens Co., Ga., d. 18 April 1833. Both are buried in Rocky Mount Cem.. Nancy Jane Johnson (2nd wife), b. ca 1815 N. C., d. after 1880, daughter of Moses & Mary Johnson (Vol. I, p. 18).

Bush, G., G. T.(?). 16-10-27 & 21-10-28. Greenberry Bush, b. ca 1823 Ala., son of William Bush who died by 1840. (Vol. I, p. 28). Nancy Jane Walls (wife - m. 6 Jan. 1848), b. ca 1828 Ga.. In 1860, his wife was M. A., b. ca 1826 Ala..

Bush, J.. 4-10-28. Joseph A. Bush, b. ca 1822 Ga., d. Feb.
1889 ("Eufaula Weekly Times & News, Feb. 28, 1889), to Ala.
by 1846. Mary A. ----- (wife), b. ca 1825 S. C., d. 6 Sept.
1888 ("Eufaula Weekly Times & News", Sept. 7, 1888), both
buried Epworth Church Cem..

Bush, L. R.. 4-10-28 & 19-11-29. Levi R. Bush bought the
land in 19-11-29 in 1848 (CR H, p. 356). He and Nathan Bush
sold it in 1851 (CR J, p. 396).

Bush, N.. 4-10-28. Nathan Bush, b. ca 1802 Ga., to Ala. by
1849. Elizabeth C. ----- (Wife), b. ca 1806 S. C.. A Nathan
Bush m. Elizabeth Butler 27 Oct. 1831 Bibb Co., Ga..

Bush, R.. 19-11-29. This may have been Richard Bush, b. ca
1804 Ga., of Macon Co., Ala. in 1843 (CR E, p. 430). Penelope
Adams (wife - m. 10 July 1832 Pulaski Co., Ga.), b. ca 1818
N. C..

Bush, Sarah. 5-9-27. She may have been the widow of William
Bush, Sr. who died by Jan. 1836 (CR A, p. 134).

Bush, W. G.. 9-9-28. William Green Bush, b. ca 1823 Ga., d.
by Aug. 1855, son of Zachariah Bush and Mary Dennis (Vol. I,
p. 25). Mary Allen (wife - m. 25 June 1845), b. ca 1828 Ala.,
m. (2) Neill Morrison 29 Dec. 1859.

Bush, Z.. 4&5-9-27 & 32&33-10-27. Zachariah Bush, b. ca
1796 Ga., d. by March 1851, possibly brother of Moses Eason
Bush (Vol. I, p. 18 & 25). Mary Dennis (wife - m. 23 Sept.
1818 Laurens Co., Ga.).

Butts, Charles. 21&29-9-26. Charles Butts, b. ca 1812 Ga.,
to Ala. by 1836. Louisa ----- (1st wife?), b. ca 1822 S. C..
Sarah A. M. Flournoy (2nd wife - m. 1 April 1858), b. ca
1824 Ala. (1860 Census).

Butts, F. C.. 13,14&15-13-28(R). Francis C. Butts, b. 25
Sept. 1821 Hancock Co., Ga., d. 9 Feb. 1859, buried in the
Ivey family cemetery, Russell Co., Ala.. Catharine -----
(wife), b. ca 1826 Ga., heir (daughter?) of James L. Daniels
who died by 1850 (OR 4, p. 82).

Butts, Jeremiah. 19-13-29(R). Dr. Jeremiah Butts, b. ca
1812 Ga., to Ala. by 1843. Ann W. Thomas (wife - m. 4 May
1837 Columbia Co., Ga.), b. ca 1817 Ga.. In 1850, E. S.
Greenwood and wife, Jane E., of Muscogee Co., Ga. gave land
to Mrs. Ann W. Butt of Barbour Co., Ala., Jeremiah Butt,
trustee (CR H, p. 668/9).

Butts, Priscilla. 3-13-26. Moses Butts, b. 23 Sept. 1782
Halifax Co., N. C., son of Moses Butts who migrated from
Wales to N. C. in 1752 (MRA, Vol. I, p. 519/20). He died

8 March 1848 Muscogee Co., Ga. (Southern Christian Advocate,
28 April 1848). Priscilla Banks (2nd wife - m. 1822 Columbia Co., Ga.), b. 20 Sept. 1802 Elbert Co., Ga., d. 2 Feb.
1853 Muscogee Co., Ga. (Southern Christian Advocate, 25 Feb.
1853), daughter of Ralph Banks & Mary Jones (MRA, Vol. I,
p. 519/20).

Butts, R.. 10-13-26. Dr. Richard Lemuel Butts of Bullock
Co., Ala., b. 1 Nov. 1824 Columbia Co., Ga., son of Moses
Butts and Priscilla Banks. (MRA, Vol. I, p. 519/20).

Butts, Solomon. 31-10-26. Solomon Butts, b. ca 1807 Ga.,
in Ala. by 1837. Sarah ----- (2nd wife?), b. ca 1820 Ala..

Byram, S. L.. 6-12-25(B). Smith L. Byram, b. ca 1813 Ga.,
in Ala. by 1836. Delilah ----- (wife), b. ca 1805 S. C..

Byrd, B.. 11,14&23-8-23 & 14-8-25. Burtis Byrd, b. 24 June
1814 N. C., d. 30 Aug. 1854 Dale Co., Ala., son of Redden
Byrd. Mary Anderson (wife), b. 17 June 1815, d. 4 March 1888
Dale Co., Ala.. (Vol. II, p. 25).

Byrd, Edw.. 13&14-8-23. Edward Byrd, b. 22 June 1815 N. C.,
d. 22 March 1895 Dale Co., Ala. (Vol. II, p. 25). Louisa
Sutton (wife), b. 8 Nov. 1818 Ga., d. 14 June 1897 Dale Co.,
Ala. (ibid), daughter of Needham B. Sutton and Elizabeth
Bryant. (Vol. I, p. 149).

Cabaniss, J.. 1-9-28. Jesse M. Cabaniss, b. ca 1809 Ga.,
in Ala. by 1836. Sarah ----- (wife), b. ca 1816 Ga..

Cade, Jas., James. 11&14-11-28. James J. Cade, b. ca 1813
Ga., to Ala. by 1836. Susan B. ----- (1st wife), b. 12 Feb.
1816 Ga., d. 21 Dec. 1861, buried Batesville Baptist Church
Cem.. Louvinia Glover (2nd wife - m. 14 April 1863 at H. G.
Glover's).

Caldwell, G.. 17-13-26(B). Dr. Graves Caldwell, b. 31 May
1824 Greene Co., Ga. (MRA Vol. I, p. 520/1), d. 8 Feb. 1899,
buried Enon Cem., Bullock Co., Ala.., son of Joshua Caldwell
of Maryland and Charlotte Beasley of Ga., grandson of John
Caldwell (ibid). Mary Ann Flournoy (wife - MRA, Vol. I, p.
520/1), b. 1825 Ga., d. June 1899, buried Enon Cem..

Calhoun, John A., J. A.. 4-11-28 & 27,28&32-12-28. John A.
Calhoun probably never lived in Barbour Co.. Sarah M.-----
(wife in Oct. 1850 - CR J, p. 98).

Calloway, D.. 21-12-25(B) & 21,22&27,13-25(B). Daniel Calloway, b. ca 1799 Ga., d. by Aug. 1864 (OR 14, p. 281/3), to
Ala. by 1836. Elizabeth ----- (wife?), b. ca 1801 N. C..

Calloway, H.. 23-13-25(B). Henry Calloway, b. ca 1805 Ga.,
to Ala. by 1836. Priscilla ----- (wife?), b. ca 1812 Ga..

Calloway, P. M.. 30&31-11-29. Rev. Pitt Milner Calloway,
b. 10 Oct. 1812 Wilkes Co., Ga., d. 29 Nov. 1898 Dale Co.,
Ala., son of Joshua S. Calloway, b. 30 May 1789 Wilkes Co.,
Ga. (DAB, Vol. III, p. 288). Ellen Wiley Jordan (1st wife -
m. 10 Dec. 1833 Talbot Co., Ga.), b. 1816 Ga., d. 27 July
1879 ("The Times & News", Aug. 7, 1879). Mrs. Mary V. Mc-
Laney (2nd wife - m. 16 Feb. 1880 where?) (DAB, Vol. III,
p. 288).

Cameron, A., A. M.. 35-13-25 & 13-13-26. Archibald M.
Cameron, b. ca 1821 Ala., living Pike Co., Ala. Aug. 1863.
He was an heir (probably nephew) of Mary and Nancy Cameron
(sisters) who died Dec. 1862 and Aug. 1863 respectively
(OR 13, p. 167/9) and son of Locklin Cameron who died by
April 1856. (OR 7, p. 530). Louisa ----- (wife?), b. ca 1822.

Cameron, L.. 2,3,10&11-13-25(B) & 2-13-28(B). Locklin
Cameron, b. ca 1785 N. C., d. by Sept. 1856, to Ala. from
N. C. after 1829. His will, written 11 Aug. 1855, mentions
a daughter in Richmond Co., N. C. (OR 7, p. 520). Christian
----- (wife), b. ca 1790 N. C..

Cameron, N.. 2-13-25(B). Nancy Cameron, b. ca 1783 N. C.,
d. 11 Aug. 1863 (OR 13, p. 167/9), sister of Locklin Cameron
and of Mary Cameron, b. ca 1783 N. C. (ibid).

Campbell, D.. 36-9-24. Daniel Campbell, b. ca 1810 S. C.,
d. by Aug. 1853 (OR 5, p. 339/40), son of William D. Campbell (Vol. I, p. 32). Cornelia M. ----- (wife), b. 19 July
1814 Ga., d. 14 Jan. 1900, buried Pine Level Baptist Church
Cem..

Campbell, R.. 24-9-24. Robert Campbell, b. 2 Aug. 1823 S. C.
d. 6 Jan. 1917, buried Pea River Presbyterian Church Cem..
Anna Bryant (wife - m. 15 Feb. 1846), b. 10 June 1820 Ga.,
d. 5 March 1885, buried same cemetery.

Campbell, Wm. D.. 25&35-9-24. William D. Campbell, b. ca
1790 S. C., d. by Dec. 1849. Elizabeth ----- (wife), b. ca
1797 S. C., d. by Jan. 1869 (Vol. I, p. 32).

Canady, Felix. 30-13-26(B). No further record.

Cannady, Joseph. 25&35-13-25(B). Joseph Cannady, b. ca
1785 N. C., to Ala. ca 1838/42. Silva ----- (2nd wife?),
b. ca 1812 N. C.. Also in this household in 1850 was
Catherine Cannady, b. ca 1770 N. C..

Cannon, P. N.. 26&34-9-26. Simeon R. Cannon, b. ca 1793
S. C., of Barnwell Dist., S. C. (DAB, Vol. III, p. 440/1).

Mary Owen Kennedy (1st wife), daughter of John Kennedy and
Elizabeth Truetlin, granddaughter of John Adam Truetlin,
Gov. of Ga. ca 1777 (DAB, Vol. III, p. 440/1). She died
6 Jan. 1844, age 57 (Southern Christian Advocate, 19 April
1844). Mrs. Penelope N. Trammell (2nd wife - m. by Nov.
1850 - OR 3, p 625), widow of James J. Trammell who died
by Aug. 1843 (OR 2, p 99).

Capel, Jas.. 1&12-9-24. James Capel, b. 25 Jan. 1800 N. C.,
d. 9 Oct. 1886, buried Pea River Presbyterian Church, to
-Ala. from Ga. by 1840. Mary ----- (wife), b. 22 Jan. 1818
N. C., d. 15 Sept. 1894, buried Pea River Presbyterian Ch.
Cem.. She was an heir of Christopher McRae of Anson Co.,
N. C. who died by 1837 and his wife, Mary, who died by
Feb. 1861 (Vol. I, p. 121/2).

Cariker, G. W.. 21&31-12-28. George W. Cariker, b. 8 May
1811 N. C., d. 23 Oct. 1856. Mary M. ----- (wife), b. 29
Dec. 1806 Ga.(1860 Census), d. 11 July 1895. Both are buried
in Batesville Baptist Church Cem..

Carmichael, A.. 26&27-13-25(B). Dr. Archibald Carmichael,
b. ca 1817 S. C.. He may have had brothers Malcolm Carmichael (b. ca 1828 S. C.) and H. W. Carmichael (b. ca 1810
S. C.). Elizabeth ----- (wife), b. ca 1828 Ga..

Carpenter, R. E. (should be A.). 24,25&26-9-24. Richard A.
Carpenter, b. 1 March 1813 N. C. (1860 Census), d. 25 Nov.
1894. Nancy Jones (3rd wife?) b. 23 June 1828 N. C. (1860
Census), d. 11 Feb. 1891. Both buried Sikes Creek Baptist
Church Cem.. In Sept. 1863, Richard A. Carpenter posted
bond as guardian of three of his children (?), Dwight,
Gillum and Jemima Ellen Carpenter, who were heirs of Anna
Byley (OR 13, p. 127 & 200). There is no other record of
her in Barbour Co..

Carol, Henry. 9-9-26. Henry Carroll, b. ca 1826 N. C..
Theresa Ann Elizabeth Fleming (1st wife - m. 29 May 1845).
Louisa M. McNair (2nd wife - m. 23 Jan. 1851).

Carr, Thos. 17-13-27. Thomas Carr, b. ca 1815 Ga., d. by
Oct. 1853 (OR 5, p. 399), in Ala. by 1833. In 1843, he borrowed money from Mary Carr of Montgomery Co., Ala. (CR E, p.
457/8). Louisa Caroline Faison (wife), b. ca 1816 Ga., dau.
of Thomas J. Faison who died by 1842 (OR 1, p. 304).

Carrol, John. 26&36-9-26. John Carroll, b. ca 1815 S. C.,
in Ala. by 1836. Elizabeth ----- (wife?), b. ca 1820 S. C..

Casey, Jas., Jr.. 33-11-24. James Casey, Jr., b. ca 1825
N. C., son of James Casey, Sr. (CR E, p. 490). Mary Bishop
(wife - m. 24 Sept. 1847), b. ca 1828 Ga. (1860 Census).

Casey, L., Lemuel. 4-8-24. Lemuel Casey, b. 26 Jan. 1813
Richmond Co., N. C., d. 3 Nov. 1886, buried Carroll Cem.,
Dale Co., Ala., son of James Casey, Sr. (CR E, p. 490).
Nancy ----- (wife?), b. ca 1816.

Carter, J. D.. 2&3-12-26. John D. Carter was of Muscogee
Co., Ga. in June 1844 (CR F, p. 182) and in Nov. 1850 (CR
J, p. 111). Zenomia D. Hoxey (wife - m. 4 Feb. 1841 Mus-
cogee Co., Ga.).

Causey, Cullen. 35-12-27. Cullen Causey, b. ca 1800 N. C.,
brother of Phillip B. Causey (OR 4, p. 634/43). Dorothy
----- (wife?), b. ca 1805 N. C..

Causey, P. B.. 13&24-12-27 & 18,19&30-12-28. Phillip B.
Causey, d. by Aug. 1849 (OR 3, p. 348). His heirs were his
brothers and sisters - one brother was from Edgecombe Co.,
N. C. (OR 4, p. 634/43). Creasey ----- (wife), b. ca 1792
N. C..

Cawthon, W. W.. 14,15&16-11-27. William W. Cawthon, b. ca
1807 Ga., d. by Sept. 1853 (OR 5, p. 353), in Ala. by 1831,
son of Josiah Dabney Cawthon, b. ca 1784 Ga., d. 1834 Henry
Co., Ala., m. (1) ----- (2) Mary Sylvester, grandson of Wm.
Cawthon, b. ca 1750,Laurens Co., Ga. by 1815, d. Telfair Co.,
Ga. ca 1817/8, m. Judith Thomas; great-grandson of William
Dabney Cawthon (Rev. Patriot) who d. Orangeburg Dist., S. C.
1786 (Cawthon family files from Ruth & Donald Philbrick,
Cape Elizabeth, Maine). Charity G. Smith (wife - m. 15 Nov.
1831 Henry Co., Ala.), b. ca 1811 Ga., daughter of Simon
Smith (ibid). On 12 Dec. 1855, she was living in Henry Co.,
Ala..

Chambers, I. H.. 24-9-24. Isaac H. Chambers, b. 1 April
1812 S. C., d. 29 Jan. 1892, in Ala.by 1836. Malinda Campbell (wife), b. 1 Feb. 1822 S. C., d. 24 Sept. 1894, daughter
of William D. Campbell (OR 17, p. 203). Both are buried in
Pea River Presbyterian Church Cem..

Chambers, L. D.. 13-9-25. Lorenzo D. Chambers, b. ca 1807
S. C., in Ala. by 1846. Mary Kinims (2nd or 3rd wife - m.
11 Oct. 1849), b. ca 1824 S. C..

Chancey, John. 12-12-24 & 12-12-25(B). John Chancey died
by June 1855 (OR 6, p. 434). Milbrey ----- (wife - OR 7,
p. 246).

Chapman, Jas.. 21,27,28&34-13-29(R). James A. Chapman was
in Russell Co., Ala. (CR L, p. 184). Elmira B. ----- (wife -
ibid).

Cheesbro, James. 25-10-28. James Cheesbro, b. ca 1799 Ct..

He received a military land grant in 25-10-28 on 7 Oct. 1851
(#5439). Anna ----- (wife?), b. ca 1810 S. C..

Chesnut, M.. 21-12-26. Mitchell Chesnut, b. ca 1806 N. C.,
to Ala. from Ga. by 1840. Sarah ----- (wife), b. ca 1816
Ga., d. July 1890 ("Eufaula Daily Times", July 2, 1890).

Childs, E. C.. 30-10-25. Elijah C. Childs, b. ca 1817 N. C..
Nancy ----- (1st wife?), b. ca 1817 N. C.. Rachel Ann Broach
(2nd wife - m. 18 Aug. 1861), b. ca 1826 Ala. (1870 Census).

Childs, J., John. 12&13-8-23 & 7-8-24. John Childs, b. ca
1800 N. C., in Ala. by 1847. Eliza ----- (wife?), b. ca
1809 N. C..

Christian, Lewis. 19-13-25(B). Lewis Christian, b. 7 May 1825
S. C., d. 18 Sept. 1896 (Christian Bible). Cyntha Sarah
Frances Spratling (wife - m. 20 July 1847 where?), b. 17
Dec. 1829 Ga., d. 25 Sept. 1896 (ibid).

Clapp, Julius R.. 31-13-25(B). No further record. He may
have been the Julius R. Clapp who m. Eleanor Howard 5 Sept.
1839 Muscogee Co., Ga..

Clark, James. 36-11-25 & 31-11-26. James Clark, b. 1791
Edgefield Dist., S. C., d. 1872, father of Whitfield Clark
(Pike Co., Ala. Obits). Harriet Wise (wife), b. ca 1795
S. C., daughter of Jacob Wise (Rev. Soldier) who died by
Nov. 1849 Barbour Co., Ala.. His will was written Sept.
1845 Edgefield Dist., S. C. (OR 3, p. 396/7).

Clements, J.. 32-11-27. James Clements, b. ca 1800 S. C.,
in Ala. by 1831. In 1839, he sold land in 26&32-11-27 to
Benjamin Clements of Darlington Dist., S. C.(CR B, p.490).
Nancy ----- (wife?), b. ca 1811 Ga..

Clyatt, Wm.. 23-13-29(R), William Cliatt, b. 1 July 1813,*
Hancock Co., Ga. (MRA, Vol. II, p. 876). Louisa Averett
(wife), b. 28 May 1824, d. 26 Feb. 1879, daughter of Matthew Averett (Cliatt Bible). Both are buried in the Averett
family cemetery).

Coaker, I. N.. 24-10-27 & 19-10-28. Isaac N. Coker, b. ca
1816 S. C., to Ala. by 1842. Elizabeth (wife?), b. ca 1810
S. C..

Cobb, J. A.. 21&22-13-26. James A. Cobb, b. ca 1817 Ga.,
d. 17 June 1898, buried Raham Baptist Church Cem., son of
Jacob Cobb who died by Feb. 1863 (OR 12, p. 861/3), brother
of Tempe Jenkins (OR 3, p. 350). Elizabeth Jane Weaver
(wife - m. 11 May 1848), b. ca 1833 Ga., daughter of Absolem
Weaver (Mar. I, p. 332).

*d. 1 Nov. 1885

Cobb, J., Jos.. 21-13-26, 4-12-27 & 33-13-27. Joseph Cobb, b. 1 Aug. 1799 Ga., d. 12 Nov. 1876, in Ala. by 1828, son of Jacob Cobb who died by Feb. 1863 (OR 12, p. 861/3), buried Ramah Baptist Church Cem.. Elizabeth Cook (2nd wife - m. 7 Feb. 1843), b. ca 1809 Ga..

Cobb, M.. 8&16-12-29. McCuin Cobb, b. ca 1813 Ga., d. by July 1853 (OR 5, p. 345). In 1838, he was of Muscogee Co., Ga. (Muscogee Co., Ga. Deed Book A, p. 110). Harriet W. Lee (wife - m. 13 Oct. 1831 Pulaski Co., Ga.), b. ca 1817 Ga..

Cochran, J.. 3-11-28 & 19-11-29. John Cochran, b. 6 March 1813 near Greenville (Cocke Co.), Tenn., d. 13 June 1873, buried Fairview Cem., Eufaula, Ala.. His first two wives were sisters (one named Mary), daughters of Alford W. Wellborn who died by Jan. 1858 in Meriweather Co., Ga. (OR 9, p. 1/2 & 6/8). His third wife was their cousin ("History of Barbour Co., Ala." by Thompson). Caroline Hopson Toney (4th wife - m. 18 Sept. 1866), b. 16 March 1847 Ala. (1860 Census), d. 20 June 1895, buried Fairview Cem., Eufaula, Ala., daughter of Washington Toney (DAB Vol. III, p. 360/1). She m. (2) ----- Bradford (Backtracking in Barbour Co., Ala.", p. 318, by Walker).

Cody, Mary. 28-13-26(B). James Cody died by March 1847 (CR G, p. 571/2). Mary ----- (wife?), b. ca 1800 Ga.. In 1850, Sarah Stinson, b. ca 1770 S. C., was enumerated in the Mary Cody household.

Cole, N. B.. 10-13-27. Noah B. Cole, b. 11 Jan. 1795, d. 1854 Caddo Par., La., son of Daniel Cole, b. ca 1760, d. 1831 Pike Co., Ala. and Mary Dubose, b. 1765 S. C., d. 1851 Pike Co., Ala. (Transactions of the Huguenot Soc. of S. C., No. 77, p. 46/69). Wealtha Taylor (wife - m. 28 Jan. 1819 Conecuh Co., Ala.),b. 1799, d. 1876 (Vol. II, p. 26/7).

Coleman, B. F.. 6-9-29. Benjamin F. Coleman, b. ca 1840 Ala., minor heir of William Coleman who died by July 1846 (OR 3, p. 12).

Coleman, W. & K.. 31&32-13-25(B). William Coleman died by July 1846 (OR 2, p. 271). Keziah ----- (wife), b. ca 1800 S. C..

Collins, C. B.. 30-13-25(B). No further record.

Collins, W., Wilson. 25,26,27,29,35&36-10-25 & 32-10-26. Wilson Collins, b. ca 1786 N. C., d. by Dec. 1875 (OR 20, p. 324/6). Elizabeth Early (wife), daughter of Jesse Early who died by 1843 (OR 2, p. 45).

Comer, J. F.. 3,4&9-12-27 & 21,28,33&34-13-27. John Fletcher Comer, b. ca 1811 Ga., d. 27 April 1858, son of Hugh

25

Moss Comer (Rev. Soldier) who moved from Va. to Jones Co., Ga.
and Anne Tripp (DAB, Vol. III, p. 387/8). Catharine Lucinda
Drewry (wife - m. 11 Nov. 1841 Jones Co., Ga.), b. 11 Nov.
1823 Ga., d. 7 March 1898 Savannah, Ga. "Eufaula Times &
News", March 10, 1898). Both are buried in Springhill Meth.
Church Cem.. She was a daughter of John Drewry & Elizabeth
Wallace of Jones Co., Ga. (DAB Vol. III, p. 387/8).

Condry, G. M.. 13-9-26. George M. Condry moved to Sumter
Co., Fla. ca 1849 (Vol. II, p. 84/5). Molcie Lee (wife -
m. 24 April 1834), b. 24 July 1811, d. 10 Sept. 1889 Sumter
Co., Fla., daughter of Arthur Lee, b. 16 Aug.1785, d. Nov.
1856 and Mary Lee, daughter of Simon Lee(Ibid).

Condry, John. 12&13-9-26 & 18-9-27. John D. Condry, b. ca
1805 S. C., d. by Jan. 1862 (OR 12, p. 90), in Ala. by 1833.
Elizabeth ----- (wife?), b. ca 1817 S. C., probably died by
Feb. 1870 (OR 17, p. 900).

Connelly, Jas. Z.. 4-11-26 & 18-12-26. Rev. James Zachariah Connelly, b. ca 1802 S. C., d. by Nov. 1866 (OR 15,
p. 144/5), probably from Newberry Dist., S. C. as son,
William Pearce Harmon Connelly was born there in 1835
("History of Methodist" p. 1138 by Lazenby). Rachel Harmon
(wife - Mrs. H. M. Martinson, Knoxville, Tenn.), b. ca 1810
S. C..

Conner, Geo. D.. 18&27-13-28. Dr. George D. Conner, b. ca
1820 S. C., probably son of George & Louisa M. Conner who
gave him the above land in 1845 (CR G, p. 319). In 1844,
they were living in Macon Co., Ala. (CR G, p. 497), later
moved to Glennville (now Russell Co.), Ala. (CR L, p. 437).
Mariah G. Brown (wife - m. 17 Jan. 1856), widow of James
R. Upshaw (m. 24 Dec. 1844). She was born ca 1830 Ga..

Cook, A.. 25-13-25(B). Archibald Cook was head of a household in the 1840 Census but his age was not given. He was
not in the 1850 or 1860 Census.

Cook, G. P.. 15-11-26. George P. Cook, b. Jefferson Co.,
Ga. (1906 Census of Confederate Veterans), son of John Cook,
Sr. (OR 9, p. 248) and Charity Turner who m. 1 July 1819
Pulaski Co., Ga..

Cook, J., John C.. 2,11&15-11-24. John Cook, Sr., d. 1
June 1858 (OR 9, p. 205). Charity Turner (wife - m. 1 July
1819 Pulaski Co., Ga.).

Cooper, A. D.. 12-10-26 & 7&18-10-27. Archibald D. Cooper,
b. ca 1801 Ga., d. by April 1860 (OR 10, p. 686), in Ala. by
1830. Elizabeth ----- (wife), b. ca 1801 N. C., d. by Oct.
1862 (OR 12, p. 472/3).

Cooper, Thos.. 23-12-29. Thomas Cooper, b. ca 1807 N. C..
Elizabeth ----- (wife?), b. ca 1819 S. C..

Cooper, Wiley L.. 5-10-27. Wiley L. Cooper, b. ca 1820
Ala., son of Archibald D. Cooper (OR 11, p. 227). Elizabeth
----- (wife?), b. ca 1824 Ala..

Copeland, John N.. 5&6-10-29. John Nelson Copeland, b. 24
Oct. 1811 Barnwell Dist., S. C., d. 20 July 1859, of Muscogee
Co., Ga. in 1837 (CR A, p. 441). Caroline Elizabeth Cannon
(wife), b. 27 Oct. 1811 Barnwell Dist., S. C., d. 17 July
1866, both buried Fairview Cem., Eufaula, Ala.. She had
married (1) ----- Garvin. She was a daughter of Simeon R.
Cannon and Mary Owen Kennedy (DAB, Vol. III, p. 440/1). See
P. N. Cannon.

Costello, ----- 1-10-25. Pierre Darcy Costello, b. 22 March
1827 near Dublin, Ireland, d. 4 Jan. 1863 Murfreesboro, Tenn.,
son of Daniel Edmond Costello and Mary McNamara of Dublin,
Ireland. She m. (2) Mr. O"Flarity in New York City (DAB,
Vol. III, p. 404/5). Cordelia Ann Lee (wife - m. 18 Dec. 1855
where?), daughter of Charles Stephen Lee and Elizabeth Mary
Broughton of Ga. (ibid).

Cotton, R.. 33-9-27. Richard Cotton was head of a household in the 1840 Census, age 50/60. In 1830, he witnessed
a deed from Joel Sims to Avent W. Cotton ⊙ Ga. (CR D, p.
179/80).

Cotton, W. W.. 10-10-26. William W. Cotton bought land in
7-10-27 from A. W. Cotton in 1840 (CR B, p. 633). In 1842,
he and Avent W. Cotton (wife Dorinda) sold land (CR D, p.
181/2).

Cowan, E. B.. 1-10-25. Ebenezer B. Cowan, b. ca 1816 Ala.,
received a military land grant in 1-10-25 in 1853 (#30121).
Catherine McIntosh (wife - m. 6 Aug. 1848), b. ca 1827 S. C.,
heir (daughter?) of Daniel McIntosh who died 23 Jan. 1866
(OR 15, p. 288/91).

Cowan, F.. 14-12-29 & 13&14-13-29(R). Franklin Cowan probably lived in Stewart Co., Ga. (CR K, p. 158). The above
land was patented by John Cowan. Amanda M. Cabaniss (wife -
m. 5 Jan. 1851 Stewart Co., Ga.).

Cowan, J. G.. 13&24-12-29. John G. Cowan, b. ca 1806 S. C.,
a Primitive Baptist Minister, ordained 21 June 1845 Barbour
Co., Ala. (Mar. I, p. 210), to Ala. from Ga. by 1844. Mary
----- (wife), b. ca 1808 N. C..

Cowan, W. L.. 23-12-27 & 4-13-27. Dr. William L. Cowan, b.
ca 1807 Tenn, d. 2 May 1859 (Vol. I, p. 139). Ann S. Pugh

(wife - lic. issued 21 Feb. 1834), b. ca 1812 Ga., d. 1869 Bullock Co., Ala., daughter of Robert Pugh and Anne Silvia Tilman (Vol. I, p.139).

Cowan, Wm. R.. 2-10-25 & 28&33-11-26. William R. Cowan, b. ca 1812 Ga., d. by Jan. 1863 (OR 12, p. 778/80), possibly related to W. R. Cowan (Rev. Soldier) who lived in Barbour Co. in 1840 (Rev. Soldiers of Ala., Vol. II). Elizabeth C. Clark (wife - m. 20 Aug. 1854), b. 19 Sept. 1833 Columbus, Ga., d. 9 Sept. 1902, daughter of James Clark ("The Clayton Record", Sept. 19, 1902). See James Clark.

Cowart, Wm.. 21&28-12-26. William Cowart, b. ca 1783 S. C., d. by Oct. 1855 (OR 6, p. 490). Susan W. Worthington (2nd wife - m. 26 Dec. 1841), b. ca 1822 N. C., heir (daughter?) of Robert Worthington who died by Dec. 1858 (OR 9, p. 470). She married (2) Jesse Robson 23 Dec. 1857..

Cowles, G. W.. 9-11-28. No further record.

Cox, E., Emanuel. 13-10-25, 16-9-26 & 18-10-26. Emanuel Cox, b. 28 July 1795 Anson Co., N. C., d. 11 June 1872, to Ala. by 1830 (Vol. I, p. 38). He served in the War of 1812 from Hancock Co., Ga.. Sarah McNeill (wife), b. 22 April 1806 Richmond Co., N. C., d. 21 Dec. 1889, daughter of John McNeill, an early settler of Barbour Co.. Both are buried in Clayton Cem.. (Vol. I, p. 38).

Cox, Nancy. 19&30-9-24. Nancy Cox is not in the early records of Barbour Co. unless she was "Jane", wife of Wm. Cox in the 1850 Census.

Cox, William. 25-9-23 & 17,27&30-9-24, 2&3-9-25 & 1-11-27. William Cox, b. ca 1785 S. C., possibly brother of Edward W. Cox, b. ca 1780 S. C.. They entered land in the same area from 1829 through 1837 (Vol. I, p. 38). Jane ----- (wife?), b. ca 1785 S. C..

Crapp, L. C.. 2&3-13-29(R). In 1843, Hampton Smith (wife Sarah), Thomas Hoxey (wife Mary R.) and Jno. Warren, all of Muscogee Co., Ga., deeded land in 2-13-29 to Louisa C. Crapp and her children of Barbour Co., Ala., John C. Davis, trustee (CR E, p. 368/9).

Crawford, A. P., Alexr.. 3-11-28 & 28&33-12-28. Dr. Alexander P. Crawford, b. 11 July 1806 Va., d. 30 Aug.1852, to Ala. by 1841. He is buried in Fairview Cem., Eufaula, Ala.. Mrs. Cassandra A. Butler (wife - m. 3 Dec. 1839 Crawfordsville (Taliaferro Co.), Ga.). She was the widow of Thomas W. Butler.

Crawford, N., Nicholas. 31-9-28. Nicholas W. Crawford,

b. 1811 N. C., d. 20 May 1888, son of Arthur Crawford (CR
C, p. 157). Lincey D. Hayes (wife - m. 22 Nov. 1843 Henry
Co., Ala.), b. 4 Dec. 1821 N. C., d. 1 Sept. 1891, daughter
of Calvin Hayes ("History of Henry Co., Ala." by Scott, p.
208). Both are buried in County Line Cem., Henry Co., Ala..

Crawford, Wm. M.. 19,20,29&30-13-26(B). No further record.

Creech, Aaron. 6-10-27. Aaron Creech, b. ca 1821 N. C..
Charity Creech (wife - m. 27 Jan. 1848), b. ca 1829 Ala..
Also in this household in 1850 was Jane Creech, b. ca 1785
S. C.. In 1850, she was granted a military land patent in
2-11-25 (#5749).

Creech, J. C.. 6-10-26. Joshua C. Creech, b. ca 1808, d.
ca 1849 (Vol. II, p. 30). Elizabeth Pynes (?) (wife), b.
ca 1820 Ga., m. (2) Levi Glass 3 March 1850.

Creech, Wm. C.. 12-10-26 & 6-10-27. William Carter Creech,
b. 4 Jan. 1810 Ga., d. 23 Feb. 1892 Butler Co., Ala.. Amanda
Elizabeth Daniels (wife), b. 19 Sept. 1820 Ga., d. 9 Sept.
1909 Butler Co., Ala. (Vol. II, p.30).

Creel, John. 29-9-27. John Creel, b. ca 1827 S. C., living
in St. Clair Co., Ala. in 1863, son of Levi Creel (OR 12, p.
912/3). Mary Sikes (wife - m. 15 Feb. 1849), b. ca 1829 S.C..

Creel, Lewis (should be Levi). 29&30-9-27. Levi Creel, b.
ca 1806 S. C., d. by March 1862 (OR 12, p. 232). Sinia -----
(2nd wife), b. ca 1803 S. C., may have gone to Texas after
1863.

Creel, Louisa. 32-9-27. She patented this land in 1844 -
no further record.

Creel, Thomas. 32-9-27. Thomas Creel, b. ca 1814 S. C..
He bought the above land from Solomon Creel (wife Mahaley)
in 1843. Levi Creel and Jackson Creel witnessed the deed
(CR E,p. 475). Louisa ----- (wife), b. ca 1816 S. C..
She may have been the Louisa Creel who patented land in
1844.

Creel, Wm.. 31-9-27. William Creel, b. ca 1815 S. C., in
Ala. by 1837. Sarah ----- (wife?), b. ca 1816 S. C..

Crews, A., Arthur. 28,29,30,31,32&33-10-27. Arthur A.
Crews, b. 28 Jan. 1792 Ga., d. 1 Feb. 1872. Mary V. King
(1st wife), b. 11 April 1796 S. C., d. 29 May 1861, both
buried New Hope Cem.. Maisy C. Walker (2nd wife - m. 12
May 1863), b. 21 Dec. 1832 Ala., d. 17 Jan. 1889, buried
Walker family cemetery, daughter of Lewis Walker and Nancy
McInnis; granddaughter of Solomon Walker (Rev. Soldier)
and Gooden Cox (Vol. II, p. 36).

Crews, John. 6-11-25 & 31-12-25. Dr. John E. Crews, b. 1 Jan. 1819 Jones Co., Ga. ("The Clayton Record", June 6, 1901), d. 2 June 1901, son of Arthur Crews and Mary King (MRA Vol. I, p. 411). Margaret E. Dubose (wife - m. 25 March 1851), b. 30 June 1831 S. C. (1860 Census), d. 15 May 1917, both buried Clayton Cem..

Crews, W. B.. 29,32&33-10-27. William B. Crews, b. 8 Dec. 1816 Ga., d. 20 July 1865. Catharine McSwean (wife - m. 8 Dec. 1842), b. 25 Feb. 1822 N. C., d. 25 Jan. 1902, both buried New Hope Cem.. She m. (2) Rev. Wm. H. Chambers 7 Jan. 1868. She was a daughter of Roderick McSwean (Vol. I, p. 127).

Crocker, J. M.. 30-10-28. John M. Coker, b. ca 1805 S. C.. Nancy ----- (2nd wife?), b. ca 1825 S. C.

Crocker, M.. 29-9-24. Monroe Crocker, b. ca 1815 Ga.. Eliza Lewis (wife - m. 22 July 1841), b. ca 1817 Ga..

Crossley, A. Estate. 29-13-25(B). Andrew Crossley, b. Darlington Dist., S. C., d. 1836 Eufaula, Ala.. He was a merchant of Pike Co., Ala. (MRA Vol. II, p. 830/1). Jane Woods (wife), b. Jefferson Co., Ga. (ibid).

Cumbie A., 34-13-25(B). Andrew Cumbie, b. ca 1804 S. C., to Ga. by 1832, to Ala. by 1846. He was ordained a Baptist Minister at Bethel Baptist Church (where?) 9 Nov. 1833, recorded Barbour Co., Ala. 3 Nov. 1846 (Mar. I, p. 246).. An Andrew Cumbie was on the Presbytery of Salem United Baptist Church, Stewart Co., Ga. on 23 Sept. 1844 when Daniel Cumbie was ordained. Recorded Barbour Co., Ala. 29 Nov. 1848 (Mar. I, p. 340). Celia ----- (wife?), b. ca 1807 S. C..

Cumbie, Jas.. 6-12-25(B). James Cumbie is not in any census of Barbour Co.. James C. Cumbie was on the Presbytery of Bethel Church in Randolph Co., Ga. 30 March 1855 (Mar. I, p. 210). James O. Cumbie was on the Presbytery of Pleasant Hill Church (Barbour Co.) 9 June 1855 (Mar. I, p. 215). James O. Cumbie m. Lucy Clyatt 5 March 1837 Stewart Co., Ga..

Cumbie, J. J.. 16-12-25(B), John J. Cumbie was ordained a Baptist Minister 17 Oct. 1841 at Teman (?) Church, Henry Co., Ga., recorded Barbour Co., Ala. 29 Jan. 1850 (Mar. I, p. 387).

Cunning, J., John. 1&2-10-28 & 35&36-11-28. He sold the above land in Jan. 1856, at which time he was of Pike Co., Ala. (CR N, p. 235). Elizabeth Ann ----- (wife - ibid).

Cunningham, D.. 27,32,34&35-11-27. Duncan Cunningham, b.

ca 1800 Cumberland Co., N. C., to Ala. by 1831, d. 1877
(Mrs. Gayla Glover, New Orleans, La.). Elizabeth McIntosh
(1st wife?). Elizabeth DeWitt (2nd wife - m. by Sept.
1845 CR G, p. 11).

Cunningham, P.. 11-10-27. Peter Cunningham, b. ca 1820
Ala., d. May 1874 ("Eufaula Tri-Weekly News", June 2,
1874). Dovey E. ----- (1st wife?), b. ca 1831 Fla..Amanda
Williams (2nd wife - m. 11 May 1854), b. ca 1836 Ala., d.
by 1875, daughter of John L. Williams; granddaughter of
William Williams who died by Nov. 1846 (Vol. II, p. 168/70).

Curenton, H.. 8-11-29. In the 1840 Census, there was an
H. Currington, age 30/40, and family. He is not in the
1850 or 1860 Census..

Curenton, W.. 21-13-29(R). W. Curenton patented the above
land in 1842 (Barbour Co., Ala. Tract Book). Wilson Cureton was an heir of Reason Cureton who died by March 1859
(Original Papers, Box 76).

Curington, J.. 16-13-26(B). No further record.

Currie, D., Danl., Daniel. 8&17-9-25. Daniel Currie, b. 5
Nov. 1796 Richmond Co., N. C., d. 11 Oct. 1867, son of Angus
Currie, Sr. (b. 1775 Scotland, d. 24 Aug. 1840) and Cath-
arine ----- (b. 1775 Scotland, d. 5 Nov. 1842). Isabella
McKinnon (?) (wife - m. 12 Sept. 1850 - OR 21, p. 190), b.
1801 N. C., d. 26 March 1881. They are all buried in Pea
River Presbyterian Church Cem.. Pea River Presby. Ch. Records.

Curry, Wm.. 12-13-27. William Curry, d. by Oct. 1858 (OR
9, p. 43), Jane A. ----- (wife). In a cemetery near Glennville (Russell Co., Ala.) is a grave of Sarah L. Ivy, b. 6
Sept. 1829, d. 27 Nov. 1864, daughter of William and Jane A.
Curry.

Danford, Danl. 25-10-24. Daniel Danford, b. ca 1825 N. C.
(1860 Census). Dorothea Jane Miller (2nd wife? - m. 26 Oct.
1845), b. ca 1820 Ga. (1860 Census), niece of John B. Mc-
Innis who died by 1865 (Vol. I, p. 113).

Danford, E.. 17-10-25. Edmund (or Edward) Danford, b. ca
1833 Ala., son of Abraham Danford (CR J, p. 180). In 1850,
he was in the household of Abraham Danford (b. ca 1782 S.C.)
and Sarah Danford (b. ca 1785 S. C.).

Danford, J.. 13-13-26. Joseph Danford, b. 15 Jan. 1813
Ga., d. 6 June 1896, in Ala. by 1841. Malinda Jane -----
(wife), b. 1818 N. C., d. 3 Nov. 1891, both buried Antioch
Church Cem..

Danford, Thomas. 19-10-25. Thomas Danford, b. ca 1810 N. C., in Ala. by 1836. In 1867, he was living in Bullock Co.,Ala. (OR 17, p. 365). Virginia Louisa Sloan (wife), b. ca 1820 Ga., daughter of John Sloan, Sr. (CR H, p. 452).

Danforth, S. A.. 29-11-29. Joshua H. Danforth, b. ca 1817 Ga., in Ala. by 1841. Sarah A. Snipes (wife), b. ca 1824 S. C., d. by Jan. 1900 Augusta, Ga., buried Fairview Cem., Eufaula, Ala. ("Eufaula Times & News", Jan. 4, 1900), heir of William H. Snipes (OR 2, p. 139) and wife Maria A. (OR 9, p. 563).

Daniel , J. L. & J. L. Estate. 24&25-13-28(R) & 19&30-13-29(R). James L. Daniel, b. 11 July 1797 Hancock Co., Ga., d. 14 April 1846. Eliza C. Butts (wife - m. 3 Dec. 1818 Hancock Co., Ga.), b. 23 July 1802 Hancock Co., Ga., d. 5 Oct. 1857, both buried in the Ivy family cemetery, Russell Co., Ala.. Also buried in this cemetery is Martha P. Daniel, d. 9 Sept. 1842, age 65, possibly the mother of James L. Daniel.

Daniel, L. L.. 10&15-13-26. Levi L. Daniel, b. ca 1817 Ga., son of John Daniel and brother of John William Daniel and Benjamin Daniel (OR 2, p. 151). Ellen E. Aspinwall (wife - m. 8 July 1845), b. ca 1827 Ga.. Also in this household in 1850 was Sarah M. Blount, b. ca 1795 N. C..

Daniel, Robert. 25-11-26. Robert Daniel died by May 1848 (OR 3, p. 201), no heirs named.

Danner, T. M.. 11,23&24-8-23. Thomas M. Danner, b. 8 May 1807 Ga., d. 16 June 1879, buried in the Danner family cemetery, probably son of Abraham Danner who died by Feb. 1839 Original Papers, Box 86). Mary A. ----- (wife), b. 9 Jan. 1813 S. C., d. 30 June 1890.

Dansby, I., Isham. 15&27-9-24. Isham M. Dansby, b. ca 1810 S. C., living in Choctaw Co., Ala. by 1855 (Vol. I, p. 42). Abigail J. McClure (wife), b. ca 1823 S. C..

Dansby, John. 1-8-23 & 6,7&10-8-24. John Dansby, b. ca 1805 S. C., probably son of Winza Dansby (Vol. I, p. 41). Sarah ----- (wife), b. ca 1817 Ga..

Davis, E.. 5&21-11-26. Elisha Davis, b. ca 1803 Ga., d. May 1872 (Original Papers, Box 358), in Ala. by 1836. Serena Bennett (wife), b. ca 1815 Ga., sister of Ryan, Redman, Orren and Elizabeth Bennett (OR 10, p. 236/7).

Davis, G., Gardner. 19,20,29&30-13-29(R). Gardner Harwell Davis, b. 1804 Upson Co., Ga., d. 4 March 1873, son of Martha Harwell Davis (DAB, Vol. III, p. 461/2). Mary Trice (wife)

b. ca 1814 Ga., d. 21 Aug. 1880, both buried Glennville Cem. (Russell Co.), Ala.. She was of a Talbot Co., Ga. family (DAB Vol. III, p. 461/2).

Davis, J., John. 13&24-13-26 & 18&19-13-27. John Davis, b. 1803 Lenoir Co., N. C., d. 31 March 1871, son of Jacob Davis and Elizabeth Howard who moved from N.C. to Telfair Co., Ga. in 1816; grandson of Ben Davis of Wales & Sallie Griffith (Mrs. Mary Beth Lightfoot, Victoria, Texas). Mary A. Mooney (wife - m. 7 Jan. 1828 Telfair Co., Ga.), b. ca 1808 Ga., daughter of William Mooney (ibid).

Davis, J. F.. 33&34-12-26. John F. Davis, b. ca 1798 Ga., to Ala. by 1831. Catherine ----- (wife?), b. ca 1804 S.C.. A John F. Davis m. Cathy Hight 29 May 1823 Wilkinson Co., Ga..

Davis, Margaret. 12-9-28. John Davis died by Nov. 1846 (OR 2, p. 329). Margaret (Griffin?) wife, b. ca 1800 S. C.. In 1821, Rachael Griffin of Fairfield Dist., S. C. gave slaves to her daughter, Margaret, wife of John Davis (CR C, p. 174). This deed was recorded in Baldwin Co., Ga. 16 Oct. 1833, in Sumter Co., Ga. 15 June 1835 and in Barbour Co., Ala. 23 Dec. 1840..

Davis, W. E.. 4-11-26. William E. Davis, b. ca 1806 Ky.. Mildred ----- (wife?), b. ca 1810 N. C..

Davis, W. K.. 18-9-29. Western K. Davis, b. ca 1824 S. C., son of John Davis who died by Nov. 1846 (OR 3, p. 300). Sarah ----- (wife?), b. ca 1823 Ga..

Dawson, J.. 14-11-25. John Dawson, b. ca 1794 S. C., to Ala. from Ga. by 1842. Keziah ----- (wife), b. ca 1806 Ga..
OR
Joseph Dawson, b. ca 1815 S. C.. Eady M. Price (2nd wife - m. 14 July 1848), b. ca 1831 N. C..

Dawson, Thos. H.. 31-13-28. Rev. Thomas H. Dawson, b. 8 April 1809, d. 19 June 1873. Annie ----- (wife), b. 18 Sept. 1827, d. 16 Oct. 1893, both buried Glennville Cem., Russell Co., Ala..

Dellafield, N.. 7&18-10-25. Nicholas Dellafield patented the above land in 1836 (Barbour Co., Ala. Tract Book) and sold it 28 Feb. 1849 (CR H, p. 638/9).

Dennard, John E.. 14-11-28. John E. Dennard, b. ca 1793/8 Ga. (1850 & 1860 Census), d. 20 Jan. 1867 (OR 16, p. 75/9). In 1841, he was of Houston Co., Ga. (CR D, p. 150). America A. ----- (wife), b. ca 1805 Va. (1860 Census). Also in this household in 1860 was Fielding Ellis, b. ca 1776 Va..

Denson, Jethro. 17-13-29(R). Jethro Denson, b. ca 1778 N.C., d. by July 1851 (OR 4, p. 115/8). Rebecca ----- (wife), b. ca 1786 N. C..

Denson, M.. 21-13-29(R). Matthew Denson, b. ca 1805 N. C., in Miss. 1831, in Ala. by 1837, son of Jethro Denson (OR 4, p. 115/8). Bethia ----- (wife?), b. ca 1810 N. C..

Dent, J. H.. 25-12-25 & 19&30-12-26. John Horry Dent, b. 1815 Newport, R. I., son of a naval officer, Commodore John Herbert Dent (b. 1782 Charles Co., Md., d. 29 July 1823 near Charleston, S. C.) and Anne Horry (Biography of Maximillan Wellborn by Hopkins). The family home of John Horry Dent was Colleton Dist., S. C. (Ala. Historical Quarterly, Vol. 25, No. 1 & 2, p. 136). Mary Elizabeth Morrison (1st wife, m. 1835 S. C.), b. ca 1818 S. C., daughter of Mrs. Mary A. Morrison who died in 1836 (Ala. Historical Quarterly, Vol. 25, No. 1 & 2, p. 136). Fanny A. Whipple (2nd wife - m. 25 July 1854), b. ca 1828 Conn. (1860 Census), d. 20 Feb. 1875 Rome, Ga. ("Eufaula News", March 6, 1875). Elizabeth Ann Dowd (3rd wife) (Ala. Hist. Quarterly, Vol. 25, No. 1 & 2, p. 36).

Deshazo, B. F.. 2&12-10-26. Benjamin Franklin Deshazo, b. ca 1822 S. C., probably son of Gracy Deshazo (b. ca 1787 S. C.). He was a full brother to William R. and Thomas J. Deshazo and a half brother to John E Deshazo (CR D, p. 342/3). Laura Creech (wife - m. 7 Feb. 1847), b. ca 1826 Ga., daughter of David Creech, b. 1773, d. by 1840 (Vol. II, p. 30/1).

Deshazo, Gracy. 30-11-25. Gracy Deshazo, b. ca 1787 S. C., possibly widow of Robert Deshazo, Sr. (Vol. I, p. 46). In 1850 and 1860, she was living with Benjamin Franklin Deshazo. This family may have come from Edgefield Dist., S. C..

Deshazo, H. P. (should be P. H.). 28-10-28. Paul Hamilton Deshazo, b. ca 1831 Ala., d. 1 Sept. 1864 New Orleans, La., son of Wilson Deshazo, b. ca 1804 Edgefield Dist., S. C., d. 27 Nov. 1892 and his 1st wife, Delilah Prescott (?), b. ca 1809 Ga. (Vol. I, p. 44). Sarah Ginwright (wife - m. 2 April 1851), b. ca 1831 N. C., d. Lakeland, Fla. (ibid).

Dewitt, A., Ann. 33&34-11-28. John Dewitt died by Feb. 1849 (OR 2, p. 214). He was formerly of Chesterfield Dist., S.C. (CR D, p. 229/30). Ann ----- (wife), b. ca 1784 S. C.. In 1850, she was in the household of John A. Moseley.

Dewitt, Saml. 1-10-28. In 1852, Elizabeth R. Dewitt, alias Elizabeth R. Cunningham, of Jackson Co., Fla. was attorney-in-fact for Samuel B. Dewitt and wife Sarah of Darlington Dist., S. C. to sell the above land.

Dewitt, W. T.. 33&34-11-28. William T. Dewitt, b. ca 1808 S. C., d. 21 July 1890 Geneva, Ala. ("Eufaula Daily Times", Aug. 8, 1890). Elizabeth (Cunningham?) (wife), b. ca 1805 S. C.. In 1852, Elizabeth R. Dewitt, alias Elizabeth R. Cunningham, was of Jackson Co., Fla. (CR K, p. 264).

Dixon, J. J.. 23-13-25(B). John J. Dixon (Dickson), b. ca 1805 Ga., a Primitive Baptist Minister. Luna ----- (1st wife?), b. ca 1807 S. C. (1860 Census), d. 27 Nov. 1863, buried Fellowship Cem., Bullock Co., Ala..

Dobbins, J. S.. 26-13-29(R). John S. Dobbins, b. ca 1813 Ga.. Evelina Williams (wife), b. ca 1813 Ga., daughter of Zachariah Williams who died 1840 (Vol. II, p. 177).

Dodson, Wm.. 6-13-25(B). No further record.

Dorman, Wm.. 16-10-25. William Dorman, b. ca 1801 S. C., d. by June 1871 (OR 18, p. 630/1), in Ala. by 1833. Penelope Smith (wife), b. ca 1814 Ga.. She was a sister of Thomas J. Smith of Ft. Bend Co., Texas. Their mother died Sandersville, Ga. and left her two children with friends. They were reunited 70 years later ("Eufaula Times & News", Oct. 23, 1883).

Doster, W.(?) B.. 4-8-25. No further record.

Dowling, E., E. G., Jr., Elias. 9-11-26 & 18&19-11-27. Elias G. Dowling, b. ca 1821 S. C., probably son of Elias and Mary Dowling. Their sixth child, Seny Lena, was born ca 1825 in Darlington Dist., S. C. ("A Dowling Family of the South", p. 69/71, by R. A. Dowling). Mrs. Lucilla S. Flournoy (wife - m. 2 Nov. 1848), b. 15 Aug. 1824 N. C., d. 24 Oct. 1885, buried Mt. Nebo Cem..

Dowling, H., Hansford. 18&19-11-27, 26,33,34&36-12-26. Hansford Dowling, b. ca 1818 S. C., d. May 1895 ("The Clayton Courier", May 25, 1895), oldest son of Elias and Mary Dowling ("A Dowling Family of the South", p. 68, by R. A. Dowling). Martha Weaver (1st wife - m. 26 Jan. 1847), b. 13 Feb. 1826 Ga., d. 6 Jan. 1887, buried Zion Chapel Meth. Church Cem., daughter of Rev. John C. Weaver who died 1872 (ibid). Nancy Harrod (2nd wife - m. 3 Dec. 1891), d. 20 Nov. 1919 (ibid).

Drewry, J., John. 16,17,21&32-13-27. John Drewry, b. 1800, d. 1 April 1857. In 1848 and 1852, he was of Jones Co., Ga. (CR H, p. 273/4 & CR J, p. 632/3). Elizabeth Wallace (wife), b. 1 Feb. 1795 Ga. (1860 Census), d. 16 Jan.1872. Both are buried in Spring Hill Methodist Church Cem..

Drewry, W. 20&29-13-27. No further record.

Dubose, A., Asa. 2,8,11&16-9-27. Asa Dubose patented land
in Barbour Co. in 1835, 1836 & 1837 (Barbour Co., Ala. Tract
Book). No further record.

Dubose, D.. 26-8-25. Deshabo D. Dubose, b. ca 1820 S. C.,
d. by Nov. 1865 (OR 15, p. 58/60), son of Jeptha Dubose;
grandson of Jeptha Dubose; great-grandson of John Dubose;
great-great-grandson of Peter Dubose who died 1736 ("Transactions of the Huguenot Society of S. C." No. 77, p. 46/69).
Milly Sheppard (wife - m. 10 Aug. 1843).

Dubose, E. E.. 23-12-28. Edwin E. Dubose, b. ca 1803 S.C.,
to Ala. by 1839. Caroline Sophronia ----- (wife), b. ca
1815 S. C.. In the estate of Polly Kennedy in March 1845,
there was a bequest to Caroline Sophronia, wife of Edwin E.
Dubose. (CR F, p. 435).

Dubose, James. 17-9-26 & 15-9-27. James Dubose, b. ca 1801
S. C., brother of Deshabo Dubose ("Transactions of the Huguenot Society of S. C.", No. 77, p. 46/69). Mary ----- (wife)
b. ca 1814 S. C..

Dubose, J., Joel. 14-10-27, 11-11-27, 1,2,3,5,7,10,11,13,
14,21&23-10-28 & 18-10-29. Joel Dubose, b. ca 1833 S. C.,
probably son of Malikiah Dubose (b. 15 March 1800 S. C.,
d. 12 Jan. 1847) and Sarah S. Floyd (b. 1802 Darlington
Dist., S. C.). ("Transactions of the Huguenot Society of
S. C.", No. 77, p. 46/69). Sarah Scisscon Dubose (b. 12
Jan. 1802, d. 14 May 1892) is buried in Mt. Aerial Cem..
In 1850, she was head of the household in which Joel Dubose
was living. Angelina Hancock (wife - m. 13 Sept. 1852).

Dubose, R., R. E.. 23,24&26-8-25. Robert E. Dubose, b. ca
1813 S. C., d. by Jan. 1870 (OR 17, p. 839), brother of
Deshabo Dubose ("Transactions of the Huguenot Society of
S. C.", No. 77, p. 46/69). Alcey Thomas (wife - m. 3 Nov.
1842), b. ca 1825 S. C..

Dubose, S. J.. 23,24&25-10-27. Seaborn J. Dubose, b. ca
1802 Ga., d. by Oct. 1873 (OR 19, p. 479/81), to Ala. from
S. C. by 1843. Zilpha ----- (1st wife?), b. ca 1810 Sumter
Dist., S. C., d. 3 Oct. 1859 -("Southern Christian Advocate",
24 Nov. 1859). Frances W. ----- (2nd wife). In Sept. 1875,
she was living in Bainbridge, Ga. (OR 20, p. 368).

Duke, D., David. 2-10-27, 34&35-11-27 & 30-12-27. David
Duke, b. 5 Feb. 1805 Clarke Co., Ga., d. 3 July 1883 Pike
Co., Ala. (John Johnston, Brundidge, Ala.), to Ala. by 1837.
Mailda Skinner (wife - m. 25 March 1824 Putnam Co., Ga.),
b. 9 March 1810 Putnam Co., Ga., d. 14 Jan. 1884 Pike Co.,
Ala. (ibid).

Duke, Wm.. 35-10-27. William Duke, b. ca 1812 Ga., to Ala.
by 1840. Margaret ----- (wife?), b. ca 1818 S. C..

Dunford, Thomas J.. 31-12-29. Thomas J. Dunford, b. ca
1820 S. C., in Ala. by 1841. Sarah ----- (wife?), b. ca
1826 Ga..

Dunn, J. M.. 11-11-26. John M. Dunn died 1840 Chambers
Co., Ala. (CR B, p. 639).

Dykes, S., Shad. 32-8-26. Shadrack Dykes, b. ca 1822 Ga..
In May 1842, he bought the above land from Abigail Dykes
(CR E, p. 35/6). In 1852, he received a military land grant
in 29-8-26 (#61936). In Aug. 1835, he was administrator of
the estate of Hiram Dykes (OR 1, p. 10). Eliza -----
(wife?), b. ca 1825 Ala..

Echols, C., Clark. 17-9-27. Clark Echols, b. ca 1817 Ga.,
to Ala. by 1842. Hester ----- (wife), b. ca 1817 Ga..
She was an heir of Acton Nash who died by Aug. 1854 (Original Papers, Box 228).

Echols, S. C.. 26-12-27. There was a Sanders C. Echols
in the 1860 Census, b. ca 1833 Ga.., wife (?) M. E., b. ca
1835 Ga.. In 1852, he bought part of the above land (CR
K, p. 371). He moved to Texas in 1865 and died at Bryan,
Texas 9 June 1882 ("The Eufaula Weekly Bulletin", June 14,
1882).

Edge, Wm.. 2-9-24. William Edge, b. ca 1800 Ga., d. by
Oct. 1871 (OR 18, p. 749/55). Cassia ----- (2nd wife),
b. ca 1798 Ga., d. 17 March 1870 (OR 17, p. 911), widow
of Joseph Henderson (Vol. I, p. 78).

Efurd, J. A.. 1-11-24. John Adam Efurd, b. 18 Feb. 1822
S. C., d. Upshur Co., Texas, son of Adam and Lucy Efurd of
Edgefield Dist., S. C. and Barbour Co., Ala. (Vol. I, p.
52). Mary Cope (wife - m. 12 Sept. 1844), b. ca 1825 N.C..

Efurd, Thos. C.. 1&2-11-24, 16&17-10-25, 3,4,7&19-11-25 &
16-10-26. Thomas C. Efurd, b. 14 Jan. 1800, d. 1860, son
of Adam & Lucy Efurd (Vol. I, p. 51/2). Mary Johnson (wife-
m. 30 Nov. 1820 S. C.), b. 24 May 1805, d. after 1860 in
Texas (Vol. I, p. 51/2).

Eidson, W., Wiley. 20&25-10-25 & 21&32-10-26. Wiley Eidson,
b. ca 1824 Ga.. Martha A. Beasley (wife - m. 21 Jan. 1849),
b. ca 1825 Ga., living Panola Co., Texas in 1880, Smith Co.,
Texas in 1883, daughter of John G. Beasley and Martha Allums
(Vol. II, p. 3/4).

Eiland, A.. 7-13-26. In 1854, Allen Eiland was of Russell Co., Ala. (CR L, p. 601). Elizabeth ----- (wife - ibid).

Elkins, J. B.. 12-9-27. John B. Elkins, b. ca 1818 S. C., to Ala. from Ga. after 1835. Julia ----- (wife?), b. ca 1823 Ga..

Elliott, J.. 15-11-26. James Elliott, b. ca 1803 S. C., in Ala. by 1836. Jane ----- (wife?), b. ca 1815 S. C..

Elmer, M.. 9-9-28 & 3,4,9&10-10-28. Mark Elmer (Elmore) patented land in 3-10-28 in 1835. Sarah Elmer patented land there in 1836 and Matthew Elmer in 1839. In 1837, Luke Elmer patented land in 10-10-28 (Barbour Co., Ala. Tract Book). In 1849, Mark Elmer was of Pike Co., Ala. (CR H, p. 660).

Emerson, B. H.. 4-10-24. Benjamin H. Emerson, b. 17 Oct. 1809 Jones Co., Ga., d. 29 June 1891 ("The Clayton Courier" July 4, 1891). Narcissa Ball (wife - m. 17 Oct. 1833 Jones Co., Ga.), b. ca 1811 Ga..

Engram, O. C.. 15-11-28. Oliver C. Engram, b. ca 1813 N. C., d. by April 1857 (OR 8, p. 196/9),to Ala. from Ga. by 1844. Mariah Louise Dennard (wife), b. ca 1823 Ga., daughter of John E. Dennard who died by Feb. 1867 (OR 16, p. 75/9).

Ethridge, R. C.. 2-9-27 & 7,8,9&18-9-28. Richard C. Ethridge,b. ca 1800 N. C., d. 1867 in Miss. (OR 18, p. 139/40), to Ala. from Ga. by 1839. Elizabeth G. Hendricks (wife - m. 5 July 1824 Crawford Co., Ga.), b. ca 1805 S.C., daughter of Mary M. Hendricks who died by Oct. 1855 (OR 6, p. 481). Mary M. Hendricks was the wife of Micajah Hendricks who died by June 1841 (OR 1, p. 185).

Eubanks, Chas. 8-13-26(B). Charles Eubanks, b. ca 1824 Ala., living in Russell Co., Ala. in Jan. 1864 when he sold land as agent for the heirs of Nancy Eubanks (CR R, p. 397).

Eubanks, N.. 7-13-26. Nancy C. -----, b. ca 1803 Ga., widow of Edward Eubanks (son Edward Thomas Eubanks is buried in Enon Cem., Bullock Co., Ala.). She died by Jan. 1864 when her heirs sold land through their agent, Charles Eubanks of Russell Co., Ala. (CR R, p. 397). An Edward Eubanks m. Nancy Bonner 13 Oct. 1819 Hancock Co., Ga..

Eubanks, T.. 5-11-25. Thomas Eubanks of Sumter Co., Ga. bought land in Barbour Co., Ala. in 1849 (CR H, p. 470/1). In Oct. 1851, Thomas Eubanks and wife, Mary, sold land in Barbour Co. (CR J, p. 463). They are not in the 1850 or 1860 Census.

Evans, J. L. C.. 28-11-24. John L. C. Evans, b. ca 1821
Ga..In 1854, he and Emanuel Evans bought land in 14-11-24
(CR L, p. 80). Martha ----- (wife - m. 20 Oct. 1847), b.
ca 1816 Ga.. She was the widow of ----- Hendrick.

Evans, Jas.. 17-10-27. James Evans, b. ca 1802 Ga., in
Ala. by 1829. He patented part of the above land in 1836
(Barbour Co., Ala. Tract Book). Melinda ----- (wife?),
b. ca 1800 Ga..

Evans, W.. 8-10-27. William Evans, b. ca 1812 Ga.. In
1852, he received a military land grand in 9-10-27 (#16924).
He had no wife in his household in 1850 but had children
ages 5 through 14, all born Ala..

Everett, J. A.. 5-13-26(B). James A. Everett of Horton
(Houston?) Co., Ga. bought land in 4,5,&8-11-27 (CR F,
p. 257).

Faison, N., Nancy. 25,26&35-13-26. Thomas J. Faison, in
Ala. by 1829, d. by Oct. 1847 (OR 3, p. 89). Nancy -----
(wife?), b. ca 1796 Ga..

Farmer, Abel. 24-9-26. Abel Farmer, b. ca 1805 N. C.,
patented the above land in 1836 and was granted a military
patent in 1851 (#7026),(Barbour Co., Ala. Tract Book).
Molsey ----- (wife?), b. ca 1810 S. C..

Farrior, Wm.. 10-9-24. William M. Farrior, b. 1808 N. C.,
d. 26 Jan. 1888. He paid the funeral expenses of Bryant
Farrior who died by Feb. 1845 (OR 2, p. 154). Sarah A. -----
(2nd wife), b. 1825 Ga., d. 10 April 1883. Both are buried
in the family cemetery.

Faulk, A. W.. 12-8-23, 6-8-24 & 31&32-9-24. Alfred Wright
Faulk, b. 30 June 1809 Ga., d. 25 June 1888, son of Henry
L. Faulk, Sr. (Vol. I, p. 57/8). Charlotte Bizzell (wife),
b. 26 Aug. 1817 S. C., d. 28 Nov. 1891, daughter of Bennett
Bizzell (Vol. II, p. 17/8). Both are buried in Faulk Cem..

Faulk, H., Sr.. 5-8-24 & 29&32-9-24. Henry Faulk, Sr.,
b. ca 1800 Ga., d. by 1870, possibly son of John Faulk of
Twiggs Co., Ga. (Vol. I, p. 62). Sarah Pryor (?) (wife),
b. ca 1800 Ga. (Vol. I, p. 62).

Faulk, H., Jr.. 20,29&32-9-24. Henry Lawson Faulk, Jr., b.
14 Nov. 1813 Ga., d. 27 July 1870, buried Faulk Cem., son
of Henry Lawson Faulk & Nancy (Kelly?), probably of Twiggs
Co., Ga. (Vol. I, p. 57/9). Sarah Jane Bizzell (1st wife - m.
29 Jan. 1845), b. 14 Jan. 1823 S. C., d. 24 April 1864,
buried Faulk Cem., daughter of Bennett and Mary Bizzell

(Vol. II, p. 17/8). Nancy L. Faulk (2nd wife - m. 18 Aug. 1865), daughter of Andrew S. Faulk (Vol. I, p. 57/9).

Faulk, Jas.. 3,4&9-9-25. "Red" James Faulk, b. 27 Dec. 1786 N. C., d. 3 May 1851. Rhoda Sellers (1st wife), b. 11 Nov. 1784, d. 8 Nov. 1847. They are buried in the family cemetery. He may have m. (2) Mrs. Mary Griffin, b, ca 1814 Ga.. (Vol. I, p. 53).

Faulk, J.. 2&11-12-25(B). Jesse Faulk, b. 9 Nov. 1822 Ala., d. 26 May 1854, buried in the family cemetery, son of "Red" James Faulk (Vol. I, p. 53/5). Nancy Head (wife - m. 25 July 1843), b. ca 1821 Ga.. She m. (2) John Sloan, Jr. 17 March 1857.

Faulk, Levi. 32-10-25. Levi Faulk, b. 15 May 1827 Ala., d. 8 Nov. 1862 Canton, Texas, son of "Red" James Faulk (Vol. I, p. 53/5). Savannah Sloan (wife), b. 20 June 1820 Ga., d. 2 Oct. 1895 Canton, Texas (ibid).

Faulk, Lorenzo. 2&3-12-25(B). Lorenzo Faulk, b.12 Sept. 1811, d. 26 April 1861, son of "Red" James Faulk. Mary L. Willis (wife), b. 4 April 1818, d. 1 March 1870, both are buried in the family cemetery. She was a daughter of Joel Willis and Elizabeth Head (Vol. I, p. 53).

Faulk, N.. 29,30,32&33-9-24. Henry Lawson Faulk, Sr., d. by 1847 (Vol. I, p. 57/8). Nancy Kelly (?) (wife), b. ca 1790 Ga..

Faulk, W. J.. 20-9-24. William J. Faulk patented this land in 1839 (Barbour Co., Ala. Tract Book). In 1849, he bought land in Barbour Co. from Francis M. Cadenhead - this deed was headed Coffee Co., Ala. (Vol. I, p. 30).

Faulk, Wm. L. (should be K). William Kendrick Faulk, b. 23 Oct.1815, d. 24 April 1872, buried Fincastle Cem., Henderson Co., Texas, son of "Red" James Faulk (Vol. I, p. 53/4). Lucretia Faulk (wife), b. 24 April 1808 Twiggs Co., Ga., daughter of "Black" James Faulk who came to Barbour Co. about 1819 and migrated to Marshall Co., Texas by 1847. (Vol. I, p. 56).

Favors, W. R.. 7&8-11-25. William R. Favors, b. ca 1823 S. C.. Tabitha Herring (wife - m. 14 Sept. 1848). The 1850 Census gives her age as 27 but the 1860 Census gives it as 44 - both say born S. C.. In 1850, there were Herring children in her household aged 6 to 14, all born in Ga.. Depending on her correct age, she could have been a widow with children when she married W. R. Favors or they could have been her brothers and sisters. Living near her in 1860 was Winneford Favors (female), b. ca 1800 S. C..

Feagin, J. M., James M.. 14,23&24-13-25(B). Also J. M.
Feagin, agent for Noah B. Cole. James Madison Feagin, b.
27 Feb. 1814 Jones Co., Ga., d. 28 Nov. 1899 Bullock Co.,
Ala., buried Fellowship Cem., Bullock Co., Ala., son of
Samuel T. Feagin and Nancy Wadsworth (Vol. II, p. 26/7).
Almira C. Cole (wife), b. 11 Dec. 1822 Covington Co., Ala.,
d. 23 Sept. 1900 Bullock Co., Ala., buried Fellowship Cem.,
Bullock Co., Ala.., daughter of Noah B. Cole and Wealtha
Taylor (Vol. II, p. 26/7).

Feagin, S. & Samuel Estate. 14,15,22&23-13-25(B). Samuel
Feagin, b. 8 Oct. 1782 Carthage, N. C., d. 5 March 1848,
buried Fellowship Cem., Bullock Co., Ala., son of Richard
Feagin (DAB Vol. III, p. 565). Nancy Wadsworth (wife - m.
13 May 1813 Jones Co., Ga.), daughter of James Wadsworth
of Jones Co., Ga. (DAB, Vol. III, p. 565).

Fenn, M.. 31-10-24 (Pike Co., Ala.), 1,2,3,10,11&15-10-26
& 34-11-26. Matthew Fenn, b. ca 1798 Ga., d. 8 Sept. 1885
(Vol. I, p. 65). Matilda Williams (1st wife), b. ca 1807
Ga., d. 3 July 1851, buried family cemetery, daughter of
William Williams who died by Nov. 1846 (Vol. II, p. 168 &
178). Martha Cordelia Weston (or Watson) (2nd wife - m.
11 Jan. 1852).

Field, B. B.. 23,28&35-11-28. Bennet B. Field , b. ca
1815 S. C., d. Nov. 1908, buried Fairview Cem., Eufaula,
Ala. ("The Clayton Record", Nov. 27, 1908). Amanda -----
(wife?), b. ca 1824 Ga..

Field, H. H.. 29,30&32-12-26. Henry Hill Field, b. ca 1803
Va., d. 1858 Caldwell Co., Texas, son of Henry Field and
Frances Hill; grandson of Henry Hill and Ann Powell of Cul-
pepper Co., Va.. Diana Slaughter (1st wife). Mary Russell
Calvin (2nd wife), b. ca 1815 Va., of Culpepper Co., Va..
(Mrs. J. C. Rogers, Jr., Rosenberg, Texas).

Finley, Jas.. 28&29-10-24. James Finley may have lived in
Pike Co., Ala.. He sold part of the above land in May 1853
(CR K, p. 447). Elizabeth ----- (wife - ibid).

Flake, S.. 13-13-28(R). Seaborn J. Flake, b. ca 1801 Ga..
He had no wife in 1850 and is not in the 1860 Census.

Flake, Wm.. 17,20&21-13-29(R). Dr. William Flake, b. ca
1800 Ga., d. 6 Nov. 1855 at the home of his son-in-law, T. K.
Appling ("Independent American", Nov. 14, 1855). He was in
Fla. in 1831, in Ga. 1837 and in Ala. 1839. Sarah Ann Chappell (wife - m. 10 Feb.1829 Putnam Co., Ga.). Two of their
daughters are buried in Glennville Cem., Russell Co., Ala..

Flewellen, E. R.. 1&2-13-27. Enos R. Flewellen, b. ca 1810

Ga. He bought the above land 1 Jan. 1859 from the heirs of
Andrew Cullen Battle - the deed was headed Troup Co., Ga..
Susan ----- (wife), b. ca 1817 Ga..

Florence, Thos. J., Thomas. 1-12-27 & 6,18&31-13-28.
Thomas J. Florence, b. 7 July 1814 Ga. (Florence Bible),
d. 3 Aug. 1886 ("Eufaula Daily Times", Aug. 5, 1886, son
of Thomas Florence (b. 5 March 1789, d. 3 June 1863) and
his first wife, Lucy Blalock (b. 5 May 1789, d. 14 March
1829) who married 11 Sept. 1806 Lincoln Co., Ga.; grandson of John Florence and Jane Lashbrook (Florence Bible).
Mary Sewell Frazier (wife - m. 18 Oct. 1837 Lincoln Co.
Ga.), b. ca 1818 Ga..(ibid).

Florence, Wm.. 8-12-28. William Florence, b. 23 Feb.
1811, son of Thomas Florence (Sr.) and Lucy Blalock
(Florence Bible).

Flournoy, H.. 5-10-27. No further record.

Flournoy, J. E. P.. 26-10-24. Joseph E. P. Flournoy, b.
31 March 1824 N. C., son of Nelson Flournoy,(b. 10 Sept.
1891 Chesterfield Co., Va., d. 20 Nov. 1848 Talbot Co.,
Ga.) m. Alcey Wright 3 Dec. 1812 (b. 8 June 1796 Anson Co.,
N. C., d. 16 June 1871 Barbour Co., Ala.); grandson of
James Flournoy (b. 23 Feb. 1763 Chesterfield Co., Va.)
who served in the Revolutionary War and was granted land
in Talbot Co., Ga. (DAR #159617 & 364175) and his first
wife, Peggy Condiff (b. 7 May 1863 Bedford Co., Va., d. 9
Oct. 1824 Anson Co., N. C.). He married (2) Elizabeth
Wright 28 Jan. 1825 Anson Co., N. C.(Mrs. Wm. Bynum, Fayetteville, N. Y.). Victoria Jeanette Lee (wife - m. 7 Nov.
1865 Elba, Ala. - ibid).

Flournoy, Josiah, Jr. & Josiah, Jr. Estate. 13,14&15-11-29.
Josiah Flournoy, Jr., b. 1819 Ga., d. 27 July 1840 (MRA,
Vol. I, p. 421/2), son of Josiah Flournoy who died by Jan.
1842 (OR 2, p. 98). Martha Rosser (wife - ibid). She married (2) Samuel A. Wales of Putnam Co., Ga. (OR 1, p. 234).

Flournoy, R. W.. 8-13-26(B). Robert W. Flournoy, b. ca
1826 Ga.. Mary ----- (wife?), b. ca 1826 Ga..

Flournoy, T., Thos., Thomas. 4-13-27, 13,23,24&26-10-28 &
2,3,4,10,11&12-11-29. Thomas Flournoy, b. 1809 Ga., d. Jan.
1859 ("Eufaula Express", Feb. 3, 1859), buried Fairview Cem.,
Eufaula, Ala., son of Josiah Flourney, Sr. and Martha Manley of Edenton, Ga.,; grandson of John Manley (Rev. Soldier)
(Vol. II, p. 99). Caroline Elizabeth Rogers (1st wife - ibid),
b. 5 May 1814 Ga., d. 23 May 1855 ("Spirit of the South",
1855), buried Fairview Cem.; daughter of Rev. Osborn and
Mary Rogers of Oxford, Ga. ("Southern Christian Advocate"

21 June 1855). Ellen M. Baker (2nd wife - m. 25 Jan. 1859),
b. ca 1813 Ga., d. 22 Oct. 1871 ("The Bluff City Times", Oct.
26, 1871), daughter of Alpheus Baker, Sr. (OR 16, p. 891/7).

Flournoy, W. A.. 9-11-26. He is not in the Barbour Co.
records unless he was William Flournoy, b. ca 1808 Fisses-
byre, Scotland (CR B, p. 255).

Flowers, Abner. 19,29&30-10-27. Abner Flowers, b. ca 1785
N, C., to Ala. from Ga. by 1831, d. by July 1852 (OR 4, p.
608/9). Rebecca ----- (wife), b. ca 1793 N. C..

Flowers, H.. 31-9-28. Harrell Flowers, b. 1826 Jones Co.,
Ga. (1906 CSA Census), d. Feb. 1905, buried White Oak Cem.
("Eufaula Times & News", Feb. 16, 1905), son of Abner Flowers
who died by July 1852 (OR 4, p. 608/9). Julia Ann Bush (1st
wife - m. 8 July 1846), b. ca 1829 Ala., d. by 1861, daughter
of Moses E. Bush and Julia Ann Calhoun (Vol. I, p. 18 & 22).
Sarah Elizabeth Harrod (2nd wife - m. 13 Aug. 1861), b. ca
1844 Ala. (1860 Census), daughter of Sarah Harrod (Vol. II,
p. 106/7).

Flowers, W.. 32-9-28. Wright Flowers, b. 9 Oct. 1819 N. C.
(1860 Census), d. 23 Nov. 1892, buried County Line Cemetery,
Henry Co., Ala., son of Abner Flowers who died by July 1852
(OR 4, p. 690). Celia F. ----- (wife), b. 2 Jan. 1832 N. C.
(1860 Census), d. 25 Nov. 1894, buried County Line Cem..

Floyd, Page. 28&33-10-26. Page Floyd, b. 22 Sept. 1816,
d. 16 April 1907; son of Theophilus Floyd (b. 12 March 1787
Horry Co., S. C., d. 19 May 1842) and Delilah Page (b. 2
Dec. 1790, d. 7 Nov. 1835) - all buried Pleasant Plains
Baptist Church Cem.. (Vol. II, p. 39), grandson of Francis
Floyd, Sr. (Rev. Patriot) of Georgetown Dist., S. C. (b. 28
May 1756, d. by Oct. 1804) and Isabel Johnston (b. 1 July
1763, d. after 1804, m. 25 Dec. 1780), daughter of Gilbert
Johnston, Jr. (b. 1725 Scotland, d. 1793 Prince George Par.,
S. C.) and Margaret Warburton (Mrs. B. W. Goss, Mansfield,
La.). Elizabeth M. Bowden (wife), b. 22 Oct. 1822, d. 2
July 1903, buried Pleasant Plains Baptist Church Cem., dau.
of William Bowden and Louie Price (Vol. II, p. 39)..

Ford, E. N.. 17-13-25(B). Eli N. Ford, b. ca 1813 S. C.,
heir of Gardner Ford who died by Oct. 1854 (OR 6, p. 210).
Jane E. ----- (1st wife), b. ca 1827 Ga.. They had two
children buried in Fellowship Cem., Bullock Co., Ala. by
1850. Harriet G. Flournoy (2nd wife?).. The Flournoy Bible
states that she married Eli N. Ford 25 July ----. She was
born 28 April 1820, daughter of Nelson Flournoy and Alcey
Wright (Flournoy Bible).

Ford, G., Gardner. 16,17&20-13-25(B). Gardner Ford, b.

1784 S. C., d. 22 Aug. 1854. Elizabeth ----- (wife), b. 1791 S. C., d. 17 May 1851, both buried Fellowship Cem., Bullock Co., Ala..

Forehand, Stephen. 9-10-28. Stephen Forehand, b. ca 1795 N. C., to Ala. from S. C. by 1839, d. ca 16 Nov. 1858 (OR 10, p. 658/9). Martha ----- (wife?), b. ca 1804 S. C.. Elizabeth Jane Myers (2nd wife - m. 17 Feb. 1858), b. ca 1832 Ga.. She had married (1) Lorenzo D. Brown 6 March 1849.

Fort, D. M. B.. 8-11-29. Duncan M. B. Fort, b. ca 1823 or 1826 N. C.. In the 1850 Census, he had no family. Isaac Fort patented land near him in 1839 (Barbour Co., Ala. Tract Book).

Foster, B.. 17-10-25. This land was patented by Beauford Foster in 1836 (Barbour Co., Ala. Tract Book). No further record.

Foster, E.. 6-9-29. No further record.

Foster, Sarah. 19-13-27. No further record.

Franklin, E.. 8,9&16-12-29. Edwin Franklin, b. ca 1819 Ga.. Sarah Ann Young Langston (wife - m. 17 Dec. 1835 Monroe Co., Ga.), b. ca 1815 Ga., daughter of Samuel W. Langston who died by Nov. 1847 (OR 3, p. 106).

Frasier, A., Addison. 12-13-27 & 7&19-13-28. Addison Frazier was living in Lincoln Co., Ga. in 1835, son of Arthur Frazier of N. C. (DAB, Vol. III, p. 613) and his 2nd wife Mary Goodrum. They came from S. C. to Lincoln Co., Ga., then to Harris Co., Ga. where he is buried. He died 12 Dec. 1829, age 68, and she died 20 May 1840, age 58 (Frazier-Florence Bible). Mary A. Florence (wife - m. 5 Feb. 1835 Lincoln Co., Ga.) (DAB, Vol. III, p. 613).

Frasier, M.. 17-13-27. Malcom Frazier patented this land in 1835 (Barbour Co., Ala. Tract Book), b. ca 1790/1800 (1840 Census).

Freeman, W., Wm.. 5,8,15,29&30-13-28 & 18-13-29(R). William Freeman, b. ca 1802 Ga.. Lucy ----- (wife), b. ca 1806 Ga.. A William Freeman married Lucy Kirk 21 Sept. 1828 Jasper Co., Ga..

French, J. P.. 19&20-11-29. Josey P. French, b. ca 1812 S. C.. Mary ----- (wife?), b. ca 1817 Ga.. A Joseph French married Mary Brown 26 June 1833 Houston Co., Ga..

Fryer, G. H. (should be W.). 20-12-27. George W. Fryer patented land in this area in 1838, 1839 & 1843 (Barbour Co., Ala. Tract Book). He was born ca 1817 S. C.. Matilda -----

(wife?), b. ca1815 S. C..

Fryer, R. H.. 4-10-26 & 33&34-11-26. Dr. Richard H. Fryer, b. 17 Aug. 1819 Laurens Dist., S. C., d. 24 May 1864 (Vol. I, p. 65). Lucinda Fenn (wife - m. 25 July 1848), b. 13 Jan. 1828, d. 25 April 1897, daughter of Matthew Fenn. She m. (2) Seaborn Jones by 1866 but probably did not stay with him (Vol. I, p. 65).

Fulton, J.. 19-9-24. John Fulton sold land in 1852 (CR K, p. 219). Mary Ann Joiner (wife - m. 22 Jan. 1847).

Gachet, J. E., Jas. E.. 1-13-25(B), 6,7&12-13-26 & 26-13-27. James E. Gachet, b. ca 1805 Ga., son of Ann Gachet of Stewart Co., Ga. (Stewart Co., Ga. Will Book A, p. 54a/56a). James E. and Charles Nicholas Gachet were sons of Dr.Charles Gachet and his 2nd wife, the widow Stubbs. Dr. Gachet was born in LaRochelle, France and migrated to Pike Co., Ga. (Two Centuri with a Willis Family", p. 299, by D. M. Willis). Levinia ---- (wife?), b. ca 1817 Ga..

Gachet, N.. 9 &16-13-26. Charles Nicholas Deleigh Gachet, b. 2 July 1822, d. 14 March 1863, son of Ann Gachet of Stewar Co., Ga. (Stewart Co., Ga. Will Book A, p. 54a/56a). Jane M. ----- (wife - m. 30 May 1844 where?), b. 31 May 1826, d. 23 Sept. 1852, both buried Enon Cem., Bullock Co., Ala..

Galloway, Jas.. 7-9-26. James Galloway, b. ca 1807 Ga.. Elizabeth Lee (1st wife), b. 18 Aug. 1815 Ga., daughter of Lovard Lee and Elizabeth McNair (Vol. II, p. 74/6). Rebecca Black (2nd wife - ibid).

Ganby (?), Z. 16-12-29 & 16-13-29(R). No further record.

Garland, E.. 2-12-28. Edward Garland, b. 11 April 1811 Louisa Co., Va., d. 4 Nov. 1875, buried Ivy family cemetery, Russell Co., Ala.. Mary Ivy (wife), b. 29 April 1821 (Ivy Bible), d. Nov. or Dec. 1893 ("Eufaula Times & News", Dec. 7, 1893), daughter of Barnabas Ivy and Alcey Davis (MRA, Vol. I, p. 426/7).

Garner, J., John. 26-8-23. John Garner, b. ca 1804 Ga. or N. C. (1850 & 1860 Census). In 1836 and 1838, Jesse Garner and Joseph Garner patented land in this area (Barbour Co., Ala. Tract Book). Jane ----- (1st wife?), b. ca 1808 Ga.. Vicey ----- (2nd wife?), b. ca 1816 Ga. (1860 Census).

Garrett, Wm. D.. 17-13-25(B). William D. Garrett, b. ca 1827 Ga. (household #2085 in 1850 Census). He was also enumerated as David Garrett (household #2092 in 1850 Census). Elizabeth ----- (wife?), b. ca 1829 Ga..

Garris, J. G.. 8-13-25(B). John Garris probably did not
live in Barbour Co.. Susan Watson (wife - m. 2 Feb. 1845).

Gary, Jas.. 25-13-26. James Gary, b. 1814 Hancock Co. or
Washington Co:, Ga., d. 1880 Raines Co., Texas, son of Wm.
Lee Gary (b. 1790 Prince George Co., Va., d. 1825 Hancock
Co., Ga.) and Elizabeth Nance Rutherford (m. 11 Nov. 1813);
grandson of James Gary (b. 1770 Prince George Co., Va., d.
1806 Hancock Co., Ga.) and Rebecca Lee; great-grandson of
William Gary (Rev. Soldier) (b. 1725, d.by 1783) (Mrs. Frank
-Martin, Eufaula, Ala.). Sarah Ellen Harper (wife - m. 10
Oct. 1839 Hancock Co., Ga.) (ibid).

Gerkey, C. F.. 25&26-11-28. Charles F. Gerke, b. ca 1814
Germany. In 1851, he received a military land grant in
19-9-29 (#10083). Sina ----- (wife?), b. ca 1814 S. C..

Gibbons, S., Stephen. 30&31-10-28. Stephen Gibbons, b. ca
1806 N. C., d. 20 Jan. 1894 (OR 27, p. 319). Eliza Sloan
(1st wife - "Henry's Heritage", p. 182, by Warren), b. ca
1806 S. C.. Caroline Matilda Miller (2nd wife - m. 30 Jan.
1877 or 18 July 1878).

Gibson, B.. 1,2,3,10,11,12&35-12-29. No further record.

Gibson, G. T.. 3-13-25(B). George M. T. Gibson, b. ca
1825 Ga., brother of William H. C. Gibson and heir of Joseph
Duckworth who died by 1835 in Jones Co., Ga., son of William
C. Gibson (b. ca 1785 Ga.) and Mary Duckworth (b. ca 1788
Ga.)(CR O, p. 290/1). They married 11 June 1807 Warren Co.,
Ga. (CR A, p. 86). Nancy ----- (wife?), b. ca 1822 Ga..

Gibson, W. H. C.. 3&10-13-25(B). William H. C. Gibson,
b. ca 1824 Ga., heir of Joseph Duckworth who died by 1835
in Jones Co., Ga. (CR A, p. 86). Sarah E. Gammon (wife -
m.18 Feb. 1858), b. ca 1840 Ala. (1860 Census).

Giddens, J.. 33-12-25. Jacob Giddens, b. ca 1793 N. C..
Eliza ----- (Wife?), b. ca 1803 N. C..

Gilchrist, D.. 25-12-27. Daniel Gilchrist, b. ca 1823
N. C., d. ca Jan. 1897, buried Palmyra Church Cem., son of
Gilbert Gilchrist (CR C, p. 12). Gilbert Gilchrist sold
his interest in land in Richmond Co., N. C. to Alexander
H, Currie of Richmond Co., N. C.(CR D, p. 338). Elizabeth
Williamson (wife - m. 13 Dec. 1847), b. 16 Sept. 1831 Ga.,
d. 14 Aug. 1904, buried Palmyra Church Cem., heir (granddaughter?) of William Head who died by Feb. 1857 (OR 9, p.
311).

Gilchrist, John. 5-12-28. John Gilchrist, b. ca1827 N. C.,
brother of Daniel Gilchrist (CR C, p. 12).

Gilchrist, M.. 4&5-12-27 & 32-13-27. Malcolm Gilchrist,
b. ca 1817 N. C., brother of Daniel Gilchrist (CR C, p. 12).
Eliza J. Head (wife - m. 31 Dec. 1846), b. ca 1826 Ga.,
daughter of William Head, granddaughter of Richard Head
(Vol. I, p. 75).

Gillinwater, A .. 8-11-29. James A. Gillinwater, b. ca
1831 Va.. Jane A. Forte (wife - m. 30 May 1850), b. ca
1833 N. C..

Gillinwater, T.. 16-11-29. Thomas Gillinwater, b. ca 1807
Va., to Ala. by 1839. Nancy H. ----- (wife?), b. ca 1814 Va.

Gillis, A., Alexr., Alexr. Estate. 36-10-26, 31-12-26 &
31-10-27. There was an Alexander C. Gillis in the 1840 Census, age 60/70. There is no estate record for him.

Gillis, D.. 30-10-26. Daniel M. Gillis, b. ca 1820 S. C.,
living in Bullock Co., Ala. in 1880. Catherine McKenzie
(wife - m. 22 Feb. 1849), b. ca 1826 A. C.. Also in this
household in 1850 was Sarah McLeod, b. ca 1790 Scotland.

Gillis, J.. 4-9-27. John Gillis, b. 23 July 1801 N. C.,
d. 30 Oct. 1884. Catherine ----- (wife), b. 7 Oct. 1802,
d. 3 Dec. 1879, both buried Louisville Cem.. Also in this
household in1850 was Christian Gillis, b. ca 1790 N. C..

Gillis, N.. 36-10-26 & 31-10-27. Neill Gillis, b. ca 1816
S. C., d. 25 March 1883. Nancy Herring (wife - m. 11 Nov.
1847), b. ca 1830 N. C., d. 1897, both buried Mt. Mariah
Cem., Shady Grove, Texas (Vol. II, p. 48).

Gilmore, W., Wm.. 3-9-27 & 34-10-27. William Gilmore, b.
ca 1807 Ga.. Elizabeth ----- (wife?), b. ca 1814 Ga. (1860
Census).

Glass, Levi. 2-11-26. Levi Glass, b. ca 1804 Ga.. Sarah
----- (1st wife - CR K, p. 15). A Levi Glass m. Sally Martin
10 Jan. 1820 Laurens Co., Ga.. Mrs. Elizabeth Creech (2nd
wife - m. 3 March 1850), widow of Joshua C. Creech, probably
nee Pynes (Vol. II, p. 30).

Glenn, M. M.. 5&8-13-29(R). Massillom McKendry Glenn, b.
8 March 1815 Abbeville Dist., S. C., d. 14 Sept. 1889, buried
Glennville Cem., Russell Co., Ala., son of Rev. James E.
Glenn (native of Franklin Co., N. C., to Cokesbury, S. C.,
to Stewart Co., Ga. 1832, to Barbour Co., Ala. 1835 - "Rus-
sell Co. in Retrospect", p. 311, by Walker) and Elizabeth
Robinson (DAB, Vol. III, p. 663/4). Barbara Wesley Herndon
(wife), b. 17 March 1820 Cokesbury, S. C., d. 9 Nov. 1897
Birmingham, Ala., daughter of Stephen Herndon & ----- Conner
(DAB, Vol. III, p. 663/4), buried Glennville Cem..

Glenn, T. S.. 30-12-28. Rev. Thompson S. Glenn, b. ca 1774
Va., probably son of Rev. James E. Glenn (Charles Tigner,
Seale, Ala.). ----- Capers (1st wife, m. 1814?) whose first
husband was Legrand Guerry who died 1811 where (?) (C. R.
Lamar, Montgomery, Ala.). Mary Catherine Hodges (2nd wife?)
(Charles Tigner, Seale, Ala.).

Glover, Hilliard. 28-12-27. Hilliard Glover, b. 1 Feb.
1812 N. C., d. 9 June 1883, buried Batesville Baptist Church
Cem.. Sarah Damascus Nash (wife - CR M, p. 220), b. 25 Nov.
1810 N. C. (Nash Bible), heir of Acton Nash who died by Aug.
1854 (OR 6, p. 408/12).

Glover, J. P.. 1-11-28 & 5-11-29. John P. Glover, b. ca
1785 N. C., to Ala. from Ga. ca 1841, d. by Sept. 1862
(OR 12, p. 500). (Mrs.?) Drucilla Evans (wife - m. 5 March
1812 Putnam Co., Ga.), b. ca 1793 Ga..

Glover, T. J.. 5&8-11-29 & 23-12-29. Thomas J. Glover, b.
ca 1820 Ga., d. by Feb. 1871 (OR 18, p. 500/2). Rachael
Vining (wife - m. 5 Oct. 1845), b. ca 1828 Ga..

Glover, W. E.. 8-12-27 & 1-11-28. William E. Glover is not
in the 1850 Census of Barbour Co.. In 1840, he was age 20/30.
Catharine Fowler (wife - m. 30 Dec. 1839 Warren Co., Ga.),
daughter of Nathan Fowler of Crawford Co., Ga. (CR P, p. 310).

Grant, J. H.. 9-11-26. John H. Grant, b. ca 1782 N. C.,
to Fla. by 1834, in Ala. by 1850, d. by Aug. 1852 (OR 4, p.
565/6). Elizabeth ----- (wife), b. ca 1793 N. C..

Grant, T. M., Thos. M.. 3,4,9&33-8-24. Thomas M. Grant, b. ca
1785 Va., to Ala. from Ga. after 1829. He patented part of
the above land in 1836 (Barbour Co., Ala. Tract Book) and in
1839 and 1840, Littleberry Grant and Larkin W. Grant patented
land close by. They are not in any early census of Barbour Co..
In 1851, Thomas M. Grant received a military land grant in
4-8-24 (#8494). Martha ----- (wife?), b. ca 1800 Ga.. She
may have been his second wife and the widow of ----- Stokes.

Grantham, Edw.. 9-9-27. Edward Grantham, b. ca 1822 N. C.,
d. near D'Lo, Miss.(Vol. II, p. 69/70). He lived in Horry
Co., S. C. before coming to Barbour Co., Ala. in 1847 (Grantham
family notes, source unknown). Molsie Johnston (1st wife),
b. ca 1813 S. C., d. 10 May 1840, daughter of John Johnston
and Mary (Molsie) Hodges (Vol. II, p. 69/70). Prudence
Johnston (2nd wife), b. ca 1821, d. 10 Nov. 1843, daughter
of John Johnston and Mary (Molsie) Hodges (ibid). Elizabeth
Grantham (3rd wife), b. 1817 N. C., d. 1875 Carroll Co.,
Miss. After the birth of their first child, they separated
(Grantham family notes). She was a daughter of Stephen
Grantham (b. 23 June 1790, d. 20 July 1858 Robson Co., N. C.)
and Celia Grimsley who d. Carroll Co., Miss., age 66 (ibid).

Graves, H., Hardy. 1&12-8-23. Hardy Graves, b. ca 1805
S. C.. Rhoda Ann Grubbs (wife - m. 7 Dec. 1847), b. 18
March 1797 S. C., daughter of William Grubbs, Sr.. She
was the widow of Robert Thompson (Vol. II, p. 53).

Green, A., Amos. 28&33-13-25(B). Amos Green, b. ca 1800
Ga.. Sarah ----- (2nd wife?), b. ca 1815 Ga.. Also in
this household in 1850 was Sophia Jennings, b. ca 1833 Ala..

Green, Thos. C.. 36-10-25. Thomas C. Green, b. 23 Oct.
1818 S. C., d. 5 Oct. 1899. Emeline ----- (wife), b. 10
June 1820 S. C., d. 20 May 1896, both buried Upper Prospect
Baptist Church Cem.. Mr. Winfred Horne says she was nee
Watkins.

Green, Wm. E.. 33-11-24. William E. Green patented the
above land in 1848 (Barbour Co., Ala. Tract Book) and sold
it in 1856 (CR O, p. 26). Mary Jane Cook (wife), daughter
of John Cook, Sr. who died 1 June 1858 (Original Papers,
Box 15, file #2). In 1872, they were of Bullock Co., Ala.
(ibid).

Greenwood, E. S.. 4-12-29. On 1 March 1850, E. S. Greenwood and wife, Jane E., of Muscogee Co., Ga. gave a slave
to Mrs. Ann Butts, Jeremiah Butts, trustee (CR H, p. 668).

Greenwood, S.. 4-13-26(R). Samuel Greenwood, b. ca 1803
Ga.. Elizabeth Randall (wife), b. ca 1812, d. 5 Oct. 1843,
sister of Dr. Randall ("The Southern Recorder", 24 Oct. 1843).

Gregory, W. B.. 20-13-27. Wilson B. Gregory, b. ca 1810
S. C., d. 2 Sept. 1886. Mahala ----- (wife), b. 1824 Ga.,
d. 26 Feb. 1877, both buried Ramah Baptist Church Cem..

Grissett, D. M., Daniel M.. 28,33&34-10-26. Daniel M.
Grissett, b. ca 1813 N. C., d. July 1892 Henry Co., Ala.,
lived Barbour Co. from ca 1832 to 1886, then to Henry Co.
("The Clayton Courier", July 30, 1892). Matilda Melvina
Brantley (2nd wife - m. by 1842), b. ca 1819 Ga. (1860
Census), d. May 1885 ("Eufaula Weekly Times & News", May
26, 1885), daughter of James Brantley who died by 1842
(OR 1, p. 320).

Grubs, A.. 18,19&20-9-24. Adam Grubbs, b. 26 April 1802
S. C., d. 4 April 1888, buried Louisville Cem., son of Wm.
Grubbs, Sr. (Vol. II, p. 53/4). Demaris ----- (1st wife)
b. ca 1798 S. C.. Nancy J. Mabry (2nd wife - m. 1 Feb.
1860), b. ca 1818 Ga. (1860 Census), d. 1897 (Vol. II, p.
54). She was the widow of Jonathan Moats (m. 30 Sept.
1845) and possibly had married first ----- Harveston. She
was an heir of Nancy Mabry (OR 23, p. 212/6) and sister of
J. W. Mabry (OR 26, p. 228/30).

Grubs, F.. 25-9-23. Friendly Grubbs, b. 16 Oct. 1817
Ala., d. 24 Nov. 1878, son of William Grubbs, Sr. (Vol.
II, p. 53 & 58). Elizabeth J. Caroline Mabry (wife), b.
16 Oct. 1817 Ga., d. 15 Feb. 1888, heir of Nancy Mabry
(OR 23, p. 212/6). Both buried Clayton Cem.. (Vol. II,
p. 58).

Grubs, J. T.. 28-12-25 & 22&27-13-25(B). John Tillman
Grubbs, b. 27 July 1824 Ala., d. 20 Oct. 1895, son of
William Grubbs, Sr. (Vol. II, p. 53 & 60). Lucitta Martin
(wife - m. 23 April 1844). After his death, she filed for
a Confederate pension in Pike Co., Ala..

Grubs, W. J.. 25-9-23 & 30-9-24. Worthy Jordan Grubbs,
b. 1 Jan. 1819, d. 2 Aug. 1890, son of William Grubbs, Sr.
(Vol. II, p. 53 & 59). Mary A. S. ----- (wife), b. 22 June
1822 Ga., d. 26 May 1900, both buried Louisville Cem.. She
was an heir of Nancy Mabry (OR 23, p. 212/6).

Grubs, Wm.. 4&25-9-25, 25&26-10-27, 6-9-28 & 30,31&32-
10-28. William Grubbs, Jr., b. 7 July 1804 S. C., d. 10
Nov. 1882, son of William Grubbs, Sr. (Vol. II, p. 53/4).
Nancy Parmer (wife), b. ca 1812 Ga., d. by July 1879, dau.
of Benjamin Parmer (Vol. II, p. 54).

Grubs, Wm. Estate. 4,17,19,20,23&30-10-25. William Grubbs,
Sr., b. 6 Oct. 1776 Chesterfield Dist., S. C., d. 26 Feb.
1849. Elizabeth ----- (wife), b. ca 1778 S. C., both buried
Bennett-Lee Cem..

Guice, S.. 12&14-13-27. Samuel Guice (or Grice) witnessed
the will of Samuel Benton in 1834 (Barbour Co. Original Papers). No further record.

Hagler, Chas.. 26-8-25. Charles W. Hagler, b. ca 1814
N. C., d. 17 March 1892 (OR 26, p. 546), son of Peter Hagler
(OR 4, p. 471/3). Nancy ----- (wife?), b. ca 1820 N. C.
(1860 Census).

Hagler, Henry. 33-12-25. Henry Hagler, b. ca 1796 N. C.,
to Ala. from Ga. by 1842, d. by June 1852 (OR 4, p. 524).
Elizabeth ----- (wife), b. ca 1805 N. C., d. by Nov. 1856
(OR 7, p. 569).

Hagler, Jackson. 35-8-25. Jackson Hagler, b. ca 1822, d.
21 Aug. 1884. Malinda Helms (wife - m. 14 March 1844), b.
ca 1825, d. 27 Feb. 1885, both buried Barsheba Cem., Dale
Co., Ala..

Hagler, John. 34-8-24. John Hagler, son of Peter Hagler
(OR 4, p. 471/3). No further record.

Hagler, Peter. 2&4-8-25. Peter Hagler, b. ca 1780 N. C.,
d. by May 1852 (OR 4, p. 470/3). Margaret ----- (1st wife).
Sarah (Cooley?) (2nd wife), b. ca 1780 N. C.,. d after 1854
(OR 7, p. 313).

Hagler, Thos.. 2-8-25. Thomas Hagler, b. 29 Oct. 1811
N. C., d. 11 Dec. 1901, buried Pine Level Baptist Church
Cem., son of Peter Hagler (O R 4, p. 471/3). Lydia -----
(1st wife), b. ca 1820 N. C.. Mary Ann Matthews (2nd wife -
m. 4 April 1856) b. ca 1831 Ala., d. 7 Jan. 1906, buried
Pine Level Baptist Church Cem., daughter of Abraham Matthews (also called Abel Mathis) (OR 18, p. 190/1).

Hagood, A.. 34-12-25. Appleton Hagood, b. 3 Dec. 1806
Clark Co., Ga. ("Henry's Heritage", p. 64 by Warren). In
1856, he was of Macon Co., Ala. (CR N, p. 184) and in 1861,
he was of Montgomery Co., Ala. (CR Q, p. 616). He died 26
Dec. 1866 Montgomery Co., Ala. ("Henry's Heritage", p. 64
by Warren), son of John Hagood,(b. 12 Nov. 1778, d. 19 Nov.
1819) and Polly ----- (b. 8 July 1790, d. 7 May 1863 (ibid).
Mary R. Lovelace (1st wife - CR N, p. 184), b. 17 Sept.1810,
d. 19 Jan. 1857, daughter of Allen Lovelace and Elizabeth
Canbon Barnet ("Henry's Heritage", p. 64 by Warren). Elizabeth C. ----- (2nd wife - CR Q, p. 616).

Hailey, Jas.. 10-11-25. James Hailey, b. ca 1802 N. C.,
to Ga. by 1831, in Ala. by 1845, d. by Aug. 1870 (OR 14,
p. 206/214). Elizabeth ----- (2nd wife), b. ca 1824.

Hall, G.. 27-11-27. Goodwin Hall, b. ca 1785 S. C.. He
had no family in 1850.

Hall, H.. 26-10-28. Hiram Hall, b. 1803 S. C., to Ala.
from Ga. after 1843. Epsey ----- (wife?), b. ca 1804 S.C..

Hall, Henry. 24-12-27. Henry Hall, b. ca 1817 S. C.,
heir of Henry Hall, Sr. who died by Nov. 1844 (OR 2, p.
195). In his household in 1850 were Daniel Hall (b. ca
1820 S. C.) and Elisha Hall (b. ca 1824 S. C.), both heirs
of Henry Hall, Sr. (ibid).

Hall, Jas. B.. 29&32-13-29(R). James B. Hall is not in any
early census. There is a child, Eugenia A. Hall, buried in
Glennville Cem., Russell Co., Ala.. She was born 1844 and
died 1845, daughter of Rev. J. B. & M. C. Hall.

Hall, J. W.. 32-12-27. John W. Hall, b. ca 1812 S. C..
In 1850 and 1860, he and William Hall were enumerated next
to each other. Mary C. ----- (wife?), b. ca 1810 S. C..

Hall, Matthew, M.. 8,10,16&17-12-25(B). Matthew Hall, b.
ca 1805 Ga.. Altha Barksdale (2nd wife - m. 4 July 1837
Talbot Co., Ga.), b. ca 1813 Ga..

Hall, R. G.. 3,8&10-12-25(B). Robert G. Hall, b. ca 1821 Ga., d. 6 Jan. 1890 Midway (Bullock Co.), Ala. ("The Clayton Courier", Jan. 18, 1890). Sarah R. ----- (wife?), b. ca 1822 Ga.. A Robert Hall m. Sarah Veasey 1 Dec. 1840 Warren Co., Ga..

Hall, W.. 16-11-27. William Hall, b. ca 1795 S. C.. In 1850, he had no wife but four children in his household age 19 to 25, all born S. C..

-Ham, Jesse. 11,13&14-9-26. Jesse Ham, b. ca 1785 S. C., to Ala. by 1825, d. by March 1854 (OR 5, p. 618). Mary ----- (wife?), b. ca 1783 S. C..

Hameter, J., Joel. 8,9,16,17,19&20-12-27. Joel Hameter, b. 4 Feb. 1807 S. C., d. 13 Nov. 1864, of Twiggs Co., Ga. in 1839 (CR C, p. 134). Elizabeth ----- (wife), b. 25 Jan. 1808 S.C., d. 10 March 1868, both buried Providence Cem..

Hamilton, Jas.. 13,23&24-10-28. James Hamilton, b. ca 1804 N. Y.. The 1870 Census shows that his parents were foreign born. He had no family in Barbour Co..

Hamock, S. J.. 30-11-27. Simeon J. (or G. or T.) Hammock, b. ca 1810 Ga.. On 10 Sept. 1851, he was granted land in 28-9-27 for military service (#7840). Caroline Jane Hammock (2nd wife - m. 15 Oct. 1843), b. ca 1824 Ga..

Hamock, T.. 12,13&14-11-27. Thomas Hammock, b. ca 1790 Ga.. In 1840, when he bought the above land, he was of Randolph Co., Ga. (CR C, p. 141).

Hammonds, H.. 35-13-25(B). Henry M. Hammonds, b. ca 1790 N. C.. Elizabeth ----- (wife?), b. ca 1800 N. C.. Also in this household in 1850 was Mary Hammonds, b. ca 1777 N. C..

Hanrick, Edw.. 32-13-25(B). Edward Hanrick was of Montgomery Co., Ala. in 1843 when he bought this land (CR E, p. 261/2).

Hardaway, R. S., Robert S.. 31-12-27. Robert Stanfield Hardaway, from Brunswick Co., Va. to Russell Co., Ala., d. 20 April 1875, son of Robert Hardaway (Rev. Soldier) of Dinwiddie Co., Va. and Sarah Hicks. In 1829, he was of Morgan Co., Ga., may also have lived in Muscogee Co., Ga.. (DAB, Vol. IV, p. 1838/41). Martha Bibb Jarratt (2nd wife) daughter of Archelus Jarratt (b. Savannah, Ga.) and Sally Booker Bibb whose first husband was Memorable Walker (ibid). Martha Bibb Jarratt was born ca 1806, d. 25 Sept. 1859 (Southern Christian Advocate", 20 Oct. 1859).

Hardwick, C. A.. 5&8-12-26(B). Charles A. Hardwick bought the above land in Feb. 1848 (CR H, p. 173) but is not in any early census of Barbour Co..

Hardwick, J., Jos.. 12-13-26(B) & 16-11-27. No further record.

Hargrove, H., Henry. 4-9-26. Henry Hargrove, b. ca 1799
N. C., d. by Nov. 1857 (OR 8,p. 448/9). In 1852, he received a military land grant in 10-9-26 (#68027). In 1853,
Lemuel Hargrove received one in 2-10-25 and John W. Hargrove received one in 3-9-26. Elizabeth ----- (wife), b.
ca 1803 N. C..

Harper, H.. 3-9-26. No further record.

Harper. W. F.. 25-13-26. William F. Harper, b.ca 1805
Ga., son of Benjamin Harper who died by Dec. 1852 in Han-
cock Co., Ga. (CR M, p. 11). Rebecca Wood (wife - m. 3
Sept. 1844 Washington Co., Ga.). Also in this household
in 1850 were Mildred Wood (b. ca 1834 Ga.) and Benjamin
Wood (b. ca 1833 Ga.).

Harper, W. H., Wm.. 5&17-12-27 & 2-10-28. William Harper,
b. ca 1795 N. C., d. by Nov. 1866 (OR 15, p. 599/601).
Margaret ----- (1st wife?), b. ca 1807 S. C.. Catherine
Sauls (2nd wife - m. 26 Nov. 1854), b. ca 1810 Ga. (1860
Census). She may have been the widow of ----- Sauls.

Harrel, J.. 4&5-11-29. Jesse Harrell died by 1857 (OR
7, p. 629) leaving no widow but minor children.

Harrelson, H.. 5-9-25. No further record.

Harris, D. W.. 28-11-25. No further record.

Harris, Henry. 4&5-12-28. In 1839, Henry Harris was of
Meriweather Co., Ga. (CR C, p. 20), possibly Henry Harris,
b. 15 May 1781 Va., d. 24 Dec. 1858 Meriweather Co., Ga.
("Southern Christian Advocate", 3 Feb. 1859).

Harris, John M.. 16-11-28. John M. Harris is not in any
early census of Barbour Co.. He sold the above land in
1853 (CR K, p. 389).

Harris, Wiley. 8-13-28(R). Wiley J. Harris was of Russell
Co., Ala. (OR 10, p. 266/8). Mary Ann E. Mitchlll (wife -
m. 28 May 1844), b. ca 1826, d. 8 Jan. 1847, buried Mitchell
Cem., Russell Co., Ala., daughter of Randolph and Avey Mitchell. He may have m. (2) Virginia Phillips 20 Feb. 1855
in Russell Co., Ala., daughter of Maj. J. Phillips ("Southern Christian Advocate", 16 March 1855).

Harrison, L. C.. 1-12-26 & 4,5&8-11-27. L. (Leonard?) C.
Harrison, b. ca 1806 Rockingham Co., Va., d. 1865 (DAB,
Vol.   , p. 763). Sarah Cook (wife - ibid), b. ca 1811
S. C..

Harrod, Jas.. 36-11-26. James Harrod, b. ca 1814 Ga..
In April 1848, he was ordained a Primitive Baptist Minis-

ter (Mar. I, p. 314). Martha ----- (wife?), b. ca 1819 Ga..

Harrod, S.. 25-11-27. Sarah Harrod, b. ca 1810 N. C., in
Ala. 1833, in Miss. 1834/6, in Ala. 1848.

Harrod, Thos. 36-11-26. Thomas Harrod died by Jan. 1862
(OR 12, p. 143). Miranda Kelly (wife - m. 16 July 1846).
They are not in any early census of Barbour Co..

Hart, J., John. 7-11-28. John Hart, b. ca 1804 N. H., to
-Ala. from R. I. by 1836, d. by March 1871 (OR 18, p. 547/52).
He and Pardon Bosworth were business partners with some con-
nection to Asa Bosworth of Providence, R. I.. Elisabeth W.
(Bosworth?) (wife), b. ca 1813 R. I..

Hartzog, David. 25-9-26. David Hartzog, b. ca 1794 S. C.,
d. ca 15 Jan. 1879 Henry Co., Ala. (Vol. II, p. 68). Rebecca
----- (2nd wife), b. ca 1814 S. C., d. Feb. or March 1891
Henry Co., Ala. ("Eufaula Times & News", March 5, 1891).
She may have been the widow of ----- Hanley or Henley.

Hartzog, F., Francis. 21&31-9-27. Francis Hartzog, b. ca
1824 S. C., probably son of George and Sarah Hartzog (Vol.
II, p. 64/5). Rebecca Zorn (1st wife - ibid). Betha Ann
Hartzog (2nd wife - m. 29 Jan. 1865).

Hartzog, Jas. Estate. 8-9-26. No further record.

Harwell, Saml., Samuel. 5-10-28 & 32-11-28. Samuel Harwell,
b. ca 1778 Va., d. by Nov. 1855 (Vol. I, p. 73). Burket ----
(wife), b. ca 1788 Va., d. by May 1862 (ibid).

Hawkins, G. S.. 1-13-28(R). George S. Hawkins was of Franklin Co., Fla. in 1846 (CR G, p. 208) and 1850 (CR J, p. 146).
Josephine Olivia ----- (1st wife - CR G, p. 208). Mary B.
----- (2nd wife - CR J, p. 146).

Hays, C.. 17-13-26(B). This may be Clarissa Hays, b. ca
1804 Ga.. William B. (or R.) Hays entered land in 17-13-26
in 1842 (Barbour Co., Ala. Tract Book). In 1848, he was of
Henry Co., Ala. (CR H, p. 656).

Hays, C. D. L.. 28-9-24. No further record.

Hays, J. L,, J. L. & Co., J. L. & R. T.. 27,28&32-9-28 &
30-11-28. Jesse L. Hays, b. ca 1823 Ala.. In Nov. 1848,
he bought the above land from Calvin S. Hays and wife Mahala
(CR H, p. 655) and from Wm. B. Hays and wife Comfort (CR H,
p. 656). All were of Henry Co., Ala.. Sarah Dansey (wife -
m. 18 March 1855).

Hays, John. 16&17-9-27. John Hays, b. ca 1809 Ga.. Jane
----- (wife?), b. ca 1824 Ga.. Also in this household in

1850 were Louisa N. Ricks (b. ca 1841 Ga.) and Mary Mobley
(b. ca 1782 Ga.).

Head, William. 2-12-27 & 34&35-13-27. William Head, b.
ca 1783 N. C., to Ala. from Ga. by 1830, son of Richard
Head (Rev. Soldier) (Vol. I, p. 75). Epsey Mosser (or
Mosses) (wife - m. 19 Dec. 1810 Jasper Co., Ga.), b. ca
1791 Ga. (ibid).

Heath, I., Isaac. 16-9-26. Isaac Heath, b. ca1787 N. C.,
d. by Dec. 1858 (OR 9, p. 469). No wife was named in his
estate.

Heath, R. (should be B.). 16-13-25(B). Britton Heath,
b. ca 1808 Ga., d. by April 1851 (CR J, p. 242). Rebecca
Digby (wife - m. 28 Dec. 1831 Upson Co., Ga.), b. ca 1812
Ga..

Helms, Aaron. 2-8-25. Rev. Aaron Helms, b. 20 June 1816
N. C., d. 20 July 1883. Mary Magdaline Whigham (wife -
m. 3 Jan. 1854), b. Nov. 1833 Ga., d. 25 Oct. 1909, both
buried in the family cemetery.

Helms, Abram. 24-8-25. Abraham Helms, b. ca 1816 N. C..
Nancy ----- (wife?), b. ca 1818 N. C.. Also in this household in 1850 was Abraham Helms, b. ca 1771 N. C..

Helms, H.. 10-8-25 & 36-10-25. Hilliard Helms, b. ca 1817
N. C.. Mahala ----- (wife?), b. ca 1819 N. C..

Helms, John. 1,12&35-8-25. Rev. John Helms, b. 22 Feb.
1811 N. C., d. 12 Aug. 1891. Hally Chaney (wife), b. 14
Feb. 1817 N. C., d. 19 Nov. 1883, both buried in the family
cemetery. She was a daughter of John and Milbry Chaney
(OR 6, p. 586/8).

Henderson, J.. 21-9-24. Joseph Henderson, b. 10 Nov. 1825
Ala., d. 13 May 1880, son of Joseph Henderson who died by
Dec. 1833 (Vol. I, p. 78/9). Margaret McDonald (wife - m.
27 Oct. 1846), b. 16 Sept. 1821 N. C., d. 4 Jan. 1881, both
buried Pea River Presbyterian Church Cem..

Henderson, John. 21-9-24. John Henderson, b. ca 1824 Ala.,
living Coffee Co., Ala. 1874, son of Joseph Henderson who
died by Dec. 1833 (Vol. I, p. 78/9). Eliza ----- (wife?),
b. ca 1826 Ala..

Hendrix, W., Sr.. 28-11-29. Whitfield B. Hendrix, b. ca
1828 S. C.. He bought the above land in 1850 from John &
Lucinda Hendrix (CR J, p. 132). Jane A. ----- (wife?),
b. ca 1834 Ala..

Henley, A.. 26-9-27. Adam Henley, b. ca 1824 S. C.. Leta

Williams (wife - m. 15 Dec. 1842), b. ca 1826 S. C..

Heron, E. M.. 35&36-10-24. Dr. Edward M. Heron, b. ca
1810 Charleston, S. C., d. May 1901, buried Fairview Cem.,
Eufaula, Ala. ("Eufaula Times & News", May 23, 1901). Mary
McNeill (1st wife - m. 4 Nov. 1841), daughter of John McNeill,
a pioneer settler of Barbour Co. from N. C. ("Eufaula Times
& News", March 7, 1891). Caroline E. A. Buford (2nd wife),
b. 1817 S. C., d. 3 Dec. 1850, buried Pea River Presbyterian
Church Cem. She was a daughter of John R. Buford of Fayette
Co., Tenn. (CR T, p. 450), brother-in-law of Samuel Jones who
died by 1852 (OR 5, p. 45/6). In 1854, the minor heirs of Samuel Jones received a legacy from their grandfather, Major Hart
of Columbia, S.C., in right of their mother (OR 5, p. 663).

Herring, G., Geo., George. 2,9,10,11,15&16-10-25 & 4-9-26.
George Herring, b. ca 1826 N. C., d. by Feb. 1852 (OR 2,
p. 161), son of William Herring who died by March 1839 (OR
1, p. 26). He probably never married.

Herring, J.. 26-10-25. John Herring, b. 2 Feb. 1789 N. C.,
d. 5 Nov. 1857, buried Bethlehem Cem.. Sarah Bowden (wife-
m. 23 May 1833 N. C. - OR 9, p. 941/2). Priscilla Henley
(2nd wife?), b. ca 1826 S. C..

Herring, W., West. 17,18,19,20,28&29-10-26. West Herring,
b. ca 1805 N. C.. In 1845, he was guardian of Mary Jane
Herring, minor heir of William Herring who died by March
1839 (OR 2, p. 208). Charity ----- (wife b. ca 1803 N.C.

Herring, William. 20&21-10-26. William Herring, b. ca
1809 N. C.. Sarah ----- (wife?), b. ca 1826 Ga.. Also in
this household in 1850 was William Lester, b. ca 1830 Ala..

Hickman, M.. 14-11-27. John Hickman died by Dec. 1848 (OR
3, p. 244). In the 1840 Census, he was age 50/60. Mary
----- (wife - ibid).

Hickman, W.(?) R.. 13-11-27. No further record.

Highnote, B.. 17-8-25 & 17-8-26. Benjamin F. Highnote,
b. ca 1796 Ga.. In July 1848, he was of Henry Co., Ala.
(CR H, p. 228). Elizabeth ----- (wife?), b. ca 1799 Ga..

Hightower, A. W.. 26-13-25(B). A. W. Hightower, b. ca
1820 Ga.. Sarah ----- (wife?), b. ca 1826 Ga..

Hightower, T. A., Thos. A.. 10,14,15&24-11-26.. Thomas A.
Hightower, b. 1804 Greene Co., Ga., d. 1896. Emma Carter Russell
(2nd wife), b. 1 April 1812 N.C., d. 20 Sept. 1858, both

both buried Mt. Nebo Cem.. Rachel M. Russell (3rd wife -
m. 16 Dec. 1858), b. ca 1816 N. C. (1870 Census).

Hill, A. S.. 25,26,27,30&36-12-29. Dr. Abraham S. Hill,
b. ca 1808 Ga. (1860 Census), d. by Aug. 1866 (OR 15, p.
440/1). In 1846, he was of Athens, Ga. and a surgeon in
the Mexican War ("The Eufaula Democrat", Nov. 11, 1846).
His only heir was his sister, Mrs. Elizabeth A. Hill, of
Clarke Co., Ga. (OR 16, p. 32).

Hill, B. M.. 12&35-12-27 & 6,7&18-12-28. Blanton M. Hill,
b. 5 May 1802 Oglethorpe Co., Ga., d. 3 Feb. 1857 Athens,
Ga., son of Miles & Tabitha Hill (Southern Christian Advo-
cate", 26 March 1857). In 1840, he was of Russell Co., Ala.
(CR H, p. 690). Miles Hill, b. 13 March 1774 Halifax Co.,
N. C., d. 4 Nov. 1844 Oglethorpe Co., Ga.,(son of Abraham
Hill), m. TAbitha Pope in 1795 ("Southern Christian Advocate", 29 Nov. 1844). Tabitha Pope, b. 11 Jan. 1778, d. 25
April 1852 Oglethorpe Co., Ga., daughter of Col. Burwell
Pope ("Southern Christian Advocate", 11 June 1852). Eliza-
beth A. Hill (wife - m. 16 June 1825 Oglethorpe Co., Ga.),
sister of Dr. Abraham S. Hill who died by Aug. 1866 (OR 16,
p. 32).

Hill, E. P.. 35-10-28. Ephriam Hill, b. ca 1807 Ga.. Ava
Minshew (wife), b. ca 1808 N.C.,daughter of Nathan Minshew
(Vol. II, p. 116/7).

Hill, F. W.. 6-9-29. Francis W. Hill, b. ca 1801 Ga..
Edney ------ (wife?), b. ca 1803 Ga..

Hill, Felix. 20-10-24. Felix Hill, b. ca 1804 S. C.. In
1853, he was granted land in 4-10-25 for military service
(#59856). Ann ----- (wife?), b. ca 1814 S. C..

Hill, J. B.. 1,12,13&24-12-29 & 7,17,18&19-12-30. Joseph
B. Hill sold land in 6-12-30 in Nov. 1849, at which time
he was of Muscogee Co., Ga. (CR J, p. 36). H. W. -----
(wife - ibid).

Hill, J. T.. 32-10-24 (partly in Pike Co., Ala.). J. T.
Hill probably lived in Pike Co., Ala..

Hobdy, H.. 32-10-24. Harrell Hobdy, b. 23 Sept. 1799, d.
21 Feb. 1865, son of Edmond Hobdy and Nancy (Harrell?) (Vol.
I, p. 84). Jennie McNeill (wife), b. ca 1798 Richmond Co.,
N. C., d. 17 Oct. 1863, daughter of John McNeill (Vol. I,
p. 84).

Hodges, E. G.. 22-11-26. Elias G. Hodges, b. ca 1812 Ga.,
In Jan, 1854, he was guardian of Sarah J. Hodges, minor heir
of George C. Hodges (OR 5, p. 487). Mary C. Perry (wife -
m. 17 July 1855), b. ca 1837 Ga. (1860 Census).

Hodges, G. C., Geo. C.. 25-12-24, 3-11-26, 1,13,23,24,25, 26,35&36-12-26 & 19,20,28&29-12-27. George C. Hodges, b. ca 1798 S. C., d. by March 1852 (OR 4, p. 373). He had a son and a daughter born ca 1827/9 in Fla., a son born ca 1836 in Ga. and a daughter born ca 1849 in Ala.. In 1838, he was of Columbus, Ga. (CR B, p. 234). In June 1833, he was trustee in a marriage agreement in Jackson Co., Fla. between John P. Booth and Martha R. W. Hodges, daughter of Richard Hodges, late of Ga. (CR E, p. 55). Sarah J. Bledsoe (2nd wife - m. 21 Dec. 1848).

Holder, A.. 2&3-11-25 & 24,27,34&35-12-25. Abraham Holder, b. ca 1810 Ga., d. by July 1853 (OR 5, p. 334). Drucilla Holliday (wife - m. 15 Sept. 1828 Warren Co., Ga.),b. ca 1813 Ga..

Holder, John. 6-10-27. John Holder, b. ca 1818 Ga., to Ala. by 1849. Mary ----- (wife?), b. ca 1824 Ga..

Holland, J. A., Joseph. 3&14-13-26. Dr. Joseph A. Holland, b. ca 1820 Ga.. Sarah A. Flewellen (wife - m. 16 April 1844 Jasper Co., Ga.), b. ca 1824 Ga..

Holland, Jesse. 34-8-25. Jesse Holland, b. ca 1798 S. C., to Ala. by 1836. Arpy ----- (wife?), b. ca 1803 N. C..

Holland, Wm.. 6-10-28. William Holland, b. ca 1810 Ga.. Mrs. Lucinda Bryant (2nd wife? - m.1 Oct. 1838 Pulaski Co., Ga.), b. ca 1825 Ga., daughter (or daughter-in-law) of Anice Bryant (1870 Census).

Holmes, N. G.. 22-10-25. Nathaniel G. Holmes, b. ca 1777 S. C.. In 1860, he was living with William and Penelope Dorman (his daughter?). Jerusha ----- (wife), b. ca 1788 S. C.. Also in this household in 1850 was Mary Ward, b. ca 1790 S. C..

Holmes, Wm.. 36-9-27. William Holmes, b. ca 1803 N. C., in Ala. by 1834. Sarah ----- (wife?), b. ca 1810 N. C..

Holoman, A. B.. 9-13-27, 15-13-28(R) & 35-13-29. Aeson B. Holleman, b. 10 Nov. 1796 Va., d. 7 June 1851, buried Fairview Cem., Eufaula, Ala.. Amanda (Birdsong?) (wife), b. ca 1821 Ga.. She m. (2) Thomas Morgan by March 1853 (OR 5, p. 194).

Holleman, E. C.. 15&22-10-28 & 35-13-29(R). Eli C. Holleman, b. 28 Dec. 1800 Va., d. 28 Aug. 1874. Samantha C. Birdsong (wife), b. 12 April 1831 Ga., d. 6 May 1896, both buried Fiirview Cem., Eufaula, Ala., granddaughter of Samuel Harwell (Vol. I, p. 73).

Holston, J. W.. 34-11-27. James W. Holston sold a lot in

Eufaula in Feb. 1845 (CR F, p. 321). Nancy C. ----- (wife - ibid).

Holt, A. A.. 22,23&26-13-28(R). Abden A. Holt, b. ca 1823 Ga., son of William Holt of Glennville, Ala. who died by May 1849 (OR 3, p. 327/9). Alsey A. Ivy (wife - m. 8 Feb. 1849), b. ca 1832 Ga..

Holt, A., Asa. 23&26-13-28(R). Asa Holt, son of William Holt of Glennville who died by May 1849 (OR 3, p. 327/9). In Oct. 1853, they were living near Auburn, Ala. ("Southern Christinn Advocate", 4 Nov. 1853). Melissa H. Glenn (wife - m. 7 Jan. 1847).

Holt, W., Wm.. 22,26,27&28-13-28(R). William Holt of Glennville, Ala. died by May 1849 (OR 3, p. 327/9). He bought land in 13-28 in April 1843 (CR E, p. 327/8) .

Hood, J. T.. 11-11-24. Joshua T. Hood, b. ca 1800 N. C., son of Bold Robin Hood (Vol. I, p. 87). Elizabeth ----- (wife?), b. ca1811 N. C..

Hooks, T. J., Thos. J.. 5-12-24(in Pike Co., Ala.) & 25&36-12-24. Thomas J. Hooks may have lived in Pike Co., Ala.. Marshall H. Hooks and Charles M. Hooks also owned land in 12-24.

Hoole, E. S.. 27-10-27. Dr. Eugene S. Hoole, b. ca 1821 S. C., d. by July 1860 (OR 11, p. 116/9). His estate named brothers and sisters in S. C.. Bertram J. Hoole, a brother, was born 1811 in Darlington Dist., S. C.. (UDC Files).

Hooten, H. T., Henry. 1-11-26 & 6-11-27. Henry T. Hooten, b. ca 1817 Ga.. He may have been from Crawford Co., Ga.. (CR H, p. 243). Rachel House (wife - m. 31 Aug. 1838 Crawford Co., Ga.), b. ca 1827 N. C..

Hopkins, J.. 11-10-26.. Andrew Jackson Hopkins, b. ca 1827 S. C.. Rachel M. Powell (wife - m. 30 July 1848), b. ca 1829 Ga., possibly daughter of George and Bashaba Powell (CR J, p. 200).

Horn, J. F.. 12-10-27. Joseph Horn, b. ca 1824 S. C., enumerated next to Willaim (D.) Horn in 1860. Sarah Jane Stewart (wife - m. 15 Dec. 1842), b. ca 1826 Fla..

Horn, Nathan. 5&16-9-26. Nathan Horn, b. ca 1806 N. C., d. 9 July 1862 (Horn Bible). Margaret ----- (wife), b. ca 1815 N. C., d. 1883 (ibid).

Horn, Wm. D.. 17&20-11-27. William D. Horn, b. ca 1819 S. C.. In 1852, he received a military land grant in

20-11-27 (#5707). Louisianna W. ----- (wife?), b. ca 1841
Ga. (1860 Census). Also in this household in 1850 and 1860
were Nancy Horn (b. ca 1800 S. C.) and Penelope Flowers (b.
ca 1785 S. C.).

Houston, E., Edward. 15,16,20&22-10-27. Edward Houston,
Sr., b.ca 1785 N. C., in Ala. by 1832. Sarah ----- (wife?),
b. ca 1805 N. C.. Also in this household in 1860 was Mary
Johnson, b. ca 1770 N. C..

Howard, J. H.. 5-9-26 & 19,20,28,29,30,31,32&33-10-29.
John H. Howard (wife Caroline),of Muscogee Co., Ga. in
1837 (CR B, p. 14), died by June 1863, still of Muscogee
Co., Ga. (OR 13, p. 36/7).

Howell, J.. 11&13-10-27. Joseph Howell, b. ca 1824 Ga..
He may have been a son of Sarah Howell, b. ca 1790 Ga..
Martha Commander (wife - may have m. 5 June 1845 Crawford
Co., Ga.), b. ca 1832 Ga..

Hudson, E.. 15-9-25. Elijah Hudson, b. ca 1789 N. C..
Elizabeth ----- (wife?), b. ca 1793 N. C..

Hudson, J., J. T., Joshua. 13&14-9-25 & 12&13-11-25
Joshua T. Hudson was age 30/40 in the 1840 Census. He is
not in any later census.

Huggins, R.. 25-12-27 & 25-12-28. Reddin H. Huggins, b.
ca 1815 Ga., d. 20 Oct. 1884 ("Eufaula Weekly Times & News"
Oct. 21, 1884). Frances McCoy (wife - m. 12 Nov. 1846),
b. ca 1826 Ga..

Hughes, Wilis. 7-9-28. Willis Hughes, b. ca 1800 S. C.,
in Ga. by 1830, in Ala. by 1850. About 1850, there is a
deed to Willis Hughes that was witnessed by Joseph Garland
Hughes and Lorenzo Dow Hughes. Julia A. ----- (wife?);
b. ca 1802 S. C..

Hunter, J. L.. 4,5,8,9&16-10-29. Gen. John Lingard Hunter,
b. 7 Nov. 1795 Charleston, S. C. (DAB, p. 872), d. 15 Feb.
1868, buried in the family cemetery near Eufaula, son of
Thomas Hunter of Scotland and S. C. and Mary Lingard Wyatt;
grandson of John Wyatt and Violetta Lingard of Charleston,
S. C. (ibid). Sarah Elizabeth Bowler (wife - m. 3 July
1817 S. C. - CR B, p. 905), b. 26 Aug. 1798 S. C.,d. 28
March 1843, buried in the family cemetery. She was a dau.
of James Henry Bowler and Sarah Bradwell Ferguson of God-
frey, S. C. (DAB, p. 872).

Hunter, M. 18-9-25. Marshall Hunter, b. ca 1800 S. C..
Sarah ----- (wife - CR M. p. 432), b. ca 1809 S. C..

Hunter, S. E.. 5-10-29. James Lingard Hunter, b. 14 April

1817 Charleston, S. C., d. 22 June 1846, buried in the Hun-
ter family cemetery. Sarah Elizabeth Shorter (wife), b. 4
Sept. 1819 Ga., d. 4 Sept. 1895, buried in the family ceme-
tery.("Eufaula Times & News", Sept. 5, 1895), daughter of
Col. Reuben C. and Mary B. Shorter (ibid). She married (2)
Wilson M. Bates 3 Feb. 1867 - his 3rd wife . He was born
3 July 1815 S. C., d. 7 Sept. 1875, buried Fairview Cem.,
Eufaula, Ala..

Hurt, G. T.. 30-12-29. George T. Hurt bought this land in
1851 (CR K, p. 394) but is not in the 1850 or 1860 Census.

Hurt, Joel E.. 2,3&4-13-29(R). In 1852, Joel E. Hurt received a military land grant in 14-13-26 (#17382). There
is no further record of him.

Hurt, John. 1-13-29(R) & 6-13-30(R). No further record.

Hyatt, Felix. 6-10-27. Felix Hyatt (Hight), b. ca 1819
Ga.. In 1872, he was living in Pike Co., Ala. (Original
Papers, Box 15, File #2). Jane Sauls (2nd wife - m. 20
Nov. 1845 Muscogee Co., Ga.), b. ca 1822 Ga.. She was the
widow of John Sauls who died by June 1840 (OR 3, p. 537).

Delilah Terry or Jerry (3rd wife - m. 23 Nov. 1851), b. ca
1825 Ga. (1860 Census). Elizabeth Stewart (4th wife - m.
13 Sept. 1863 - Mrs. Caroline Price, Lampasas, Texas), b.
ca 1826 Ga. (1850 Census Pike Co., Ala.).. She was the
widow of James M. Cook (Box 15, File #2 Original Papers).

Ivey, B.. 1&2-12-28, 13,22,23,24,26,27&36-13-28(R), 6-12-29,
31-13-29(R). Barna Ivy, b. 22 Sept. 1795 N. C., to Ala.
from Ga. by 1838, d. 21 Nov. 1856, buried in the family
cemetery in Russell Co., Ala., son of Robert Ivy who died
in Baldwin Co., Ga. (MRA, Vol. I, p. 533/5). Alcey Davis
(wife - m. 12 Dec. 1816 - Ivy Bible), b. 9 Dec. 1800, d.
1886, daughter of Malachi Davis (b. 22 Jan. 1777, d. 20
Sept. 1806) and Mary ----- (b. 22 Jan. 1777 Lenoir Co.,
N. C., d. 27 Aug. 1854) - they married 9 Feb. 1800 (Ivy
Bible). Note: there must have been an error in the birth
date of Malachi Davis or his wife, Mary.

Ivy, Dowsey. 9-11-29. Dowsey Ivy bought this land in 1840
(CR B, p. 878). He may have married Ann Miller 3 Sept.
1836 Baldwin Co., Ga..

Ivy, M.. 4&9-12-28(R). Malachi Ivy, b. 22 Jan. 1818 Ga.,
d. 14 Sept. 1895, buried Perote Cem., Bullock Co., Ala.,
son of Barna Ivy and Alcey Davis (Ivy Bible). Caroline J.
McTyere (1st wife - m. 1844 Russell Co., Ala.), daughter
of John & Elizabeth McTyere, formerly of Barnwell Dist.,
S. C.. ("Southern Christian Advocate", 24 Sept. 1847.)

Matilda A. Gunn (2nd wife - m. 1854), b. Madison Co., Ga.,
d. 1857 (MRA, Vol. I, p. 533/5). Sarah J. Curry (3rd wife -
m. 26 Aug. 1850), b. 6 Sept. 1829, d. 27 Nov. 1864, buried
in the Ivy family cemetery. She was a daughter of William
and Jane A. Curry. Samantha A. Dendey of Denby (4th wife -
m. 9 Nov. 1858 Harris Co., Ga.), b. 5 Sept. 1829, d. 22
Dec. 1910, buried Perote Cem., Bullock Co., Ala.. Note:
Sarah A. Curry probably died 1853, not 1864.

Jackson, A.. 4-12-29. Albertus E. Jackson bought land in
Glennville (now Russell Co., Ala.) in 1840 (CR C, p. 456).
He bought the above land in 1842 (CR E, p. 12). He is not
in any Barbour Co. census. Mary Ann ----- (wife - CR G, p.
24).

Jackson, J. A.. 31-13-26. Jordan A. Jackson, b. ca 1820
Ga., possibly a son of Jacinth Jackson (Vol. I, p. 88).
Elizabeth L. ----- (wife?), b. ca 1827 Ga..

Jackson, J. N.. 31-13-26. Jasper N. Jackson, b. ca 1824
Ala., possibly son of Jacinth Jackson (Vol. I, p. 88/9).
Mary A. ----- (wife?), b. ca 1829 Ga..

Jackson, J. W., J. W. W.. 2,3,9,10&11-9-25 & 1,30,31&35-
10-25. John W. W. Jackson, b. 1812 Ga., d. 1 Feb. 1899,
Elizabeth Lee (wife), b. 1 Oct. 1810 Ga., d. 27 July 1888,
both buried Orion Cem., Pike Co., Ala.. She was a daughter
of Needham Lee, Sr. and Lydia Pryor (Vol. II, p. 78/9).

Jackson, Jefferson. 32&33-13-29(R). Jefferson Franklin
Jackson, b. 23 Nov. 1821 Pike Co., Ala., d. 27 March 1862
Montgomery, Ala. (DAB, p. 893), son of Jacinth Jackson
(b. 16 Oct. 1796, d. 5 Sept. 1869 Sumter Co., Ala.) and
Prudence Allums (b. 1797, d. 1857 - John Johnston, Brundidge, Ala.), m. 26 May 1814 Baldwin Co., Ga.; grandson
of Randle Jackson, b. 1763 Brunswick Co., Va., d. 1838)
and Elizabeth Kendall (b. 1776, d. 1854) (John Johnston,
Brundidge, Ala.). Eleanor Clark Noyes (wife - m. 2 Feb.
1848 Boston, Mass.), daughter of Daniel Noyes and Eleanor
Clark; granddaughter of Ephriam Noyes and Sarah Dike who
married 1779 Bridgewater, Mass. (DAB, p. 893).

Jackson, M.. 5-8-24. Margaret Jackson bought this land
in Feb. 1850 (CR H, p. 612). No further record.

Jackson, S.. 19-9-24. Starling Jackson, b. ca 1816 N. C.,
in Ala. by 1838. Margaret ----- (wife?), b. ca 1815 N. C..

James, E.. 5-10-28. Rev. Edwin James, b. 13 Feb. 1790
Darlington Dist., S. C., d. 15 April 1856, son of Enos and
Anna James ("Southern Christian Advocate", 19 June 1856).
In 1840, he was ordained a deacon in the Methodist Church
at Glennville (CR C, p. 316). Mary Britt (wife), b. ca

1803 S. C., daughter of Daniel and Mary Britt of Darlington
Co., S. C. (Edwin James, Dallas, Texas).

James, J. B.. 13-10-27, 24-11-27 & 19-10-28. John Boswell
James, b. 16 July 1819 S. C., d. 13 April 1892. Mary Elizabeth Bizzell (wife - m. 8 May 1845), b. 8 Feb. 1828 Ala.,
d. 24 June 1881, both buried Faulk Cem.. She was the dau.
of Bennett Bizzell (Vol. II, p. 17 & 21).

James, Wm. M.. 4&5-9-28. William M. James, b. ca 1809 S. C.,
Ann Ross (wife), b. ca 1808 S. C., probably daughter of
Henry Ross (source unknown).

Jarratt, T. K., Thos. K., Thomas K.. 3,4&5-12-26 & 31,32,33-
13-26 (all but 3-12-26 in Bullock Co.). Thomas K. Jarratt is
not in any early census of Barbour Co.. He sold some land in
Oct. 1844 and his signature was attested in Montgomery Co.,
Ala. (CR G, p. 126).

Jenkins, D., Danl.. 2&35-13-25(B). Daniel Jenkins, b. 31
Oct. 1790 N. C., d. 7 May 1877. Nancy ----- (wife), b. 25
June 1797 N. C., d. 16 Aug. 1863, both buried in Bethsadie
Cem..

Jenkins, J.. 17-13-26(B). This may be John Jenkins, brother
of Haley G. Jenkins (b. ca 1800/10 - 1840 Census, d. by Feb.
1846 without issue - OR 3, p. 110/1). His only heirs were
his widow, Temperance, and the following brothers and sisters:
1. Nancy Jenkins of Jefferson Co., Fla. (CR H, p. 340 & 624/5).
2. Martha, wife of John Walker, of S. C.
3. Lucinda, wife of William Walker, of S. C.
4. Sarah, wife of Isaac Pate. In 1847, she was of Greenville
   Dist., S. C. (OR 3, p. 110/1); In 1847, she was of Forsyth Co., Ga. (CR H, p. 341/2) and in 1856, she was of Gil-
   mer Co., Ga. (CR H, p. 624/5).
5. Charles R. Jenkins. In 1847, & 1856, he was of Dallas Co.,
   Ala. (CR H, p. 339 & 624/5).
6. John Jenkins. In 1847 & 1856, he was of Houston Co., Ga.
   (ibid).

Jenkins, R.. 35-13-25(B) & 25-13-26. Elder Riley Jenkins,
b. 10 July 1820 N. C., d. 2 Dec. 1898. Lucretia ----- (wife),
b. 4 April 1825 N. C., d. 28 Jeb. 1912, both buried Bethsadie
Cem..

Jernigan, H. W.. 6-13-26(R) & 24-13-29(R). Henry W. Jernigan, b. 16 June 1806, d. 1 June 1849 (or 1 Jan. 1856 -
"History of Stewart Co., Ga."), buried Glennville Cem.,
Russell Co., Ala.. Caroline Sarah Mildred Gachet (wife -
m. 22 May 1828 Jones Co., Ga.), b. 8 July 1807, d. 7 May
1880, buried Enon Cem., Bullock Co., Ala., daughter of
James E. and Ann Gachet ("History of Stewart Co., Ga.").

Jernigan, Wm.. 28&29-10-28. William M. Jernigan, b. 12
Sept. 1823 Ala., d. 1 July 1902, probably son of Milly
(Emily) Jernigan (b. ca 1790 N. C., d. Feb. 1867). Martha
Deshazo (wife - m. 12 March 1845), b. 30 Nov. 1826 Ga., d.
25 July 1896, all buried Mt. Aerial Cem.. She may have
been a daughter of Wilson Deshazo (b. ca 1804 Edgefield
Dist., S. C., d. 27 Nov. 1892) and his 1st wife, Delilah
Prescott (Vol. I, p. 90/1).

Johns, F.. 1-8-23, 36-9-23, 1&6-8-24, 6-9-24 (Pike Co.) &
30,31&36-9-24. Francis Johns, b. 12 Dec. 1800 S. C., d.
2 Nov. 1881. Nancy Faulk (wife - m. 15 June 1843), b. 1
Aug. 1805 Ga., d. 2 Oct. 1883, both buried in the Johns
family cemetery. She may have been a widow when she married Francis Johns (CR E, p. 342/5).

Johnson, B.. 32-12-28. Bynum Johnson, b. ca 1821 S. C..
His land joined that of Jonathan D. Johnson. Martha -----
(wife?), b. ca 1828 S. C..

Johnson, D., David. 3&10-11-25. David Johnson, b. ca 1822
S. C.. Mary A. Holder (1st wife - m. 3 Feb. 1848), b. ca
1832 Ga.. Haney Ann Lindsey (2nd wife - m. 30 Oct. 1857),
b. ca 1836 Ala. (1860 Census). She had married (1) U. L.
Creech 28 Aug. 1851.

Johnson, I., Isham. 14,15&23-11-24 & 14-12-24. Isham
Johnson, b. ca 1804 S. C.. Mahala ----- (wife?), b. ca
1805 S. C..

Johnson, J. D.. 4-11-28 & 32&33-12-28. Jonathan D. Johnson, b. ca 1814 S. C.. Mary Sylvester (wife), b. ca 1810
S. C., widow of John H. Peake (Mrs. Helen Foley, Eufaula,
Ala.). Also in this household in 1850 was Rachel Johnson,
b. ca 1780 Va..

Johnson, J. F., Jesse. 9,12&13-11-25 & 6-11-26. Jesse F.
Johnson, b. 11 June 1806 S. C., d. 1854, son of Stephen
Johnson and his 1st wife, Mary (Lindsay?) (Vol. I, p. 93/4).
Sarah ----- (wife), b. ca 1807 S. C..

Johnson, J. W.. 11-12-28. John Washington Johnson, b. ca
1822 Ga., d. Jan. 1879 ("The Times & News", Jan. 30, 1879),
probably a son of Andrew N. Johnson who died ca 1840/6 in
Leon Co., Fla. (Vol. I, p. 99), wife Mary. There was a
Mary Johnson (b. ca 1798 Ga.) in this household in 1850.
Louisa Ball (wife - m. 18 Aug. 1844), b. ca 1827 S. C.,
daughter of Wm. R. Ball. In 1833, Jane Shield of Beaufort
Dist., S. C. deeded her estate to Louisa Ball and her
brother and sister (Vol. I, p. 2).

Johnson,L. A. T.. 32-12-27. Lewis A. T. Johnson, b. 23
March 1817 S. C., d. 7 Aug. 1891 La., son of Stephen Johnson

64

and Rosanna Williams (Vol. I, p. 93 & 96). Patience Elizabeth Norton (1st wife - m. 3 Dec. 1837), b. ca 1818 S. C.,
d. 10 May 1863, daughter of William and Lucretia Norton
(Vol. I,p. 96). Eliza Jane Burleson (2nd wife - m. 8 Oct.
1865).

Johnson, R. S.. 18&19-13-26(B). R. S. Johnson, b. ca 1809
Va.. Asinith ----- (wife?), b. ca 1815 Ga..

Johnson, Timothy. 15-11-25. Timothy Johnson, b. ca 1798
N. C., son of Philip Johnson (Vol. I, p. 94). Elizabeth
Johnson (wife), b. 7 March 1799 S. C., daughter of Stephen
Johnson and his 1st wife, Mary (Lindsay?) (Vol. I, p. 93/4).

Johnson, Turner. 5-11-25. Turner Johnson, b. ca 1832 Ga.
(1860 Census). Margaret Earp (wife - m. 1 Sept. 1853), b.
ca 1835 Ga. (1860 Census).

Johnston, A.. 31-10-26. Alexander Johnston, b. 24 Oct.
1814 S. C., d. 15 Oct. 1891, son of Stephen Johnson,(b. 11
Nov. 1776 Newberry Dist., S. C., d. 20 Aug. 1836) and his
2nd wife, Rosanna Williams (b. 17 Jan. 1785, d.18 Jan. 1837);
grandson of Capt. Jeremiah Williams (Rev. Soldier) (1755-
1830) and Nancy Jane Graham (b. 30 Jan. 1756, d. 11 April
1829) (Vol. I, p. 93 & 96). Elizabeth Collins (1st wife -
m. 19 Dec. 1838), b. ca 1825 Ala.' (Vol. I, p. 96). Catherine F. Lott (2nd wife - m. 23 Feb. 1859), b. ca 1830
Ala. (Vol. I, p. 96).

Johnston, Elizabeth. 13-12-28. Isham Johnston d. by Nov.
1846 (Vol. I, p. 99). Elizabeth ----- (wife), b. ca 1800
Ga. (ibid). In 1850, she was living with her son, Richard
M. Johnston, b. ca 1830 Fla..

Johnston, J., John. 28-9-27 & 21,22&28-10-27. John Johnston, b. ca 1784 Horry Co.,(M) C., d. 3 Sept. 1853 (Vol. II,
p. 69). Mary (Molcie) Hodges (wife), b. ca 1796 Horry Co.,
S. C., d. 1879 (ibid).

Joiner, N.. 9&35-9-23(Pike Co.,Ala.), 25&36-9-23, 36-9-25
& 11-10-26. Nathan Joiner, b. ca 1802 S. C., to Ala. by
1835. Cinthia ----- (wife?), b. ca 1803 S. C..

Jones, A., A. E.. 15,22,27&28-10-27. Aerial E. Jones, b.
ca 1820 N. C., in Ala. by 1841, in Fla. by 1849, back to
Ala. by 1850, son of Aerial Jones (b. ca 1780/90 - 1840
Census). He moved to Texas ca 1881 ("The Clayton Courier",
March 19, 1881). Matilda Baker (wife - m. 17 Jan. 1841),
b. ca 1824 N. C..

Jones, H., Henry. 2-9-24 & 2-9-25. Henry Jones (Rev. Soldier), b. 9 Feb. 1762 Dinwiddie Co., Va., d. 15 May 1851,

buried Louisville Cem., son of Henry Jones and Winnie Elder.
She married (2) Robert Lenoir ("History of Barbour Co., Ala."
by Thompson). Sallie Lightfoot (1st wife - m. 16 Dec. 1786
Brunswick Co., Va.), daughter of Henry and Mary Lightfoot
(ibid). Mary Hogan (2nd wife - m. in N. C.) (ibid). Ellender
Payne (3rd wife - m. Covington Co., Ala.) (Vol. I, p. 124).

Jones, J. A.. 12-13-28(R). James A. Jones, b. ca 1815 S. C..
Mary A. ----- (wife?), b. ca 1820 Ga..

Jones, J. B.. 24-10-27. A John B. Jones entered much land
in Barbour Co. in 1827 and may have been a land speculator.
By 1832, he and his wife, Elizabeth, were living in Lowndes
Co., Miss. (Vol. I,p. 102).

Jones, J. W.. 10&15-10-27. James W. Jones, Jr., b. 17 April
1810 N. C., d. 28 July 1862, buried Rocky Mount Cem.. Maria
----- (1st wife?), b. ca 1818 N. C.. Susannah S. ----- (2nd
wife - m. by 1860), b. 19 Oct. 1817 N. C., d. 31 Oct. 1895
buried Rocky Mount Cem..

Jones, Josiah. 18-13-28 & 36-13-28(R). No further record.

Jones, R.. 22-9-24. Russell Jones, b. ca 1816 N. C., to
Ala. by 1837. Elizabeth McDonald (wife - m. 13 Jan. 1846),
b. ca 1827 N. C..

Jones, S.. 30-11-27, 27,28&29-12-27 & 16&17-12-28. Seaborn
Jones, b. ca 1815 S. C.. In 1849, Seaborn Jones of Edgefield Dist., S. C. was granted land in 27-12-27 (Original
Land Grants). Jane ----- (wife), b. 17 March 1825 Edgefield Dist., S. C., d. 6 March 1857, buried Providence Cem..

Jones, Wm.. 31-9-28. William Henry Jones, b. ca 1822 Ga.,
son of Henry Lightfoot Jones (b. 16 Sept. 1791 Ga.) and
Mary Elizabeth Marcus (b. ca 1805 Ga.); grandson of Henry
Jones (Rev. Soldier) and of Daniel Marcus (Rev. Soldier)
who died Bienville Par., La. ("History of Barbour Co., Ala."
by Thompson). Rebecca Westbrook (wife - m. 17 Nov. 1844),
b. ca 1830 N. C., daughter of John Westbrook (OR 9, p. 954).

Jones, W. M.. 32-8-28. Possibly William Jones, b. ca 1811
Va.. Elizabeth ----- (1st wife?), b. ca 1811 Ga.. Mrs.
Nancy A. Futch (2nd wife - m. 3 Oct. 1859), b. ca 1828 N. C.
(1860 Census).

Jordan, J.. 18-13-29(R). Rev. Junius Jordan, b. 14 Sept.
1813 Lunenberg Co., Va., d. 4 Dec. 1894, son of Miles Jordan and Harriet Pettus (tombstone inscription). Frances
Harriet Weyman (1st wife - m. 1 Dec. 1836 Muscogee Co., Ga.)
b. 1813 Ga., d. 6 Nov. 1871, both buried Fairview Cem.,
Eufaula, Ala., daughter of Edward and Eliza Weyman (tombstone inscription). A second wife, name unknown, b. ca

1826, d. Oct. 1891 ("Eufaula Times & News", Oct. 29, 1891).

Jordan, M.. 8-9-28. Membrance Jordan, b. ca 1800 S. C., to Ala. from Ga. by 1848. Melinda ----- (2nd wife?), b. ca 1815 Ga..

Justice, Eli. 30-13-25(B). Eli Justice in not in any early census of Barbour Co.. He may have married Mrs. Ann A. E. Justice 25 Sept. 1859 (Mar.IV, p. 485).

Keener, -----. 20-12-27. This land was patented by John F. Keener in 1846 (Barbour Co., Ala. Tract Book). He was born ca 1810/20 (1840 Census).

Kelly, W. C.. 17-9-25. William C. Kelly, b. ca 1810 S. C.. Elizabeth ----- (wife?), b. ca 1816 S. C.. Note: In Jan. 1845, William Lister gave land in 17-9-25 to his daughter, Charlotty, wife of William Kelly (CR F, p. 286). In April 1852, William C. Kelly and wife, Charlotte, sold land (CR K, p. 293).

Kenemore, John. 13-12-25(B). John C. P. Kenemore, b. ca 1813 S. C.. Nancy G. Thornton (wife - marriage agreement 16 Dec. 1845 - CR G, p. 369). Both signatures were attested in Russell Co., Ala.. Also in this household in 1850 was Jane V. Crapps, b. ca 1833 S. C.. She was a daughter of John J. Crapps who died by Sept. 1835 in Talbot Co., Ga.. His will was recorded in Barbour Co., Ala. 11 June 1845 (OR 2, p. 201). She married Henry Sims by March 1852 (OR 4, p. 350/1).

Kennedy, Danl. 23-9-27. Daniel Kennedy, b. ca 1817 Scotland. Nancy McLean (wife - m. 4 Feb. 1844), b. ca 1819 S. C..

Kennedy, D.. 4&5-12-25(B). David J. Kennedy, b. ca 1825 N. C., heir of John Kennedy who died by Nov. 1865 (OR 15, p. 99). Harriet Shelby (wife - m. 25 May 1851), b. ca 1830 N. C. (1860 Census).

Kennedy, J., John. 17-12-25(B) & 16&17-12-26(B). John Kennedy, b. ca 1788 N. C., d. by Nov. 1865, no wife named (OR 14, p. 624).

Kennedy, J. M.. 10-12-25 & 10-13-25(B). John M. Kennedy, b. ca 1817 N. C., d. by Dec. 1866 (OR 15, p. 487), heir of John Kennedy who died by Nov. 1865 (OR 15, p. 99). Mary ----- (wife), b. ca 1825 Ala.. She married (2) Jason Cargill (OR 15, p. 487).

Kennedy, Jos., Joseph. 26&27-13-25(B). Joseph T. Kennedy, b. 1829 N. C., d. 1889, heir of John Kenndey who died by Nov. 1865 (OR 15, p. 99). Mary M. A. Williamson (wife -

m. 18 Jan. 1857), b. 8 Oct. 1838 S. C. (1860 Census), d. 29
Jan. 1906, both buried Ramah Primitive Baptist Church Cem.,
Pike Co., Ala..

Kennedy, Thos. 3&16-11-26. Thomas Kennedy, b. ca 1811 N. C.,
in Ala. by 1834. Catherine ----- (wife?), b. ca 1810 S. C..

Kennedy, W. R.. 19-12-25(B). William R. Kennedy, b. ca
1820 N. C., heir of John Kennedy who died by Nov. 1865 (OR
15, p. 99). Clary S. Thigpen (wife - m. 2 Dec. 1847), b.
ca 1828 N. C., heir of Joseph Thigpen who died by Oct. 1856
(OR 7, p. 616).

Kent, G.. 2,3,16,22&32-11-27. Guilford Kent, b. ca 1808
Ga.. Sarah Adeline Chany (1st wife - m. 26 April 1848).
She was the widow of David Spear - m. 19 Nov. 1843. She
died by July 1849 (OR 3, p. 338). Susan Brown (2nd wife -
m. 21 Feb. 1850), b. ca 1825 N. C.. Mary T. Stewart (3rd
wife - m. 20 Aug. 1857).

Key, Thomas A.. 7-10-29. Thomas A. Key, b. ca 1813 Ga..
Eliza ----- (2nd wife?), b. ca 1825 Ga..

Kiels, N.. 20&29-9-25. Niecy Kiels, b. ca 1791 S. C.. In
1850, he was in the household of Elias M. Kiels, b. ca 1818
Ala.. In 1834, Niecy Kiels was administrator of the estate
of Isaac Kiels (OR 1, p. 5). In 1858, Elias M. Kiels was
an heir in the estate of William D. Kiels (OR 9, p. 303/5).

Kilpatrick, E.. 35-12-25(B). Easler Kilpatrick, b.ca 1819
S. C., in Ala. by 1836. Emily ----- (2nd wife?), b. ca
1823 N. C..

Kilpatrick, Jesse. 6-9-27. Jesse Kilpatrick, b. ca 1818
S. C.. Nancy ----- (1st wife - CR G, p. 415), b. ca 1832
Ala.. Harriet L. Floyd (2nd wife - m. 16 Sept. 1852), b.
ca 1833 S. C. (1860 Census).

Kilpatrick, W.. 13,14&23-11-24. Warry Kilpatrick, b. ca
1791 S. C.. In 1850, he was living with what must have been
his children, including one named Easler Kilpatrick (b. ca
1831 Ala.). Also in this household (listed last) was Elizabeth Kilpatrick, b. ca 1794 S. C..

Kilpatrick, W. H. 1-10-26 & 34-10-28. William H. Kilpatrick, b. ca 1807 S. C., in Ala. by 1834. Elizabeth
----- (wife - CR F, p. 271), b. ca 1808 S. C..

Kilpatrick, Wm. R.. 6-9-27. William R. Kilpatrick, b. ca
1825 S. C.. Elizabeth Jane Benson (1st wife - m. 25 Dec. 1845),
d. by Jan. 1848 (CR H, p. 81). Rebecca ----- (2nd wife), b.
ca 1835 Ala..

King, A., A. H.. 34-13-25(B). Abner H. King, b. ca 1819
Ga., d. by Aug. 1864 (OR 14, p. 293), heir of Henry King
who died by Nov. 1854 (OR 6, p. 263). Elizabeth Lewis
(wife - m. 4 Nov.1841), b. 10 May 1820 N. C., d. 18 April
1877, buried Fellowship Cem., Bullock Co., Ala., daughter
of Elvy Lewis (OR 11, p. 218/9).

King, Arrington. 34-10-24. No further record.

King, H.. 15&21-12-25(B) & 19-13-26(B). Henry King ,b. 1
March 1792, d. 1 May 1854, buried family cemetery, Bullock
Co., Ala.. In 1839, he was of Upson Co., Ga. (CR G, p. 143).
Abi ----- (wife - OR 6, p. 27). There is an item in the
"Southern Christian Advocate", 27 Nov. 1846 - Mrs. Nancy
King, wife of Henry King of Barbour Co., Ala., died 15
Sept. 1846, age 53.

King, R. H.. 22-12-25(B). Robert H. King, b. ca 1825 Ga.,
heir of Henry King who died by Nov. 1854 (OR 6, p. 263).
Mary ----- (wife?), b. ca 1832 Ga..

King, T.. 18&19-13-25(B). Theophilus C. King, b. 1827 Ga.,
d. 1876. Elizabeth G. Harper (wife - m. 16 Dec. 1847), b.
1827 Fla., d. 1894, both buried Spring Hill Methodist Church
Cem.. She was an heir of William Harper who died by Oct.
1857 (OR 16, p. 466). Also in this household in 1850 and
1860 was Lurana King, b. ca 1805 Ga..

King, T. W., Tandy W.. 3-11-25 & 22-12-25(B). Tandy W.
King, b. ca 1828 Ga., son of Henry King(OR 6, p. 228) who
was born 1 March 1792, died 1 May 1854, buried in the family
cemetery. Tillitha ----- (1st wife - m. ca 1850), b. ca
1829 Ala.. Mary Ann Louisa Efurd (2nd wife - m. 31 Jan.
1854), b. 27 Nov. 1833 Ala., daughter of Thomas C. Efurd
and Mary Johnson; granddaughter of Adam and Lucy Efurd
(Vol. I, p. 51/2).

King, W.. 25,28&35-10-25. William King, b. 2 May 1811
N. C., d. 7 Aug. 1890, buried Bethlehem Cem.. Mary -----
(2nd wife?), b. ca 1816 S. C.. Also in this household in
1850 and 1860 were Chloe A. Herring (b. ca 1838 Ala.) and
Sarah Baker, b. ca 1780 S. C. (in 1860 only).

King, Winey. 25-9-23. Gary King, b. 18 Sept. 1801, d. 28
Jan. 1844 (Vol. II, p. 114/5). Wineford (Winey) Minshew
(2nd wife), b. ca 1810 Ga., daughter of Jacob Minshew, Sr.
(Vol. II, p. 114/5). She married (2) Elisha Rumley by Sept.
1849 (OR 3, p. 390) and (3) Isaac H. Harrell 29 July 1855.

Knight, H. S. C.. 10-8-25. Harbert S. C. Knight, b. 1 April
1824 Barbour Co., Ala. (then Pike Co., Ala.), d. 2 Dec. 1879.
Mary L. Zitterow (wife - death certificate of son, Ira Lan-
der Knight), b. ca 1826 Ga., d. 15 Nov. 1880, buried Bethel

Hardshell Baptist Church Cem..

Knight, W. J.. 9-8-25. William J. Knight, b.3 March 1829
Ala., d. 28 April 1894. Angeline ----- (wife), b. 25 Nov.
1844, d. 29 Sept. 1897, both buried Blue Springs Assembly
of God Cem..

Knight, Wm.. 15-8-25. William Knight, b. ca 1797 N. C.,
in Ala. by 1829, possibly died April 1882 ("Eufaula Times
& News", April 11, 1882). Mary A. ----- (wife?), b. ca
1800 Md..

Laird, L. J.. 13-11-28 &18&19-11-29. Lewis J. Laird, b.
ca 1812 S. C.. Eliza ----- (wife), b. 1820, d. 31 Aug. 1849,
buried Fairview Cem., Eufaula, Ala.. She was an heir of
William D. Kiels. In 1858, her two children were living
with Henry W. Laird in Coffee Co., Ala. (OR 9, p. 303/5).

Lamar, H. Estate. 20&29-13-29(R). Harmong Lamar, b. 22
Oct. 1798, d. 1 Jan. 1844, buried Glennville Cem., Russell
Co., Ala., son of John Lamar and ----- Appling, 5th in
descent from Thomas Lamar, Sr. who emigrated from France
to Virginia (DAB, Vol. IV, p. 1004). Harmong Lamar wrote
his will in Bibb Co., Ga. in Aug. 1843 - it was probated in
Barbour Co., Ala. in April 1844 (OR 2, p. 126). Martha
Ann Young (wife), daughter of William Young of Baltimore,
Md. and Augusta, Ga. (DAB Vol. IV, p. 1004).

Lampley, Ira. 23&24-10-25. Ira Lampley, b. ca 1818 N. C..

Lampley, Jacob. 1&2-9-24 & 6&7-9-25. Jacob Lampley, b. ca
1782 S. C., d. 17 Aug. 1859. Hannah ----- (wife), b. ca
1792 S. C., d. 8 July 1855, both buried Louisville Cem..

Lampley, J. M.. 1&2-8-23, 28-9-24, 36-10-24, 8-9-25, 12&18-
10-25, 11-11-25, 8-9-26 & 32-10-26. Note: some of this land
may have belonged to Ira Lampley or to the firm of I. & J.
Lampley. John M. Lampley, b. 1819 N. C., d. 1867 Kings Co.,
N. Y. (OR 16, p. 503/7). Milly P. Warren (wife - m. 22 June
1847), b. 1832 Ala., d. 1915, both buried Fairview Cem.,
Eufaula, Ala.. She was a daughter of Thomas Warren, Sr.;
granddaughter of Thomas Warren who died by 1821 Edgefield
Dist., S. C. (Vol. I, p. 167).

Lampley, J. R.. 2-9-24. Jonathan R. Lampley, b. ca 1821
N. C.. Catherine A. Shipman (wife - m. 16 Oct. 1845), dau.
of James Shipman (Vol. I, p. 145), probably widow of -----
Whiddon.

Lane, J. P.. 6-11-25. James P. Lane was of Macon Co., Ga.
in 1850 (CR J, p. 54). He and Sarah A. Lane (wife?) sold
the above land in Dec. 1850 (CR J, p. 233).

Laney (Larey?), J.. 4-9-26. John R. Larey (or Laney), b. ca
1823 Ga.. Emeline Cooper (wife - m. 18 Sept. 1851), b. ca
1831 Ala. (1860 Census), daughter of Archibald D. Cooper who
died by April 1860 (OR 10, p. 686).
                              OR
John W. Laney, b. ca 1821 N. C. (1860 Census). Harriet A.
----- (wife?), b. ca 1827 Vt. (1860 Census).

Langston, S. Estate. 18-12-29. Samuel W. Langston, b. ca
1787, d. 19 Sept. 1847 ("The Eufaula Democrat", Oct. 6, 1847)
He was in the militia in Jones Co., Ga. in 1813. Patty Cabaniss (1st wife - m. 22 Dec. 1816 Jones Co., Ga.). (Mrs.?)
Sarah Murphy (2nd wife - m. 16 Nov. 1835 Monroe Co., Ga.).

Laseter, J. C.. 32-11-27. There was a James Laseter in the
1840 Census, b. ca 1790/1800, with a family. No further record.

Lasseter, M.. 19,29,30-10-28. Matthew Lasseter,b. ca 1788
N. C., d. 11 Nov. 1880 ("The Clayton Courier", Nov. 13, 1880)
Henrietta ----- (1st wife?), b. ca 1784 Md., possibly nee
Parmer. Mary Grubbs (2nd wife - m. 24 Sept. 1857), b. ca
1803 Ga., daughter of William Grubbs, Sr. (Vol. II, p. 60).
She married (1) ----- McDowell (2) John Sloan, Sr. 22 July
1849 (3) Benjamin Parmer 1 Oct. 1856 .

Lasseter, M. M.. 7-11-27. Matthew Monroe Lasseter, b. ca
1328 Ga., d. by Jan. 1865 (OR 14, p. 370/1), son of Matthew
Lasseter (Mar. I, p. 304/5). Jane Bishop (wife - m. 30 Dec.
1847), b. 5 Jan. 1831 Ala., (Bishop Bible), daughter of William Bishop and Nancy Pitts (OR 6, p. 107).

Lasseter, T., Thos., Thos. J.. 12&13-11-27 & 17&30-10-28.
Thomas J. Lasseter, b. ca 1810 Ga.. Margaret ----- (2nd
wife?), b. ca 1821 Ga..

Lawless, J.. 8-13-27. Jones Lawless, b. ca 1788 Ga.. He
sold the above land in Dec. 1853 (CR L, p. 52). There was
a Jones Lawless in the 1830 Census of Meriweather Co., Ga.
Cynthia ----- (wife), b. ca 1805 Ga..

Lawson, H.. 19-11-29. No further record.

Lee, A.. 29-12-27. Andrew V. Lee, b. ca 1810 S. C., in Ala.
by 1837, son of Timothy Lee and Elizabeth Muldrough (Vol.
II, p. 86). Nancy McLeod (wife - m. 3 June 1836), b. 3 July
1813 S. C., d. 30 Jan. 1892 or 1897, buried Clairette, Tex.
(Vol. II, p. 108).

Lee, Arthur. 20&29-9-27. Arthur Lee, b. 16 Aug. 1785, d.
Nov. 1856 (Vol. II, p. 84). Mary Lee (wife), b. 16 Nov.
1786, d. 27 Nov. 1852, both buried Adamsville Cem., Sumter
Co., Fla., daughter of Simon Lee (ibid).

Lee, E.. 20-9-27. Timothy Lee, b. 3 July 1772, d. 22 May 1845. Elizabeth Muldrough (wife - Vol. II, p. 84), b. 23 Oct. 1781, d. 20 Jan. 1848, both buried in the Lee family cemetery.

Lee, F.. 31-13-28(B). Ferdinand Lee, b. ca 1798 S. C., in Ga. by 1838, in Ala. by 1839. Susan ----- (wife?), b. ca1798 S. C..

Lee, J. B.. 4-9-27. James Lee, b. ca 1807 S. C., in Ala. by 1838, son of Timothy Lee and Elizabeth Muldrough (Vol. II, p. 86). Sarah ----- (wife?), b. ca 1809 S. C..

Lee, Jas. A.. 23-9-27. James A. Lee, b. ca 1820 S. C.. In 1847, he was appointed trustee of the property (slaves) of Amanda Cynthia Cook, wife of Henry S. Cook and daughter of Ferdinand Lee (CR G, p. 470/1). In 1850, he was enumerated in the household of Ferdinand Lee, b. ca 1798 S. C.. Mary ----- (wife?), b. ca 1832 Ala..

Lee, Jesse. 9-12-29. Jesse Lee, b. ca 1806 Ga. (1860 Census). He bought the above land in Nov. 1850 (CR J, p. 326) but is not in the 1850 Census of Barbour Co.. Sarah Ann ----- (wife), b. ca 1831 Ga. (1860 Census). Also in this household in 1860 was John Thomas, b. ca 1803 Ga..

Lee, L., Lovard. 13-9-25 & 7&18-9-26. Lovard Lee, Sr., b. 25 Sept. 1791 S. C., d. 1 Nov. 1870. Elizabeth McNair (daughter of Gilbert McNair of Cochran, Ga.?) (1st wife), b. 22 March 1795 Ga., d. 7 March 1855, both buried in the family cemetery. Sarah Jane Polk (or Pope) (2nd wife - m. 26 June 1859), b. ca 1843 Ala.. She married (2) J. M. Danford (Vol. II, p. 75).

Lee, Lovard, Jr.. 32-10-25. Lovard Lee, Jr., b. 10 Nov.
1817 Augusta, Ga., d. 6 June 1896, son of Needham Lee, Sr.
and Lydia Pryor (Vol. II, p. 78 & 82). Susan Emeline Lovelace (wife - m. 24 Oct. 1842), b. 25 Oct. 1823 Ga., d. 6
Jan. 1877, both buried Clayton Cem..

Lee, N., N.Jr. & N.Jr, Trustee. 21,29&32-10-25. Needham
Lee, Jr., b. 28 Aug. 1813 Ga., d. 24 Feb. 1887, son of
Needham Lee, Sr. and Lydia Pryor (Vol. II, p. 78/9). Eme-
line Lewis (wife - m. 19 Nov. 1835), b. 8 Oct. 1816 N. C.,
d. 4 May 1871, both buried Louisville Cem., daughter of
Elvy Lewis (OR 11, p. 218/9).

Lee, N.Sr., Needham, Sr.. 29-10-25. Needham Lee, Sr., b.
6 Sept. 1786 Barnwell Dist., S. C. ("Southern Christian
Advocate", 25 Feb. 1853), d. 28 Nov. 1852, buried in the
family cemetery. Lydia Pryor (1st wife - Vol. II,p. 78).
(Mrs.?) Sarah Ann Sloan (2nd wife - m. 16 Oct. 1850), b.
9 Aug. 1811 Ga., d. 30 Aug. 1881 Lake City, Fla. (ibid).

Lee, R.. 28-9-27. Robert Lee, b. 11 Dec. 1822 S. C., d. 7
June 1903, buried Pond Bethel Cem., son of Timothy Lee and
Elizabeth Muldrough (Vol. II, p. 87). Mary Pary Parmer
(1st wife - m. 15 Dec. 1842), b. ca 1820 Ga., d. 24 Oct.
1884, daughter of Jacob Parmer and Martha Stripling (Vol.
II, p. 135/7). Ida Griffin (2nd wife - m. 27 Sept. 1887),
b. 30 Oct. 1869, d. 25 Nov. 1957, buried Pond Bethel Cem..
She married (2) John Foy Adams (Vol. II, p. 87).

Lentithon, E.. 20,25&26-11-28. Eugene Lentithon and
Frederick Martin, merchants of New York City 31 May 1843
(CR E, p. 358). Emily D. ----- (wife - CR J, p. 149).

Leonard, J. C.. 27&34-13-26. In Dec. 1855, James C. Leonard
and James F. Marshall of Talbot Co., Ga. bought part of the
above land (CR N, p. 39). There was a James C. Leonard in
the1830 Census of Talbot Co., Ga..

Lewis, D.. 36-12-24. Daniel G. Lewis, b. ca 1822 Ala..
Lucy Ann Efurd (wife - m. 5 Oct. 1843), b.3 Feb. 1824 Ala.,
daughter of Thomas C. Efurd and Mary Johnson; granddaughter
of Adam Efurd (Rev. Soldier) (Vol. I, p. 50/2).

Lewis, Elvy. 10,11&15-12-25. Elvy Lewis, b. ca 1790 Va.,
d. by Sept. 1860 (OR 11, p. 218/9). Nancy ----- (wife), b.
ca 1796 N. C..

Lewis, H.. 29-9-24. Hanson Lewis, b. ca 1825 Columbus Co.,
N. C. (1906 CSA Census), d. Oct. 1895 ("The Clayton Courier",
Nov. 2, 1895), son of William Lewis (OR 10, p. 310/3). Mary
A. Bizzell (wife - m. 11 Dec. 1860), b. 12 June 1832, d. 1
Dec. 1912, buried Pea River Presbyterian Church Cem., dau.
of Harrison F. Bizzell; granddaughter of Bennett Bizzell
(Vol. II, p. 17/8).

Lewis, J. J.. 14-12-25(B). Joseph J. Lewis, b. ca 1826
N. C., son of Elvy Lewis. Elizabeth ----- (wife?), b. ca
1836 Ga..

Lewis Neecy. 30&31-12-25. Neecy Lewis, Sr., b. ca 1810
N. C., d. 6 June 1886. Rebecca E. Thigpen (wife), b. 5
June 1820 Ala., d. 17 May 1886, both buried in the family
cemetery in Bullock Co., Ala.. She was an heir of Joseph
Thigpen who died by Dec. 1856 (OR 7, p. 616).

Lewis, Sarah. 5-10-26. Daniel B. Lewis patented this land
in 1829 and 1830 (Barbour Co., Ala. Tract Book). He died
by July 1833 (Vol. I, p. 104). Sarah ----- (wife), b. ca
1775 S. C.. (ibid).

Lewis, T. G.. 5-11-25. No further record.

Lewis, W., Wm., Wm. H(?). 19,20,29&30-9-24. William Lewis,
b. ca 1790 N. C., d. by Nov. 1859 (OR 10, p. 310/3), Catherine ----- (wife), b. ca 1800 N. C..

Lewis, Zachary. 29&30-9-24. Zachariah M. D. L. Lewis, d.
by Aug. 1855 (OR 4, p. 438/9), son of William Lewis (OR 10,
p. 310/3). Jane Edge (wife - m. 8 March 1855), b. ca 1839
Ala.. She married (2) Marvin Green 25 Dec. 1859.

Lightner, J. M.. 11-10-26. John M. Lightner, b. 26 July
1824 Ga., d. 28 May 1858, buried in the family cemetery,
son of Michael Lightner (OR 15, p. 526/33). Martha McCarty
(wife - m. 16 May 1844), b. ca 1830 S. C..

Lightner, M., Michael. 3&4-10-26, 34-11-26 & 36-12-26.
Michael Lightner, b. Oct. 1794 S. C., to Ala. from Ga. by
1830, d. 19 Sept. 1866. Sophia ----- (1st wife), b. Oct.
1801 Ga., d. 6 June 1853, both buried in the family cemetery. Martha Holly (2nd wife - m. 6 Sept. 1853), b. ca
1830 Ala. (1860 Census).

Lightner, S. F.. 9-10-26. Samuel F. Lightner, b. 29 May
1828, d. 13 Nov. 1904, son of Michael Lightner (OR 15, p.
526/33). Mary T. Cotton (wife - m. 21 Dec. 1854), b. 29
May 1832, d. 22 May 1919, both buried in Clayton Cem..

Lightner, T. S.. 9&10-10-26. Thomas S. Lightner, b. ca
1823 Ga., son of Michael Lightner (OR 15, p. 526/33).
Nancy Bishop (wife - m. 16 July 1845), b. 28 May 1823 Ala.
(Bishop Bible), daughter of William Bishop (OR 6, p. 107).

Lindsey, J., Jeptha. 4&6-11-25 & 32&33-12-25. Jeptha
Lindsey, b. ca 1808 N. C., in Ala. by 1834. Tabitha Rouse
(1st wife - m. 1831 Duplin Co., N. C. - Mrs. Eoline Jack,
Dallas, Texas).. Lydia Ann Creech (2nd wife - m. 5 Aug.

1846). She had married (1) Noel Register 18 Oct. 1837 in
Henry Co., Ala.. She was a daughter of David Creech (Vol.
II, p. 30/1).

Lister, T. B. & W.. 17-9-25. William Lister died by April
1848, wife Mary Ann. He had sons Thomas, W. B., Joshua and
David and many daughters (OR 3, p.197/8). In 1846, he
deeded the above land to his grandsons, Thomas B. and William P. Lister (CR H, p. 196/7), sons of Joshua Lister
(OR 3, p. 197/8). Thomas B. Lister was born ca 1826 Ala.,
William P. Lister was born ca 1830 Ala..

Little, J., Josiah. 13&14-11-24. Josiah Little, b. ca
1800 N. C., to Ala. from S. C. by 1832, d. by Feb. 1882
(Original Papers, Box 447). Ann ----- (1st wife?), b. ca
1803 N. C.. Kitsey ----- (2nd wife), b. ca 1826 N. C.
(1860 Census).

Locke, J., Jesse. 35-11-27 & 17,18&20-11-29. Jesse Locke,
b. 22 Feb. 1813 Ga., d. 3 Aug. 1896, son of Richard Locke
and Elva Davenport (MRA, Vol. I, p. 440). Richard Locke
was born 12 Feb. 1791, died 26 Jan. 1864. Sarah Ann Amanda
Beauchamp (2nd wife), b. 3 April 1822 Ala., d. 31 May 1890,
all buried Perote Cem., Bullock Co., Ala.. She was a dau.
of William Beauchamp; granddaughter of Littleton Beauchamp
(Rev. Soldier) (Vol. I, p. 4/5).

Loftin, J.. 3-12-29. There is no J. Loftin in the early
records of Barbour Co.. However, in the 1870 Census,
James Loflin was enumerated in 12-29, age 23, born Ala.

Long, C. P.. 32-13-27. Charles P. Long (or Commodore P.
Long), b. 1819 Richmond Co., N. C. (MRA, Vol. I, p. 442/3),
d. by Oct. 1873 (OR 19, p. 505). Martha Streeter (1st wife)
d. 1847 (MRA, Vol. I, p. 442/3). Amanda Maddox (2nd wife -
m. 20 April 1851), b. 25 Sept. 1831 Ga., d. 26 Sept. 1857,
daughter of J. P. Maddox, buried Spring Hill Methodist Ch.
Cem.. Amanda C. Wilson (3rd wife - m. 26 Aug. 1858), b. 3
Feb. 1839 Ga. (1860 Census), d. 27 Jan. 1913, also buried
Spring Hill Methodist Church Cem.. She may have been a
daughter of Archilles Wilson.

Long, Charles. 27-8-25. Charles Long, b. ca 1811 N. C., d.
by Jan. 1868 (OR 16, p. 633/5). Elizabeth Hagler (wife), b.
ca 1814 N. C., daughter of Peter Hagler (OR 4, p. 471/3),
Also in this household in 1850 was Margaret Long, b. ca
1780 N. C..

Long, J.. 5-9-25. There was a J. B. B. Long (b. ca 1800/10)
and family in the 1840 Census, also a James M. Long (b. ca
1800/10) and family. No further record of either.

Long, N. W.. 1-13-26(R) & 4,5,6,7,8,9,10&17-13-27.
Nimrod W. Long, b. 1800 Baldwin Co., Ga., d. 1875 Columbus,
Ga., lived Houston, Twiggs and Upson Cos., Ga. and Russell
Co., Ala. (DAB, Vol. IV, p. 1067/8). He had a military land
grant in 1-13-26 in 1851 (#7923). Catherine Davis (1st
wife - m. 22 March 1821 Baldwin Co., Ga.). She died 1840
and he married 3 more times, names unknown.

Lott, A., Arthur. 4,5&6-9-26 & 32-10-26. Arthur Lott,
b. ca 1790 S. C., to Ala. from Ga. by 1844, d. by Aug.
1859 (OR 10, p. 166/71). Bidsey McGaines (2nd wife - m.
7 Jan. 1842), b. ca 1803 Ga., d. by July 1868 (OR 16, p.
957/9).

Lovelace, E. Estate. 23-9-24. Everett Loveless died by
Oct. 1840 (OR 1, p. 61). Nancy Faulk (wife - Vol. I, p.
61), d. by 1847, daughter of Henry Lawson Faulk, Jr. (Vol.
I, p. 61).

Lovit, J. & Nancy. 20&23-8-25 & 20&29-9-26Joshua Lovitt
d. by April 1845 (OR 2, p. 240). Nancy ----- (wife). In
Dec. 1852, she bought land in Dale Co., Ala. (OR 5, p. 55).
By Jan. 1856, she may have moved to Holmes Co., Fla. (OR 7,
p. 380).

Lowe, Robert. 8-9-27. Robert N. Lowe, b. ca 1808 N. C.,
to Ga. by 1843, in Ala. by 1847, d. by April 1863 (OR 12,
p. 954/5), son of Bird Lowe of Rockingham Co., N. C. (Rockingham Co., N. C. Will Abst., Vol. I, p. 56) and brother of
John W. S. Lowe (ibid, p. 73). Mary H. ----- (wife - m.
3 Aug. 1832 - OR 13, p. 283), b. ca 1809 Va..

Lowman, G. W.. 6-11-27. George W. Lowman, b. ca 1823 S. C.,
d. by May 1861 (OR 11, p. 843), heir of John Jacob Lowman
(OR 11, p. 307/9). Julia Keziah Treadwell (wife - m. 28
July 1846), b. 1820 S. C., d.1907, buried Fairview Cem.,
Eufaula, Ala.. In 1860, they were enumerated in separate
households. She m. (2) Arba Sterns 4 Aug. 1861.

Lowman, H.. 29-13-29(R). No further record.

Lowman, J.. 36-12-26. Joseph Lowman, b. ca 1805 S. C., to
Ga. by 1847, in Ala. by 1850, d. by Oct. 1853 (OR 5, p. 358).
Mary H. ----- (wife), b. ca 1808 S. C..

Lowman, J. J.. 6&8-11-27. John Jacob Lowman, b. 4 Dec.
1793 S. C., to Ala. from Ga. by 1836, d. 29 March 1860,
buried Providence Cem.. He had a daughter born ca 1836
Hancock Co., Ga. ("Southern Christian Advocate, 2 Feb. 1855)
Mary Évans (1st wife - m. 12 Nov. 1814 - "Southern Christian
Advocate", 7 June 1860), b. 22 March 1801 S. C., daughter of
H. & S. Evans, buried Providence Cem.. Eliza J. Williams

(2nd wife - m. 11 Dec. 1855), b. ca 1814 N. C. (1860 Census).
She had m. (1) Wm. B. Saunders 15 Feb. 1842. In 1850, she
was living in the household of Turner Williams, b. ca 1783
N. C..

Lowman, J. L.. 17&18-11-27. James L. Lowman, b. ca 1822
S. C., heir of John Jacob Lowman (OR 11, p. 307/9). Martha
E. Lowman (wife - m. 9 Feb.1854), b. ca 1839 S. C..

Lowman, Wm. H.. 3,4,5,8,9&10-11-27. William H. Lowman, b.
ca 1816 S. C., to Ala. from Ga. by 1845, d. by Jan. 1862
(OR 12, p. 79), heir of John Jacob Lowman (OR 11, p. 307/9).
Mary T. Everett (wife), b. ca 1818, d. 10 Oct. 1849, buried
Providence Cem., daughter of Turner and Mary Everett ("Sou-
thern Christian Advocate", 9 Nov. 1849).

McAlpin, A. S.. 22-13-26. Alexander S. McAlpin, b. ca 1810
N. C., d. by June 1866 (OR 15,p. 358). In Jan. 1857, he was
of Russell Co., Ala. (CR N, p. 423). Frances ----- (wife?),
b. ca 1830 N. C.. In April 1867, she was living in La.
(OR 16, p. 242/5).

McAskill, Mary. 36-13-26 & 31-13-27. In Dec. 1840, Daniel
McAskill and wife, Mary, sold land in 31-13-27 to John Mc-
Askill (CR E, p. 83/4). No further record.

McBride, J., John. 4&5-11-29. John McBride, b. ca 1777 Ga.,
d. by Oct. 1852 (OR 4, p. 652). Rachael ----- (wife), b.
ca 1782 Ga.. Also in this household in 1850 was Sophia
Carlisle, b. ca 1778 S. C..

McBride, Mary. 22-12-29. John McBride, Jr. d. by Jan. 1842
"late of Muscogee Co., Ga." (OR 2, p. 227). Mary Ann McBride
(wife - m. 8 Sept. 1829 Crawford Co., Ga.?), b. ca 1813 Ga.,
daughter of John McBride who died by Oct. 1852 (OR 4, p. 652).
She married (2) Samuel Vining 17 June 1853 - he had married
her sister, Jane McBride, 3 Dec. 1827 Crawford Co., Ga..

McBride, S., Saml. 13&14-12-29. Samuel McBride, b. ca 1805
Ga., in Ala. by 1839, son of John McBride who died by Oct.
1852 (OR 4, p. 652). His first wife may have been Sara P.
Cowan, m. 22 Feb. 1825 Crawford Co., Ga.. Mary ----- (2nd
wife - m. 2 June 1850), b. ca 1828 Ga., probably the widow
of ----- Morris.

McCall, A.. 1-8-24 & 1-9-24. Judge Alexander McCall per-
formed a marriage in Barbour (then Pike) Co. in 1826 (Cox
Bible).

McCall, C.. 31&33-9-25. Charles McCall, heir of Daniel Mc-
Call (OR 12, p. 193). In 1862, his residence was unknown.

McCall, D.. 7-11-26. Daniel McCall, b.ca 1798 N. C., in Ala. by 1824, d. by Sept. 1860 (OR 11, p. 214). Mary ----- (wife?), b. ca 1803 Ga..

McCall, G.. 4&5-9-24 & 1-10-25. Gilbert McCall, b. 19 March 1821 Cumberland Co., N. C., d. 8 April 1903. His heirs were the children of his brother, Daniel A. McCall (OR 30,p. 273). Adeline Warren (wife - m. 24 Sept. 1846), b. 25 Aug. 1827, d. 18 Jan. 1894, both buried in the Warren family cemetery. She was a daughter of Burris Warren and Lucinda Efurd; granddaughter of Thomas Warren of Edgefield Dist., S. C.. (Vol. I, p. 166/7).

McCall. H.. 33-9-25 & 7-11-26. Hartwell McCall, b. ca 1824 Ala., heir of Daniel McCall (OR 12, p. 193). In Feb. 1862, his residence was unknown.

McCall, Paul. 31&32-9-25. Paul McCall, b. ca 1814 N. C.. Mary M. Baxter (wife), b. 7 Jan. 1821 S. C., d. 5 Jan. 1855, buried Pea River Presbyterian Church Cem., daughter of James and Mary Baxter - of Lowndes Co., Ala. ca 1830, to Green Co., Ala. by 1837 (father probably died there), family to Barbour Co. (Pea River Presbyterian Church Records).

McCarty, Wm.. 7-13-26(B). William Allen McCarty, b. 23 March 1819 Tenn., d. 19 April 1904 Anniston, Ala. ("History of Methodism" by Lazenby). Belinda W. Conner (1st wife - m.1838 - ibid), d. 6 Oct. 1852 Macon Co., Ala., daughter of Dr. F. Conner of S. C. ("Southern Christian Advocate", 5 Nov. 1852). Cornelia Susanna Glenn (2nd wife - m. 6 Dec. 1854 near Auburn, Ala. - "Southern Christian Advocate, 22 Dec. 1854). Mary Emma Rivers (3rd wife, m. 1860 - "History of Methodism" by Lazenby).

McCraney, Malcom. 27-10-26. Malcolm McCraney, b. 1 July 1807 N. C., to Ga. from S. C. by 1838, in Ala. by 1846, d. 30 June 1885. Arabella ----- (wife), b. 8 Sept. 1809 S.C., d. 27 Sept. 1893, both buried Pleasant View Presbyterian Church Cem..

McCrary, Jas.. 26,27,28&33-11-26. James McCrary, b. ca 1800 S. C., d. by Nov. 1852 (OR 4, p. 667). In Nov. 1848, Thomas McCrary of Green Co., Ala. gave power-of-attorney to James McCrary of Barbour Co., Ala. to collect his share of the estate of Ann McCrary of Edgefield Co., S. C.. Rebecca ----- (wife), b. ca 1812 S. C..

McDonald, Arch'd. 30-12-28. Archibald McDonald deeded the above land to his sons Archibald, Joshua, John Crofford and James Gabriel McDonald in 1848 (CR H, p. 315).

McDonald, R.. 5-9-25. Angus R. McDonald, b. ca 1816 N. C., d. after 1880. The 1880 Census shows that his parents were born in Scotland. Mary ----- (wife?), b. ca 1825 S. C..

McDonald, C.. 30-11-29. Colin McDonald, b. ca 1785 N. C..
Elizabeth McPhail (wife), b. ca 1802 N. C., sister of Edward C. McPhail (OR 7, p. 511).

McDonald, D. B.. 14-9-24. Daniel B. McDonald, b. ca 1786
N. C., d. 11 May 1854, possibly brother of Malcolm McDonald.
Mary ----- (2nd wife?), b. 24 May 1800 N. C., d. 15 Sept.
1871, both buried Pea River Presbyterian Church Cem..

McDonald, H. W.(?). 25-9-26. No further record.

McDonald, M.. 8,9&16-9-24. Malcolm McDonald, b. ca 1796
N. C., d. 1871, son of Daniel McDonald; grandson of Mal-
colm McDonald; great-grandson of John McDonald (Pea River
Presbyterian Church Records). Martha McRae (wife), b. 4
Aug. 1804 N. C., d. 4 Jan. 1877 or 1879, both buried Pea
River Presbyterian Church Cem.. She was a daughter of
Daniel McRae and Sarah McKenzie from Scotland to Richmond
Co., N. C..

McDonald, M. P.. 30-11-29. Alexander McDonald, b. Elbert
Co., Ga. ca 1791, to Jasper Co., Ga. then to Barbour Co.,
Ala.("Southern Christian Advocate", 11 Sept. 1846), d. by
Dec. 1846. He had a sister, Mrs. Elizabeth Hardy, of Tenn.
and a brother James McDonald who died in New York (OR 2, p.
322). Martha P. Hudson (wife - m. 22 March1821 Elbert Co.,
Ga.), b. ca 1805 Ga., d. 29 Nov. 1869 (OR 17, p. 865/9).

McDonald, Mary. 29-10-24 (partly in Pike Co., Ala). See
D. B. McDonald. In 1860, she was living in the household
of John McDonald (b. ca 1824 N. C.).

McDonald, N.. 25&36-11-27. Neil McDonald, b. ca 1795 N. C.,
d. by Oct. 1851 (OR 4, p. 119). Hugh McDonald bought land
in 36-11-27 in 1838 (CR B, p. 535) and in 1841 (CR C, p.
372). Mary A. R. Harrison (wife - m. 17 Feb. 1842), b. ca
1818 S. C., d. after 1870. In 1850, L. L. Harrison (b. ca
1836 Ga.) and Charles Harrison (b. ca 1838 Ga.) were in this
household, so it it possible that she was the widow of -----
Harrison.

McDougald, D.. 9-12-26, 12,15,20,25&29-11-28, 36-12-28,
25-12-29 & 9&15-13-29. Daniel McDougald of Columbus, Ga.
sold land in Barbour Co. ca 1852 and died before making a
deed (Russell Co., Ala. Court Minutes 1847-1855, p. 148).
Ann Eliza ----- (wife - ibid). She may have been Eliza
Alexander, m. 22 Dec. 1831 Putnam Co., Ga..

McDougald, J.. 12-12-25(B). No further record.

McEachern, D. C.. 31-10-26. Daniel C. McEachern, b. 7
March 1821 Richmond Co., N. C., d. 17 March 1894, son of
Gilbert McEachern and Catherine Cameron (Vol. II,p. 94).
Sarah Lee (wife - m. 18 July 1850), b. 8 March 1830, d.
Aug. 1884 Leesburg, Fla. (Vol. II, p. 94), daughter of
Lovard Lee and Elizabeth McNair (Vol. II, p. 75).

McGehee, A., Abner. 27,28&34-11-29. Abner McGehee, b.
ca 1807 Ga., d. by June 1873 at Indian Springs, Ga. where
he had gone for his health (OR 19, p. 409/11). In 1839,
he was of Randolph Co., Ga. (CR B, p. 693). Louisa Lamar
(1st wife - m. 11 Dec. 1832 Putnam Co., Ga.), b. ca 1809
Ga.. Caroline ----- (3rd wife), b. ca 1822 N. C. (1870
Census). In 1873, she was living in Butts Co., Ga..
(OR 19, p. 409/11).

McGehee, Alfred. 5-11-29. Alfred McGee, b. 2 Sept. 1810
Ga., d. 7 Sept. 1881. Martha Lacy (wife - m. 4 Dec. 1834
Monroe Co., Ga.), b. 15 Dec.1807 Ga., d. 5 Jan. 1891, both
are buried in a small family cemetery called "Handshake
Cem.".

McGehee, E. M.. 35-9-27 & 33-13-29(R). Edward M. McGehee,
b. ca 1815 Ga.. Mary ----- (wife?), b. ca 1825 Ga..

McGilvray, D., Duncan. 1&12-9-26 & 6-9-27. Duncan McGilvray, b. ca 1814 N. C., d. Feb. 1890 ("Eufaula Daily Times,
Feb. 8, 1890), probably never married. In 1850 and 1860,
John McGilvray (b. ca 1816 N. C.), Daniel MdGilvray (b. ca
1818 N. C.), Malcolm McGilvray (b. ca 1820 N. C.) and Mary
McGilvray (b. ca 1785 Scotland) were in his household, probably his brothers and his mother.

McGilvray, Jas., James. 6-9-27 & 31-10-27. James McGilvray, b. 1789 (?) Scotland, d. 27 Aug. 1863. Anna McNeill
(wife - m. 4 July 1846), b. 1817 N. C., d. 6 April 1881,
both buried Old Scotch Cem.. She was a daughter of Daniel
and Abigail McNeill (OR 4, p. 64).

McGilvray, Janet. 17-13-27. In March 1848, Martin McGilvray deeded his share of the estate of John McGilvray to
Mrs. Janet McGilvray = she died by March 1856, leaving her
entire estate to Roderick C. Chisholm and his sister, Janet
(Vol. I, p. 108).

McGilvray, John. 31-10-27. John McGilvray, b. 1798 Scot.,
d. 27 Oct. 1857. Margaret Gillis (wife), b. 1813 Scotland,
d. 20 Jan. 1885, both buried in Old Scotch Cem.. She received an equal share (1/9) of the estate of Hugh Gillis
who died by 1833, as did Sarah Gillis (b. ca 1815 Scot.)
and Christian Gillis (b. ca 1810 Scot.), who were living
with her in 1850.

McGilvray, M., Martin. 36-9-25 & 30&31-9-26. Martin Mc-
Gilvray, b. ca 1802 Scotland. Sarah Gillis (2nd? wife -
Vol. I, p. 107), b. ca 1817 N. C..

McGreggor, N.. 20-9-25. N. McGregor bought this land in
April 1852 (CR K, p. 293). He is not in any early census
of Barbour Co..

McInnis, H., Hector. 22,27,35&36-9-24. Hector McInnis,
b. 10 Feb. 1801 N. C., d. 14 Feb. 1850 (Vol. I, p. 111/2).
Janet McInnis (wife), b. 4 March 1805 N. C., d. 4 Feb.
1870, both buried Pea River Presbyterian Church Cem.. She
was a daughter of Duncan McInnis who died by 1857 (ibid).

McInnis, John. 23&26-9-24, 30&35-8-25 & 23&33-9-25. John
McInnis, b. 1794 Richmond Co., N. C., d. 9 March 1870, heir
of Duncan McInnis who died by 1857(Vol. I, p. 110). Christian
----- (wife), b. 1806 Richmond Co., N. C., d. 29 May 1887,
both buried Pea River Presbyterian Church Cem.. (ibid).

McInnis, Miles. 22&23-9-24. Miles McInnis, b. 1796 Richmond Co., N. C., d. 15 July 1876, heir of Duncan McInnis
who died by 1857 (Vol. I, p. 110). Sarah (McInnis?) (1st
wife), b. 5 June 1790 Richmond Co., N. C., d. 11 April 1861
(ibid). Sarah A. McDonald (2nd wife - m. 8 April 1862), b.
5 June 1826 N. C., d. 20 Feb. 1895, all buried Pea River
Presbyterian Church Cem..

McIntosh, D.. 17&20-13-27. Daniel McIntosh, b. ca 1780
Scotland, d. 23 Jan. 1866 (OR 15, p. 265/6). Sarah -----
(wife), b. ca 1800 S. C..

McIntosh, J. G.. 4-12-27 & 33-13-27. John G. McIntosh, Jr.,
b. 1820 S. C., d. Aug. 1900, buried Spring Hill Methodist
Church Cem. ("Eufaula Times & News", Aug. 9, 1900). In 1850,
he was living in the household of Margaret McIntosh (b. ca
1800 Scotland) - she was an heir of Hugh Gillis who died by
1833 (Vol. II, p. 45/6).

McKay, Donald. 29-9-25. Donald McKay, b. ca 1812 Scotland,
d. by Nov. 1854 (OR 6, p. 194). Winney McRae (wife), b. ca
1815 N. C., daughter of Alexander McRae; granddaughter of
Phillip McRae who died ca 1824 N. C. (Vol. I, p. 119/21).

McKenzie, D., Dan'l, Daniel. 26&27-8-23, 13&14-8-25, 4,8&18-
9-25, 26,27,31&33-10-25, 28-9-26, 21&28-12-26, 21&28-12-27 &
31-12-29. Daniel McKenzie, b. 25 Nov. 1805 N. C., d. 19 Jan.
1886, son of Kenneth McKenzie who emigrated to Richmond Co.,
N. C. in 1784 from Scotland (Vol. II, p. 99). Amanda Burch
(wife), b. ca 1820 Ga., d. 1869, both buried Bethlehem Cem..
She was a daughter of Jesse Burch who died by 1857 in Caddo
Par., La.. (Vol. I, p. 16).

McKenzie, J. K. (or H.). 22-11-27. John H. McKenzie, b. ca
1825 S. C.. Nancy McLeod (wife - m. 16 Nov. 1848), b. ca
1825 S. C., daughter of Katie McLeod, b. ca 1805 S. C. (1880
Census).

McKenzie, W. A.. 19-11-29. William A. McKenzie, b. ca 1811
England. Martha ----- (wife?), b. ca 1825 Tenn., d. 8 March
1875 Opelika, Ala., buried Eufaula, Ala. ("Eufaula News",
March 9, 1875).

McLean,Alexr. 12-9-26. Alexander McLean, b. ca 1823 Scotland.
Sarah ----- (wife?), b. ca 1827 S. C..

McLean, Colon. 10-8-26. Colon McLean, b. ca 1806 N. C. (1860
& 1870 Census say born ca 1800 N. C.). Catherine ----- (1st
wife), b. ca 1810 N. C.. Christian ----- (2nd wife?), b. ca
1805 S. C. (1860 Census).

McLean, D., Danl, Daniel. 12,13,24&30-9-26 & 23-9-27. Daniel
McLean, b. ca 1797 Scotland, d. by 1854 leaving his estate to
his brothers and sisters: John McLean, Hugh McLenn, Sibby Mc-
Lean and Christian, wife of John Cameron (in 1855, they were
in Alexandria, Canada).

McLean, James. 23-9-27. James and Hugh McLean bought this
land in Jan. 1842 (CR F, p. 260). James McLean is not in
any early Barbour Co. Census. Hugh McLean was born ca 1782
Scotland, died 1 Aug. 1880, buried Pond Bethel Cem.. He
was a brother of Daniel McLean who died by Jan. 1855 (OR
6, p. 515/8).

McLean, J.. 27&34-8-26. John W. McLean, b. 1795 N. C., d.
5 May 1870. Margaret Curry (wife), b. 1 Nov. 1798 N. C., d.
5 Feb. 1870, both buried Pea River Presbyterian Church Cem..
She was a daughter of Angus and Catherine Curry (Vol. I, p.
117/8).

McLean, John. 1-11-24, 19&30-9-25, 6-11-25 & 30-9-27. John
McLean, b. ca 1788 Scotland. Catherine ----- (wife?), b. ca
1812 Scotland.

McLendon, Frank. 5-13-25(B). Francis McLendon patented the
above land in 1837 (Barbour Co., Ala. Tract Book). He is
not in any early census of Barbour Co..

McLendon, John. 13-13-29(R) & 18-13-30(R). John McLendon,
b. 22 Aug. 1797 Ga., in Ala. by 1823, d. 18 Aug. 1882.
Mary ----- (wife), b. ca 1808 Ga., d. 16 Feb. 1853, both
buried in the family cemetery in Russell Co., Ala..

McLendon, J. G., John G.. 5-9-24, 32&36-10-24, 5-9-25 &
31&32-10-25. John G. McLendon, b. ca 1804 S. C., d. ca 24

March 1881 Milan Co., Texas (OR 33, p. 24/5), nephew of
Mary, wife of Christopher McRae (Vol. I, p. 121) who was
in his household in 1850, b. ca 1775 N. C.. Elizabeth
(McLeod?) (wife?), b. ca 1823 N. C..

McLendon, M. M.. 4-9-25. Martin M. McLendon borrowed money
from Lauchlin Currie & Co. in Aug. 1841 and put up two cotton
gins as security (CR C, p. 411). No further record.

McLeod, Alex. 27-11-27. Alexander McLeod, b. ca1814 N. C.,
d. 14 July 1891 Terrell Co., Ga., heir of Angus McLeod
(Vol. II, p. 106). Catherine McIntosh (1st wife), b. 13
June 1820 Kershaw Dist., S. C., d. 9 June 1856. Catherine
Stewart (2nd wife - m. 5 Jan. 1862), b. 22 April 1833, d.27
Aug. 1887 - all buried in Palmyra Cem. (Vol. II, p. 106).

McLeod, Angus. 24&25-11-27. There were two men by this name
in Barbour Co. in 1850 and both owned property:
Angus McLeod (possibly a brother of Daniel McLeod who died by
1842 - see John McLeod), b.ca 1781 Scot., d. by 1868 (Vol. II
p. 106). Margaret ----- (wife?), b. ca 1782 Scotland, living
with Mary Winslett in Pike Co., Ala. in 1860 (Vol. II, p. 106
She was an heir of Angus McLeod who died by 1868 (OR 26, p.
286/8).
                            OR
Angus McLeod, b. ca 1823 N. C., d. Nov. 1864 in the Civil War
buried Ft. Gaines, Ga., heir of Norman McLeod who died by
Jan. 1842 in Anson Co., N. C. (Vol. II, p. 112). In 1850,
Mary McLeod (b. ca 1790 N. C.) was living with Angus McLeod.
Josephine Brown (wife), b. ca 1830 Ga., d. Durant, Okla.
(Vol. II, p. 112).

McLeod, D., Daniel D.. 24,25&26-11-27 & 27-12-28. Daniel
D. McLeod, Sr., b. 1783 Isle of Skye, Scotland, d. 1856, in
Robeson Co., N. C., then Kershaw Dist., S. C., then Barbour
Co., Ala. (Vol. II, p. 108), son of Alexander McLeod who
migrated from Scotland to N. C. (MRA, Vol. I, p. 443/4).
Mary Catharine Douglass (wife - m. Robeson Co., N. C.), b.
1789 N. C., d. 14 Oct. 1853, both buried Palmyra Cem.. In
1838, Margarite McLeod also owned land in 24-11-27 but she
is not in any early census of Barbour Co..

McLeod, John. 26-11-27. John McLeod, b. ca 1820 S. C., d.
ca Oct. 1886. He was an heir of Angus McLeod who died by
1868 (Vol. II, p. 106/7). In Sept. 1853, he was granted a
military land patent in 33-11-27 (#30161). Jane Cunningham
(wife - m. 26 May 1842), b. 8 Jan. 1825 Ala., d. 2 May 1901,
both buried Palmyra Cem., daughter of Duncan Cunningham
(Vol. II, p. 107).

McLeod, John. 27-12-28. John McLeod, b. ca 1808 N. C., d.
by Jan. 1857, heir of Daniel McLeod who died by 1843 (Vol.

II, p. 103). Sarah ----- (wife), b. ca 1815 Ga., possibly
died after 1870 (ibid).

McLure, R.. 7-10-27. Richard Rankin McLure, b. 1 Nov. 1783,
d. 19 Oct. 1858, son of John McLure of Scotland and Beaver
Creek, Kershaw Dist., S. C. ("History of Pike Co., Ala." by
Farmer, p. 125). Mary Young (wife), b. 17 Nov. 1788, d. 9
June 1848, both buried Brundidge Cem., Pike Co., Ala..

McLure, Thos. C.. 17-9-24. Thomas C. McLure, b. ca 1800
S. C., son of Richard Rankin McLure ("History of Pike Co.,
Ala." by Farmer, page 125). Mary ----- (wife?), b. ca 1804
S. C..

McMillan, A., Alexander. 8,17&18-10-28. Alexander McMillan,
b. ca 1803 N. C., d. by Nov. 1855 (OR 6, p. 573). He was
living alone in 1850 and no heirs were named in his estate.

McMillan, Danl, Daniel. 27&28-13-25(B). Daniel McMillan,
b. ca 1799 Scotland, to Ala. from N. C. by 1836, d. by Nov.
1851 (OR 4, p. 160/1). Mary ----- (wife), b. ca 1798 N. C..

McMillan, John. 5&8-12-25(B). John McMillan, b. ca 1834
Ala., son of Daniel McMillan (OR 4, p. 343). On the 1854
Tax List, his property was turned in by his guardians,
Finley and Mary McMillan.

McMurray, S. F.. 11-10-26. Samuel F. McMurray, b. ca 1804
Ga.. About 1836, William M., Robert and Samuel F. McMurray
bought land in 16-9-24 (CR A, p. 366). In Dec. 1837, when
Elisha Davis and wife, Sina, sold land in 9-10-26, Samuel F.
McMurray signed a quit claim (CR B, p. 468). He may have
been in Twiggs Co., Ga. in April 1828 when Rachel Beal had
a suit in court against him and NancyMcMurray ("Abstracts
of Some Documents of Twiggs Co., Ga.", p. 11, by Eleanor D.
McSwain). Mary ----- (wife), b. ca 1802 Ga.. In the 1840
Census of Barbour Co., W. M. Murray (W. McMurray?) had a
female in his household age 70/80. He was age 30/40.

McNab, A. C.. 22-10-25. Archibald C. McNab, b. ca 1814
Scotland (1860 Census) bought this land in March 1852(CR
K, p. 140). Mrs Piercy Andrews or Anderson (wife - m. 24
Sept. 1848), b. ca 1806 N. C. (1860 Census).

McNab, D.. 10-9-24. Duncan McNab, b. ca 1796 Scotland, to
Ala. from S. C. after 1844, d. 12 July 1859 ("Southern Christian Advocate", 11 Aug. 1859). Isabella ----- (wife), b. ca
1810 N. C., d. 7 Aug. 1888, buried Fairview Cem., Eufaula, Ala.

McNab, D. & J.. 13-12-26 & 17,18,19&20-12-27. Also see John
McNab. Duncan McNab, b. 1815 Scotland, d. 31 March 1855,
buried Fairview Cem., Eufaula, Ala.. He died at New Orleans,
La. but was a resident of Jefferson Co., Texas (OR 7, p. 97).

84

McNab, Jno. 19-12-27. John McNab, b. 1807 Scotland, d. 16
Feb. 1890 Eufaula, Ala., to Fayetteville,N. C. in 1818, to
Eufaula in 1837 ("Eufaula Daily Times", Feb. 18, 1890). He
and Duncan McNab were brothers and probably sons of Duncan
McNab who died 12 July 1859. Jane Graham (wife - "Backtrack-
ing in Barbour Co., Ala.", p. 157, by Walker), b. ca 1815
Isle of Islay, Scotland, d. 2 May 1869 Eufaula, Ala..

McNair, J. P., John P.. 13-9-25. John P. McNair, b. ca
1810 N. C., d. by Nov. 1857 (OR 8, p. 494). Ann C. ------
(2nd wife - m. 1850 Conecuh Co., Ala. - OR 8, p. 494), b.
ca 1820 Ala.. She was the widow of ----- Jay.

McNair, John. 18,19&20-10-25 & 5-12-25(B). John McNair, b.
ca 1822 Ga.. Mary Ann Cadenhead Grubbs (wife - m. 23 July
1847), b. 10 Sept. 1816 Ga.. She was the widow of Wineford
Grubbs (m. 14 July 1835). The birth record of her two oldest
sons by Wineford Grubbs (James Jefferson Grubbs and John
Tilman Grubbs) is in the family Bible of John Cadenhead. He
was born 1 Oct. 1776 in Pitt (?) Co., N. C., m. (1) Mattie
Whitehurst of Ga. 30 Dec. 1798 Oglethorpe Co., Ga.. She
died 13 Nov. 1803 and he married (2) Pheba Foster 2 Dec.
1806 in Ga.. They moved to Ala. in 1827 and she died 16
March 1843 (Cadenhead Bible).

McNeal, Hector. 1-8-25. Hector McNeill, b. ca 1813 N. C..
Mary ----- (wife?), b. ca 1814 N. C..

McNeil, A.. 16-11-28 & 8-11-29. Anderson McNeil, b. ca
1803 Ga.. He was of Muscogee Co., Ga. in Nov. 1848 when
he bought the land in 8-11-29. Elizabeth ----- (wife?),
b. ca 1814 Ga.. She may have been Elizabeth Thomas, a
second wife, m. 23 Sept. 1841 Muscogee Co., Ga..

McNeil, Daniel. 10-10-27. Daniel McNeil, d. by Feb. 1848
(OR 3, p. 149). Abigail ----- (wife), b. ca 1775 N. C.
(1860 Census).

McNeil, Nancy. 15-9-24 & 6-9-25. John McNeil, b. Richmond
Co., N. C., d. ca 1823 Pike (now Barbour) Co., Ala.. Nancy
Martin (wife), b. ca 1785 Richmond Co., N. C. (source un-
known).

McNeil, R.. 10-10-27. Roderick McNeil, b. ca 1815 N. C.,
heir of Daniel McNeil who died by Feb. 1848 (OR 3, p. 149).
Flora Cunningham (wife - m. 7 April 1842), b. ca 1826 Ala.,
d. 19 Oct. 1886 ("Eufaula Daily Times", Oct. 21, 1886).

McPhail, E., E. C.. 15,21,28&31-12-29. Edward C. McPhail,
b. ca 1815 N. C., d. by Feb. 1856 (OR 6, p. 648), probably
never married. He had brothers Michael McPhail (d. by March
1853 - OR 5, p. 150), Alexander McPhail of Cumberland Co.,

N. C., Davis and Daniel McPhail of Harrison Co., Texas and sisters Mrs. Effie Williams and Mrs. Colon McDonald, both of Barbour Co., Ala..

McRae, A. D., Alexr. 5&6-9-25. Alexander D. McRae, b. ca 1815 N. C., d. by Nov. 1860 (OR 11, p. 344). Elizabeth McRae (wife - m. 15 Dec. 1853), b. ca 1830 N. C. (1860 Census), probably daughter of John R. McRae.

McRae, A. K., Alexr. K.. 2&3-9-24. Alexander Keane McRae, b. ca 1823 Anson Co., N. C. (1906 CSA Census), son of John R. McRae and Comfort Keane (Vol. I, p. 123/4). Winney Elder Jones (wife), b. 3 Nov. 1835 ("History of Barbour Co., Ala." by Thompson), daughter of Henry Jones and his second wife, Ellender Payne (Vol. I, p. 123/4).

McRae, C.. 1&12-9-24. Christopher M. McRae, b. 27 Dec. 1819 N. C., d. 23 May 1883. Abigail ----- (wife), b. 8 Feb. 1820 Anson Co., N. C., d. 27 Oct. 1895, both buried Pea River Presbyterian Church Cem..

McRae, C. C.. 16-9-24. Christopher C. McRae, b. 18 Dec. 1823 Anson Co., N. C., d. 18 Nov. 1861. Nancy A. Campbell (wife - m. 8 Aug. 1850), b. 26 June 1832 Anson Co., N. C., d. 28 May 1910, both buried Pea River Presbyterian Church Cem..

McRae, F., F. A.. 13,14&23-9-24. Farquhar A. McRae, b. 1796 N. C., d. 11 Dec. 1858, son of Phillip McRae who died in N. C. ca 1824 and Christian McLeod who died in Barbour Co., Ala. by 1844 (OR I, p. 119). Mary McRae (wife), b. 1796 N. C., d. 25 May 1854, both buried Pea River Presbyterian Church Cem.. She was a daughter of Christopher McRae who died by April 1837 Anson Co., N. C. - his will was recorded in Barbour Co., Ala. 31 March 1840 (Vol. I, p. 119 & 121).

McRae, F. C.. 6,22,26,27&35-9-24 & 19-9-25. Farquhar C. McRae, b. ca 1817 Ala., probably son of William McRae (b. 8 Jan. 1798 N. C., d. 10 Dec. 1886, buried Pea River Presbyterian Church Cem. - Vol. I, p. 123). Mary Ann E. Cameron (wife - m. 27 July 1854).

McRae, G. W.. 11-9-24. George Washington McRae, b. 24 Apr. 1811 Anson Co., N. C., d. 5 April 1878. Christian McLeod (wife - m. 20 Feb. 1845), b. 18 Feb. 1814 N. C., d. 3 April 1889, both buried Pea River Presbyterian Church Cem..

McRae, J., John. 1,2&12-11-25. John McRae, b. ca 1816 S. C.. Virginia ----- (1st wife?), b. ca 1825 Ga.. C. G. ----- (2nd wife?), b. ca 1839 Ga. (1860 Census).

McRae, John A.. 11,12&13-9-24. John A. McRae is not in any
early census of Barbour Co.. In Feb. 1835, Duncan McRae and
wife Catherine sold the above land to John A. McRae of Lowndes
Co., Ala. (CR A, p. 82). In June 1835, Alexander McRae borrowed money from John A. McRae of Lowndes Co., Ala. (CR A,
p. 83).

McRae, J. C., John C.. 10,11,14&15-9-24. John C. McRae, b.
18 Feb. 1806 Anson Co., N. C., d. 11 April 1891. Janet
McLeod (wife - m. 21 Sept. 1826 Anson Co., N. C.), b. 26
Feb. 1806, d. 6 June 1868, both buried Fairview Cem., Eufaula,
Ala.. She was a daughter of Norman and Mary McLeod (Vol. I,
p. 122).

McSwean (McSwain), D., Danl, Daniel. 24,33&34-8-26 (partly
in Henry Co., Ala.). Daniel McSwean (McSwain), b. ca 1776
Scotland. In 1847, 1848 and 1849, Angus McSwean, Daniel
McSwean and Daniel McSwean, Jr. all patented land in 33&34-
8-26. In Jan. 1859, Daniel McSwean gave a slave to his son,
Daniel McSwean of Dale Co., Ala. (CR P, p. 232). Mary -----
(wife?), b. ca 1778 N. C.. In 1860, she was living with
Malcolm McSwean (1860 Census).

McSwean, R.. 33-13-26(B). Roderick McSwean, b. ca 1812
N. C.. Catherine ----- (wife?), b. ca 1816 N. C..

McSwean, R. C.. 1&2-9-26 & 6-9-27. Roderick C. McSwean,
b. 1791 Isle of Skye, Scotland, to Ala. by 1829, d. 28 Jan.
1862. Mary Gillis (wife), b. 1795 Richmond Co., N. C., d.
16 Dec. 1861, both buried Louisville Cem..

Mabry, Jas. W.. 8-9-25. James Walton Mabry, b. ca 1825
Forsyth, Ga., son of Allen Mabry (MRA, Vol. I, p. 445/6).
He died 26 Jan. 1894 ("The Clayton Courier", Feb. 3, 1894).
Mary Ann Calloway (wife - m. 23 Aug. 1855), b. ca 1832 Ala.
(1860 Census), moved to Dothan, Ala. in 1895 ("The Clayton
Courier" Nov. 30, 1895).

Mabry, S., Seth. 15&22-11-24, 7&8-9-25 & 15-11-25. Seth
Mabry, b. ca 1821 Ga., d. 1 Feb. 1882 ("Eufaula Times &
News", Feb. 7, 1882) probably never married. Son of Allen
Mabry and Nancy Sherer who married 4 Jan. 1813 Lincoln Co.,
Ga.. She was born 23 Dec. 1781, d. 16 Dec. 1881 ("The
Eufaula Weekly Bulletin", Dec. 17, 1881); grandson of Joshua
Mabry and Mourning Harwell who married 10 Sept. 1770 Bruns-
wick Co., Va. (she died 1807 Wilkes Co., Ga.); great-grand-
son of Joshua Mabry and Lucretia Jones. Also grandson of
James Sherer who died by 1815/6 Wilkes Co., Ga. (The Mabry
Family in Ga. by Rev. D. E. Collins).

Madox, J. P.. 26,35&36-13-26. John P. Maddox, b. ca 1809

Ga., to Fla. by 1835, to Ga. by 1839 and to Ala. by 1842.
He was a brother-in-law of James J. Trammell who died by
Aug. 1843 (OR 2, p. 99). Eliza Ann ----- (wife), b. ca
1814 Ga..

Mallard, P. C.. 22-9-27. Peter C. Mallard sold land in.
21-9-27 in Dec. 1850 (CR J, p. 131). No further record.

Malone, G.. 4-11-29 & 33-12-29. Green Malone, b. ca
1807 S. C. (1850 Census) or ca 1796 Va. (1860 Census),
d. by Aug. 1861 (OR 11, p. 946/7). He was a Methodist
Minister. Mrs. Louisa S. Torrence (1st wife - m. 4 Aug.
1840 - "Southern Christian Advocate", 21 Aug. 1840),
widow of Ebenezer Torrence (OR 1, p. 25). She was born
ca 1801, died 14 Jan. 1849 ("The Eufaula Democrat", Jan.
23, 1849). Julia T. Abney (?) (2nd wife), b. ca 1830 Fla.

Maloy, D.. 28-13-25(B). Duncan Malloy, b. ca 1797 S. C..
In Feb. 1842, he bought land in 29-13-25, at which time
he was of Macon Co., Ala. (CR E, p. 551). Mary -----
(wife?), b. ca 1810 Ga..

Man, G.. 13-10-27 & 7-10-28. Gilbert Mann, b. ca 1774
S. C., d. 11 July 1854. His only heir was his son, Robert
Mann (Vol. I, p. 130).

Man, R.. 22-12-26. Robert Mann, b. ca 1805 S. C., son of
Gilbert Mann (Vol. I, p. 130). Harriet Bennett (?) (wife),
probably daughter of Luke and Elizabeth Bennett (Vol. II,
p. 10).

Marley, H. J.. 21-9-26. Horatio J. Marley, b. ca 1800
N. C.. Dianna ----- (1st wife?), b. ca 1813 N. C.. Nancy
Texas Lewis (2nd wife - m. 30 Dec. 1869), b. 12 Oct. 1844,
d. 15 March 1912, daughter of John Lewis (b. 1 March 1810,
d. 8 July 1873) and Epsey Suwanee Wood (b. 17 Feb. 1817,
d. 6 Jan. 1886) who married 12 Jan. 1837 in N. C.. (Vol.
II,p. 192).

Martial, J. F.. 34-13-26. James F. Marshall, b. 10 June
1820, d. 15 June 1887. He and James C. Leonard, both of
Talbot Co., Ga., bought the above land (CR N. p. 39). Ella
Clifford Weaver (wife), b. 26 Aug. 1846, d. 25 Feb. 1937,
both buried Ramah Baptist Church Cem... She was a daughter
of Absolom Weaver who died 26 July 1889 (OR 25, p. 319/20).

Martin, E.. 22&23-12-29. Ezekiel Martin, b. ca 1816 Ala.
(?). Elizabeth ----- (wife?), b. ca 1826 Ala. (?).

Martin, F.. 17-13-26(B). Felix Martin, b. ca 1814 Ga..
Nancy ----- (wife?), b. ca 1823 Ala. (?).

Martin, J. L.. 17,18,19&20-10-28. James L. Martin, b. ca

1790 S. C., to Ala. from Ga. by 1843, d. by Sept. 1852
(OR 4, p. 594). Sarah Smith (wife - m. 31 March 1821 Jasper Co., Ga.), b. ca 1805 Ga..

Martin, J. T.   21-11-26.   John T. Martin, b. ca 1815 S. C.,
son of D. Martin and Mary Efurd; grandson of John & Lucy
Efurd (Vol. I, p. 51). Hepsey Worthington (wife - m. 11
May 1845), b. 24 Sept. 1825 N. C., d. 27 July 1866, buried
Warren family cemetery.

Martin, M. D..   1-8-24 & 27,28&33-9-24.   Martin D. Martin,
b. ca 1811 Richmond Co., N. C. (MRA, Vol. I, p. 448), d.
by March 1860 (OR 10, p. 677/9). Margaret McRae (wife), b.
ca 1819 N. C., d. 1891 (MRA, Vol. I, p. 448).

Martin, Robert.   6-11-28.   Robert Martin, b. ca 1798 Ga..
Charlotte (2nd wife?), b. ca 1796 Ga..

Martin, S..   17&18-13-27.   Sylvester Martin, b. ca 1815
N. C., to Ala. from Ga. by 1847, later moved to Henry Co.,
Ala. (OR 26, p. 276).   Delia ----- (1st wife?), b. ca 1817
Ga..   Susan Williamson (2nd wife - m. 2 Sept. 1852), b. ca
1826 N. C. (1860 Census), daughter of Charles Williamson
who died 1867 (OR 26, p. 276).

Martin, Wm..   28&33-9-24.   There was a William Martin (b.
ca 1790/1800) in the 1840 Census with a family. He is not
in any later census nor is there an estate record for him
in Barbour Co..

Massy, N..   10-11-25.   Nathaniel D. Massey, b. ca 1823 Ga.
(1860 Census).   Ruthy ----- (wife?), b. ca 1828 Ga.. (ibid).

Mathews, A..   11-9-25.   Abel (or Abraham) Mathis (or Matthews), b. ca 1802 N. C., in Ala. by 1833, d. 13 April 1870
(OR 18, p. 191/3).   Jincey ----- (wife?), b. ca 1815 N. C..

Mayo, John.   29&30-9-26.   John Mayo, b. ca 1799 S. C., to
Ala. from Ga. by 1843. He received a military land grant
in 10-9-25 in 1851 (#11648).   Olive ----- (2nd wife?), b.
ca 1814 Ga..

Meadle, Eldridge.   10&11-12-25(B).   Eldridge Medley, b. ca
1806 N. C..   Mary ----- (2nd wife?), b. ca 1813 Ga..

Meadley, H..   36-13-25(B).   Hansel Medley, b. ca 1810 N. C..
In 1850, his household consisted of himself, Judith Medley
(b. ca 1782 N. C.), Jemima Medley (b. ca 1812 N. C.) and
Milly Medley (b. ca 1815 N. C.). Judith Medley was probably his mother but there is nothing to show if either
Jemima or Milly was his wife. He sold land in 1851 but no
wife signed the deed.

Meadley, Roderick. 33-13-26(B). No further record.

Meadley, Wm.. 30-13-26(B). William Medley married Ellen
Cook 20 Jan. 1842 in Barbour Co. but is not in any census.

Miles. A. B.. 29&32-11-27. Abram Baldwin Miles, b. ca
1808 Ga., d. 15 Feb. 1890 Eddy, Texas ("Eufaula Daily Times"
Feb. 21, 1890). Nancy Locke (2nd? wife), b. ca 1830 Ala.,
daughter of Richard Locke (MRA, Vol. I, p. 440/2). See
Jesse Locke.

Miller, A. T.. 24-12-27. Asa T. Miller, b. ca 1805 N. C..
Elizabeth B. Tarver (wife - m. 1 Dec. 1846), b. ca 1829.

Miller, D. C.. 36-12-25 & 30&31-12-26. Dr. David C. Miller,
b. ca 1818 S. C.. He sold the above land in Oct. 1854 (CR
O, p. 649). Mildred ----- (wife), b. ca 1826 Ga..

Miller, G. S.. 2&3-11-25. George W. S. Miller, b. ca 1810
Ga. (1860 Census). Temperance ----- (1st wife - CR L, p.
441). Martha A. ----- (2nd wife?), b. ca 1823 Ga. (1860
Census).

Miller, I. L.. 25-11-25 & 20-12-26. Irwin L. Miller, b.
1818 Orangeburg Dist., S. C., d. 29 Dec. 1899 ("Eufaula
Times & News", Jan. 4, 1900). He and his family moved to
Texas about 1855, then after the Civil War they moved to
Brazil, South America until about 1896. Sophia Ferguson
Hunter (wife), b. ca 1828 S. C., d. 24 Jan. 1890, buried
in the Hunter family cemetery. She was a daughter of John
L. Hunter ("Eufaula Daily Times", March 25, 1890).

Miller, J. C.. 36-12-26. No further record.

Miller, J. H.. 24&25-10-25, 3&4-9-26 & 19,29,30,31,34&35-
10-26. John H. Miller, b. ca 1812 S. C.. Ann C. Ott (wife)
b. ca 1819 S. C., sister of Edward S. Ott and Mary M. Treadwell (OR 15, p. 155/8).

Miller, Lewis. 24&34-10-27. Lewis Miller, b. 8 May 1803
N. C., d. 10 May 1895. Hettie Parmer (wife), b. 16 Aug.
1810 Ga., d. 20 July 1885, both buried Rocky Mount Cem..
She was a daughter of Benjamin Parmer (Vol. II, p. 132/3).

Miller, M.. 15-9-27. Martin Miller, b. ca 1812 N. C., d.
28 Aug. 1889 ("Eufaula Weekly Times & News", Aug. 29, 1889).
Jane ----- (2nd wife), d. 26 Dec. 1888, age 76, buried
Belcher Bethel Cem..

Mims, C. C.. 16-13-29(R). No further record.

Minshew, Jacob. 8-8-24. Jacob Minshew, b. ca 1808 N. C.,

son of Jacob Minshew, Sr. (Vol. II, p. 114/5). Mary Dansby (wife), b. ca 1817 S. C., daughter of Winza Dansby of Pike Co., Ala. (Vol. I, p. 41/3).

Minshew, J., John. 24,27&34-8-23. John M. Minshew, b. ca 1800 N. C., in Ala. by 1826, moved to Rusk Co., Texas (Vol. II, p. 114),son of Jacob Minshew, Sr. (ibid). Harriet ----- (wife), b. ca 1810 Ga..

Minshew, N.. 18-8-24. Nathan Minshew, b. ca 1803 N. C., d. by July 1860 (Vol. II, p. 117). Elizabeth Moreland (?) (wife), b. ca 1816 N. C. (ibid).

Mitchell, Americus C.. 3,4,9,10,13,16&17-13-28(R) & 6,7& 18-13-29(R). Americus C. Mitchell, b. 18 Nov. 1819 Ga.. d. 21 Jan. 1891, son of Julius Caesar Bonaparte Mitchell (CR G, p. 24/5). Mary Elizabeth Billingslea (wife - m. 4 Sept. 1841 Jones Co., Ga.), b. 2 Nov. 1823 Ga., d. 7 July 1895, both buried Glennville Cem., Russell Co., Ala..

Mitchell, Benjamin. 15-13-27. Dr. Benjamin J. J. Mitchell, b. 15 Nov. 1820 Ga., d. 8 June 1855, buried in the family cemetery in Russell Co., Ala.; son of James and Elizabeth M. Mitchell (tombstone inscription). James Mitchell died by March 1841 (OR 1, p. 126). Sarah G. ----- (wife? - OR 6, p. 532).

Mitchell, C.. 17-13-28. Julius C. B. Mitchell, b. 24 July 1795, d. 30 Jan. 1848. Catherine Daniel (wife - m. 1817 Hancock Co., Ga.), b. 4 March 1799 Hancock Co., Ga., d. 19 July 1880, both buried Glennville Cem,, Russell Co., Ala..

Mitchell, Randolph. 18-13-29(R). Randolph Mitchell,b. ca 1800 Ga., d. by April 1858 (OR 9, p. 53/4). He may have been a son of James Mitchell who died by March 1841 (OR 1, p. 126). Avey ----- (1st wife). Martha Denson (2nd wife - m. 7 Aug. 1840 Harris Co., Ga.), b. ca 1820 N. C., daughter of Jethro Denson who died by 1851 (OR 4, p. 115/8).

Moats, J.. 3-11-26. Jonathan Moats, b. ca 1796 S. C., d. 1855 (OR 26, p. 228/30). Nancy Ann Mabry (2nd wife - m. 30 Sept. 1845), b. ca 1818 Ga., d. 1897. She was the widow of ----- Harveston and an heir of Nancy Mabry (OR 23, p. 212/6). She married (3) Adam Grubbs 1 Feb. 1860.

Moats, Wm.. 18&19-9-24. William Moats, b. ca 1824 Ala., in Miss. ca 1844/6, in Ala. by 1848. Sarah ----- (wife?) b. ca 1825 Ala..

Moffett, H.. 11-13-25(B) & 7&17-13-26(B). In Nov. 1852, Henry Moffett and wife, Lorinda, of Russell Co., Ala. sold the land in 11-13-25 (CR K, p. 413).

Moody, J.. 9-11-28. John Moody, b. ca 1823 S. C.. In 1850, he was in the household of Henry Urquhart - no further record.

Moore, J. C.. 6-13-25(B). John C. Moore, b. ca 1833 Madison (?), Ga. d. 8 Jan. 1884 ("The Eufaula Weekly Bulletin", Jan. 9, 1884). In 1848, John Gill Shorter was his guardian (OR 3, p. 244). Martha V. Flournoy (wife), b. ca 1839 Ala. (1860 Census), heir of Thomas Flournoy who died by June 1863 (OR 13, p. 67).

Moore, James. 7-11-29. James C. Moore patented land in 17-11-29 in 1840 (Barbour Co., Ala. Tract Book). No further record.

Moore, W.. 35-13-25(B). William M. Moore, b. ca 1827 N. C.. Martha ----- (wife?), b. ca 1825 N. C..

Morgan, J. C.. 9-10-27. James C. Morgan, b. ca 1823 Ga., heir of Simon S. Morgan who died by Jan. 1833 Monroe Co., Ga. (OR 1, p. 102). Nancy Elizabeth Kirkland (wife - m. June 1855 in Ga. - CR M, p. 358), daughter of David B. Kirkland who died Dec. 1855 Randolph Co., Ga. (ibid).

Morris, Jas.. 10&11-11-25. James Morris, Sr., b. ca 1790 N. C., d. by Oct. 1865 (CR 14, p. 602/3). Gatsey A. ----- (wife?), b. ca 1798 N. C..

Morrison, D., Danl, Daniel.. 16-10-27 & 26-11-27. Daniel Morrison d. 7 Dec. 1846, age 64. Catharine ----- (wife), b. 1788 Scotland, d. 23 April 1855, both buried Fairview Cem., Eufaula, Ala..

Morton, Lucy. 1-13-25. Lucy Morton bought this land in May 1842 (CR E, p. 501). No further record.

Morton, W., Wm.. 1,2&3-13-25(B) & 17-13-26(B). William Morton, b. 2 Oct. 1804 Ga., d. 1885. Eliza B. ----- (wife), b. 17 Feb. 1812 Ga., d. 12 Dec. 1884, both buried Enon Cem., Bullock Co., Ala.. Also buried in this cemetery is Julia Ann, wife of Thomas Morton, died 24 April 1851, age 32, In 1854, Thomas Morton was of Macon Co., Ala. (CR L, p. 257).

Moseley, F. M.. 9-13-25(B). Francis Marion Moseley, b. 4 Oct. 1815 Ga., d. 22 Aug. 1869, buried Fellowship Cem., Bullock Co., Ala.. Mary Ann Watson (wife), b. ca 1815 Ga., daughter of Peter Watson. She may have moved to Tyler, Texas (Vol. I, p. 170/1).

Moseley, Wm.. 9-13-25(B). No further record.

Mosher, Wm.. 22-11-28. William H. B. Mosher, b. ca 1823

Rhode Island. Mariah A. Hill (wife - m. 16 Feb. 1854), b. ca 1835 S. C. (1860 Census), daughter of Martin M. Hill (Mar. 4, p. 141).

Mothershead, Levi. 3-10-24. Levi Mothershead, b. ca 1805 S. C.. Lucy ----- (wife?), b. ca 1803 S. C..

Myers, Jas.. 10-11-25. James Myers, b. ca 1790 S. C.. Elizabeth ----- (wife), b. ca 1804 S. C..

Nancy, S.. 7-8-24. Sylvester Nance, b. ca 1825 S. C.. Catherine ----- (1st wife), b. ca 1823 S. C.. She was an heir of David Powell who died by Sept. 1854 (OR 6, p. 232/3). Martha ----- (2nd wife), b. ca 1836 Ala.. (1880 Census).

Nash, Acton. 7-10-29. Acton Nash, b. ca 1764 Va., d. by Aug. 1854 (OR 6, p. 408/9). He married in Wilkes Co., Ga. in 1799 and probably was in Twiggs Co., Ga. before coming to Barbour Co., Ala.. Margaret Strozier (wife - m. 12 Aug. 1799 Wilkes Co., Ga.), b. ca 1767 Ga..

Nash, M. B.. 28-11-25. Milton B. Nash was of Russell Co., Ala. in 1838 (CR B, p. 705). Melissa Moore (wife - m. 25 Feb. 1847), possibly his second wife.

Newman, Saml.. 2-13-25(B). Samuel Newman is not in any early census of Barbour Co.. He was a son-in-law of Bartholemew Fields, a Rev. Soldier who died at the home of Samuel Newman in Dale Co., Ala. in March 1845 ("Southern Christian Advocate", 25 July 1845).

Niece, H.. 10-11-25. Henry Niece, b. ca 1810 S. C.. He did not report owning any real estate in the 1850 Census. In April 1839, David Neece deeded land in 1-11-25 to Elizabeth Neese (CR B, p. 501) - they may be the family connected with this land.

Niece, Jacob. 5-11-25. The 1854 Tax List includes J. Niece estate, John Niece, guardian. In 1853, John Niece and wife, Mary, sold land in 9-11-25 (CR K, p. 676). None of these are in any early census of Barbour Co..

Nobles, A.. 17-11-28. Archibald Nobles, b. ca 1809 N. C.. Eliza Jane ----- (1st wife - CR K, p. 422), b. ca 1813 Ga.. Nancy Ann Murry (2nd wife - m. 5 July 1857) .

Nolin, Avery. 6,24&26-10-27 & 28-10-28. Avery Nolin, b. ca 1805 S. C., in Ala. by 1828, d. after 1870. He received a military land grant in 26-10-28 in 1851 (#13559). It is very likely that Avery, Daniel and James B. Nolin were brothers. Melinda ----- (wife), b. ca 1806 S. C.. Also in this household in 1850 was Benjamin McKenney, b. ca 1794 S. C..

Nolin, D.. 13-10-27. Dennis Nolin, b. ca 1815 Ga.. Martha
E. J. Dubose (wife - m. 2 June 1850), b. ca 1828 S. C.. Also
in this household in 1850 was Mary Nolin, b. ca 1783 S. C..

Nolin, Danl. 23-10-27. Daniel Nolin, b. ca 1807 S. C., d.
31 March 1873 (OR 19, p. 732/3). Elizabeth ----- (wife), b.
ca 1815 Ga., d. 17 March 1874(ibid).

Nolin, J., J. B., James. 24&25-10-27 & 17&18-10-28. James
B. Nolin, b. ca 1800 S. C., in Ala. by 1827. Mary -----
.(wife?), b. ca 1810 S. C. (1860 Census).

Nolin, W. S. (should be S. W.). 25-10-27. Simpson W. Nolin,
b. ca 1825 Ga. (1860 Census). Ruthy Jane Bullock (wife - m.
15 Jan. 1850), b. ca 1830 Ala. (1860 Census).

Norton, D. A.. 6&7-11-27 & 29-12-27. Daniel Asbury Norton,
b. ca 1813 S. C., d. 1897 La., son of William Norton, Jr.
and Lucretia Harrelson; grandson of William Norton (Rev.
Soldier) and of Josiah Harrelson (wife Mary Vick), all of
Horry Co., S. C. (Vol. II, p. 120 & 124). Lucinda Johnson
(wife), b. 30 April 1811, daughter of Stephen Johnson and
Rosanna Williams (ibid).

Norton, J. R., Jas. R.. 21,22&28-10-26. James Russell
Norton, b. 21 Dec. 1804 S. C., d. 24 Sept. 1886, brother of
Daniel Asbury Norton. Margaret C. Johnston (wife), b. 4
Oct. 1808, d. 30 July 1864, both buried Pleasant Plains
Baptist Church Cem., daughter of John Johnston and Molcie
Hodges (Vol. II, p. 120/1).

Norton, J. K., John K.. 27-11-27 & 29-12-27. John Kennedy
Norton, b. ca 1816 S. C., brother of Daniel Asbury Norton.
Christian McLeod (wife - Vol. II, p. 124/5).

Norton, J. W.. 5-11-27. Rev. John W. Norton, b. 22 Jan.
1794 S. C., d. 15 March 1862, buried Providence Cem., son
of William Norton (Rev. Soldier) of Horry Co., S. C. (Vol.
II, p. 120 & 126). A son, Lewis Fletcher Norton, was born
1820 Moore Co., N. C. ("Southern Christian Advocate", 5
Jan. 1844). Nancy A. Phillips (wife), b. 8 July 1802 N. C.,
d. 8 June 1853, buried Providence Cem. (Vol. II, p. 126).
She was a daughter of Lewis D. and Charity Phillips ("Southern Christian Advocate", 22 July 1853).

Norton, W. V.. 15&22-10-26. William Vick Norton, b. 6 May
1807 Horry Dist., S. C. ("Southern Christian Advocate", 3
Aug. 1849), d. 12 June 1849, buried Tabernacle Cem., brother
of Daniel Asbury Norton. Isabella Floyd (wife), b. ca 1810
S. C., daughter of Theophilus Floyd and Delilah Page (Vol.
II, p. 39).

Odom, H. S.. 24-11-27. Hubbard S. Odom, b. ca 1809 Ga..

Marinda Ann ----- (wife - CR F, p. 45), b. ca 1822 Ga..

Odom, Jas.. 13-11-27. James Odom, b. ca 1805 S. C., to
Ala. from Ga. by 1839. Clarissa ----- (wife?), b. ca 1807
Ga..

Oliver, J.. 33-13-25(B). John L. Oliver, b. ca 1790 Ga.
(1860 Census says born N. C.). Elizabeth ----- (wife?),
b. ca 1795 Ga..

Oliver, M., McDonald. 2-11-25, 4&19-12-25(B) & 10-11-26.
McDonald Oliver, b. ca 1828 Ga., d. 28 July 1864, buried
Fairview Cem., Eufaula, Ala.. He was an heir of Wiley
and Milbrey Oliver (OR 5, p. 335). Nancy ----- (wife),
b. ca 1833 Ga..

Oliver, W., Wiley. 31&36-9-23, 19,29,30, 31&32-12-25 &
2-11-26. Wiley Oliver, b. 15 Oct. 1802 Ga., d. 29 April
1853. Milbrey ----- (wife), b. 8 Jan. 1808 Ga., d. 30
Oct. 1853, both buried in the White family cemetery.

Orr, Jas.. 22&27-10-27. James Orr, b. ca 1821 Ireland, d.
by 1858 (Vol. I, p. 22/3). Jane Bush (wife - m. 20 Aug.
1846), b. 4 April 1830 Ala., d. 27 Jan. 1907, buried in
Rocky Mount Cem., daughter of Moses E. Bush and Julia Ann
Calhoun. She m. (2) Herbert Tiller 8 Jan. 1867 (Vol. I.,
p. 18 & 22/3).

Ott, E. S.. 34-12-27. Edward S. Ott, b. 1 Jan. 1815
Orangeburg, S. C., d. 2 April 1882, son of William Ott
(Alston Bible). Anne Amanda Alston (wife - m. 29 July
1846 Columbus, Ga. - Alston Bible), daughter of William
H. Alston (ibid). She was born 2 March 1827 Elberton, Ga.,
d. 1 Jan. 1913, both buried Fairview Cem., Eufaula, Ala..

Ott, Wm., William. 1,2,4,11&12-11-27. William Ott, b.
28 Oct. 1789 S. C., d. 26 June 1857, buried Miller Cem.
(Alston Bible). He was from Orangeburg Dist., S. C.
("Southern Christian Advocate",13 Aug. 1857). Catharine
----- (1st wife - m. 13 June 1813 - Alston Bible), widow
of Jacob Dantzler of S. C. who died 28 Aug. 1812 (Alston
Bible). She was born ca 1785 Orangeburg Dist., S. C., d.
9 March 1847 ("Southern Christian Advocate", 12 & 19 March
1847). Sarah Ann Lawhorn (2nd wife - m. 28 Sept. 1854).

Owens, T. C.. 23-13-27. Thaddeus C. Owens, b. ca 1822
Decatur Co., Ga., son of Whitman H. Owens. T. C. Owens
moved to Butler Co., Ala. in 1856, died 1889 in Miss. on
a tour (MRA, Vol. I, p. 569/70). Emily E. Dennard (wife)
b. ca 1827 Ga., daughter of Jared Dennard (ibid).

Owens, W. H.. 15,23&25-13-27 & 30-13-28. Whitman Hill
Owens, b. ca 1794 N. C., to Ala. from Ga. after 1839,

d. 1870 Henry Co., Ala., son of William Owens who died 1839
Decatur Co., Ga. ("Henry's Heritage", p. 64, by Warren).
Eliza Ann Hare (1st wife), b. 12 Nov. 1795 Sumpter Dist.,
S. C., d. 9 Nov. 1854, buried Glennville Cem., Russell Co.,
Ala., daughter of Edmond Hare and Mary Scott (ibid). Nancy
A. ----- (2nd wife), b. ca 1810 Ga. (1860 Census).

Owens, W. J.. 29-13-26(B). William J. Owens, b. ca 1810
Ga., d. by 5 Feb. 1859 (OR 9, p. 864/7), lived at Midway,
Ala.. Elizabeth A. ----- (wife), b. ca 1815 Ga. - she may
have been his second wife.

Padget, E.. 2-10-24. In Sept. 1851, Elijah Padget was of
Muscogee Co., Ga. (CR J, p. 383).

Padget, Josiah. 1-11-26. Josiah Padget, b. ca 1826 S. C..
He and Luke Padget bought this land from Henry Padget in
March 1843 (CR E, p. 34/5). In Jan. 1846, Luke Padget
sold his share to Penelope Padget (CR G, p. 167) - she was
born ca 1785 S. C., possibly the widow of Henry Padget.
Mary Ann Glass (wife - m. 9 April 1847), b. ca 1829 Ga..

Palmer, Dan'l. 12-12-25(B). No further record.

Palmer, M. G.. 7-13-25(B). Matthew G. Palmer, b. ca 1817
Ga.. Susan Ann ----- (wife?), b. ca 1829 Ga.. In Jan. 1855,
Elizabeth Ely of Macon Co., Ala. gave slaves to her daughter,
Susan Ann, wife of Matthew G. Palmer.

Parish, Spivey. 33-11-24. Spivey Parish bought this land
in Aug. 1849 (CR J, p. 90). No further record.

Parker, C. A.. 28-12-25. Cader A. Parker, Sr., b. ca 1809
N. C. (1860 Census), a Primitive Baptist Minister, ordained
3 May 1834 Stewart Co., Ga. (Mar. 4, p. 60). In Dec. 1851,
he was still of Stewart Co., Ga. (CR J, p. 488). Louisa C.
----- (wife?), b. ca 1806 Ga. (1860 Census).

Parker, E. M.. 35-10-24. Edward M. Parker, b. ca 1825 Ga.
He and Sherrod Parker bought this land in Oct. 1850 (CR J,
p. 115). They were enumerated next to each other in the
1850 Census and immediately following Stephen Parker (b. ca.
1787 Ga.). Martha ----- (wife?), b. ca 1827 Ga..

Parker, M. B.. 13,29&32-13-28. Milo B. Parker, b. 24 May
1804 Hancock Co., Ga., d. 20 May 1855 Glennville, Ala..
Missouri Thomas (1st wife), b. 12 Sept. 1811 Ga., d. 3 July
1850, both buried in the Mitchell family cemetery, Russell
Co., Ala.. She was a daughter of DAvid and Mary Thomas.
Mrs. Sarah Ann Perry (2nd wife - OR 7, p. 151 ¬ m. 10 Mar.
1851 Bibb Co., Ga.).

Parker, W.. 9&10-9-24. Walter L. B. Parker, b. ca 1824 Ga..
Ann McRae (wife - m. 7 Feb. 1850), b. ca 1822 N. C.. She
transferred her membership from a Methodist Church in Anson
Co., N. C. to Pea River Presbyterian Church in Barbour Co.,
Ala. in 1855 (Pea River Presbyterian Church records).

Parmer, B.. 30-9-27. Benjamin Parmer, Sr., b. ca 1781 Md.,
to Ga. by 1806, in Ala. by 1839, d. 28 Jan. 1857. He served
in the War of 1812 from Jones Co., Ga.. Nancy ----- (2nd
wife), b. ca 1822 S. C., d. 28 Oct. 1855 ("Spirit of the
South", Nov. 13, 1855). Mary Grubbs (3rd wife - m. 1 Oct.
1856), widow of John Sloan, Sr.. She was born ca 1803 Ga.,
married (3) Matthew Laseter 24 Sept. 1857 (Vol. II, p. 132).

Parmer, Benj., Benjamin. 13,14,26&36-10-27. Benjamin
Parmer, b. ca 1800 N. C.. According to the 1850 Census,
he was in Ala. by 1832, in Miss. by 1838 and back in Ala.
by 1850. Although he lived in the same part of Barbour
Co. as the other Parmer families, there is nothing in the
records to show any relationship. He usually spelled his
name Benjamin Palmer. Nancy ----- (2nd wife?), b. ca 1820.

Parmer, Jacob. 33-10-27. Jacob Parmer, Sr., b. ca 1794 Ga.,
d. 2 Oct. 1866 (Vol. II, p. 135). Martha Stripling (wife -
m. 30 Dec. 1812 Jones Co., Ga.), b. ca 1795 S. C., d. 1883
("The Eufaula Weekly Bulletin", June 6, 1883).
OR
Jacob Parmer, b. ca 1826 Ga., son of George W. Parmer and
Rightly Kent who married 6 June 1815 Jones Co., Ga. (Vol.
II, p. 141/2). Adeline Baker (wife - m. 4 Oct. 1849), b.
ca 1826 S. C., daughter of James Baker, Jr.. (ibid).

Parmer, Jefferson. 4&9-10-25. Jefferson Parmer, b. ca
1800 Ga., son of Benjamin Parmer, Sr. (Vol. II, p. 132).
He probably never married.

Parmer, L. B. J.. 35&36-10-27. Littleberry B. J. Parmer,
b. ca 1818 Ga., son of George W. Parmer and Rightly Kent
(Vol. II, p. 141/2). He was in Dale Co., Ala. in 1868 and
in Henry Co., Ala. in 1870. Elizabeth Horn (wife), b. ca
1820 Ga., widow of ----- Winslett). Also in this household in 1850 was Judy Horn, b. ca 1748 Va..

Parmer, Z. W.. 25-10-27. Zachariah Wesley Parmer, b. ca
1820 Ala., in Texas by 1857, son of Benjamin Parmer, Sr.
(Vol. II, p. 132/3). Jane Tindall (wife - m. 16 June 1842).

Parremore, W. E.. 31-12-28. William E, Parramore was of
Stewart Co., Ga. in Nov. 1851 (CR J, p. 501).

Parsons, John. 4-10-28. John L. Parsons, b. 20 Sept. 1805
Ga. (1860 Census), d. 1862 CSA, son of Jeremiah Parsons,

(b. 20 Sept. 1776 N. C., d. 19 Oct. 1820) who married Sarah
G. Granead 24 June 1802 (source unknown). Benetta Stanley
(1st wife - m. 7 Sept. 1830 where?) - she died 12 May 1835
(ibid). Elizabeth Pate (2nd wife - m. 6 April 1836 where?)
Mrs. Lincie Ann Coates Worrell (3rd wife - m. 11 Jan. 1857),
b. 5 Jan. 1825 Ga. (1860 Census), widow of Elisha Worrell.

Passmore, J. R. A.. 8-9-25. John Robert Allen Passmore,
b. 26 Sept. 1828 Ga., d. 20 Sept. 1900, son of John Passmore (Pike Co., Ala. Deed Book A, p. 15/6) who died by
.Nov. 1842 (Original Papers, Box 240). Georgiann Dickinson
Norton (wife - m. 20 May 1867), b. 2 Oct. 1842 Ala., d. 8
May 1902, both buried Louisville Cem.. She was a daughter
of Rev. John W. Norton and Nancy A. Phillips, granddaughter
of William Norton (Rev. Soldier) (Vol. II, p. 120, 126 & 131).

Pasmore, L., Lemuel. 1&2-9-25 & 35-10-25. Lemuel Passmore,
b. ca 1801 Ga., d. Aug. 1893 ("The Clayton Courier", Aug.
12, 1893). He may have been a son of John Passmore (Pike
Co., Ala. Deed Book A, p. 15/6).

Passmore, M., Mary. 9-9-25. John Passmore died by Nov.
1842 (Original Papers, Box 240). He lived in the part of
Barbour Co. that was cut from Pike Co. in 1832. Mary -----
(wife), b. ca 1796 Ga., d. 27 April 1879 ("The Times &
News", May 6, 1879).

Pate, Wm.. 29-9-24. William Pate, b. ca1808 Ga., in Ala.
by 1832. Lenora ----- (wife), b. ca1810 Ga., heir of William Lewis who died by Nov. 1859 (OR 10, p. 310/3).

Patisals, Joshua. 2-11-28 & 9&30-11-29. When he bought
this land in 1836, he was of Houston Co., Ga. (CR A, p.
354) and died there by Sept. 1858 (CR P, p. 205).

Patrick, H. R.. 4-8-24. No further record.

Patterson, M. A.. 5-9-25. Rev. M. A. Patterson, b. ca
1810 N. C., to Ala. from Ga. by 1848, to Union Co., Ark.
in 1858. He was a Presbyterian Minister. Ann ----- (2nd
wife), b. ca 1826 N. C.. She may have been Ann McRae, m.
1 Dec. 1844 Early Co., Ga..

Paullin, Lewis. 5-10-29. In Feb. 1851, Lewis Paullin and
wife, Clementine, of Early Co., Ga. sold the above land
(CR J, p. 353).

Pearson, B. F.. 28-13-26(B). Benjamin Franklin Pearson,
b. ca 1812 N. C., d. by Oct. 1869 (OR 17, p. 605). He came
to Barbour Co. about 1840 from Cumberland Co., N. C., son
of Herbert Pearson and Martha Ann Rogers (DAB, Vol. IV, p.
1333/4). Harriet Maria Dismukes (wife), b. ca 1823 N. C.,
d. after 1891 (OR 26, p. 218), daughter of William Dismukes and Mrs. Elizabeth Ward Pickett (widow of Joseph
Pickett); granddaughter of George Dismukes (Rev. Soldier)

who came to America from France with LaFayette (DAB, Vol.
IV, p. 1333/4).

Pearson, C. R.. 4&8-12-26 & 32&33-13-26(B). Clinton R.
Pearson, d. ca 1860 Holmes Co., Miss. (OR 26, p. 217).
Hubbard (Herbert) Pearson bought the above land in Nov.
1835 and transferred it to Clinton R. Pearson in July 1841
(CR C, p. 355). In 1891, Robert H. Pearson of Jefferson
Co., Ala. filed claims against the U. S. Govt. for the
estate of his father, B. F. Pearson, and the estate of
his uncle, Clinton R. Pearson (OR 26, p. 217).

Peck, Ira. 12&13-12-25(B), 8&24-11-26, 30-9-27, 5,7,8,9,
11,12&15-10-27 & 19&30-9-29. Ira Peck never lived in Barbour Co.. In Jan. 1839, when he bought land in 12-12-25,
he was of Twiggs Co., Ga. (CR B, p. 427). He was a merchant in Twiggs Co., Ga. from the early 1820's until about
1860, having come there from New England (possibly Conn.).
Shortly before the Civil War, he sold all of his property
and returned to the North ("Abstracts of Some Documents of
Twiggs Co., Ga.", p. 244, by E. D. McSwain). Penelope
----- (wife - CR F, p. 16/7).

Peck. W. A.. 13-11-26. No further record.

Peterson, Batte. 23,25&26-12-26. Dr. Batte Peterson, b.
ca 1818 Ga., in Ala. by 1841. There was another Batte
Peterson who married Sarah Pinckard 24 May 1836 Monroe
Co., Ga. - he was in Macon Co., Ala. in 1850. Louisa Jane
Watson (wife). In Dec. 1858, Batte Peterson was guardian
of his minor children, Martha Ann and Sarah Eugenia, who
had been left bequests by Douglas Watson and L. J. Watson,
both of Monroe Co., Ga. (OR 9, p. 484).

Petty, B. F.. 1&11-10-26, 30,31,32&33-11-26 & 5-10-28.
Benjamin Franklin Petty, b. 2 Sept. 1806 New York, d. 3
Sept. 1876. Eveline Belmont Lewis (1st wife), b. ca 1818,
d. 23 Aug. 1842, both buried Clayton Cem.. She was a dau.
of Charles and Juliet Lewis. Catherine Smith (2nd wife -
m. 20 Feb. 1845), b. ca 1828 Tenn.. Mary A. Lee (3rd wife -
m. 27 June 1854), b. 8 Sept. 1836 Ala., d. 20 March 1892,
buried Clayton Cem.. She was a daughter of Needham Lee,
Sr. and Lydia Pryor (Vol. II, p. 78/9).

Petty, C., Chas.. 1&2-10-25, 36-11-35 & 8,9&17-10-26.
Charles Petty, b. ca 1820 New York, d. 27 April 1869, buried
Clayton Cem.. Narcissa Clark (wife - m. 20 Oct. 1842), b.
ca 1824 S. C., d. Feb. 1902 Arkadelphia, Ark. ("The Clayton
Record", Feb. 28, 1902).

Phillips, Burrel. 5-8-24. Burrel Phillips, b. ca 1823 Ga.,
possibly a son of Isham Phillips (b. ca 1785 N. C.) d. Jan.
1894, buried Faulk Cem.. Caroline M. Ivy (wife - m. 20 Feb.
1859), b. ca 1843 Ala. (1860 Census).

Phillips, C. S.. 5-8-24. Caroline S. Phillips, b. 30
March 1823 Ga., d. 10 April 1905. She was a daughter of
Jesse Sutton and Mary Bryant. She m. (1) Henry H. Phillips
who died 21 Oct. 1844 (2) Arrington H. H. Phillips 18 Nov.
1860 (Vol. I, p. 149/50).

Phillips, Council. 24-8-25. Council Phillips was in the
1840 Census, b. ca 1800/10. When he sold the above land
in July 1852, he was of Dale Co., Ala..

Phillips, H.. 14-13-26. There is no H. Phillips in the
early records unless it is Hester Phillips, b. ca 1781 N.C..

Phillips, H. H.. 5&6-8-24. Henry H. Phillips d. 21 Oct.
1844 and is buried in the family cemetery. He was a brother to Kinchen W. Phillips who died by Dec. 1843 - other
brothers lived in Lawrence Co., Ga. (OR 2, p. 55). Caroline S. Sutton, b. 30 March 1823 Ga., d. 10 April 1905,
buried Elam Cem.. She married (2) Arrington H. H. Phillips
18 Nov. 1860. His first wife was her sister, Martha Sutton.
They were daughters of Jesse Sutton who died 3 June 1860
(Vol. I, p. 149/50).

Picket, Thos. C.. 18-13-25(B). Thomas C. Pickett, b. ca
1795 S. C., to Ala. from Ga. after 1839. In May 1842, he
was administrator of Lazarus N. Pickett (OR 1, p. 297). In
May 1857, he contracted to support Thomas J. H. Pickett for
the rest of his life in return for slaves (CR N, p. 347/8).
Mary ----- (wife), b. ca 1800 Ga..

Pierce, L. L.. 7-9-26. Lovard L. Pierce, b. ca 1825 Ga..
Ann Jane ----- (wife), b. ca 1830 Ga..

Pinkerton, C.. 33-9-28. Catherine Pinkerton, b. ca 1790
Ga., probably widow of David Pinkerton (CR F, p. 97/8).

Pipkin, H.. 11-12-25(B) & 29-13-26(B). Haywood Pipkin, b.
ca 1812 N. C., to Ala. from Ga. by 1839, d. Sept. 1893 at
Midway, Ala. ("The Clayton Courier", Oct. 7, 1893). His
first wife may have been Emily Jones, m. 29 Sept. 1833 (or
1835) Newton Co., Ga.. Eliza Cameron (2nd wife - m. 4 Jan.
1849), b. ca 1821 N. C., daughter of Lauchlin Cameron who
died by April 1856 (OR 7, p. 530).

Pippin, C.. 21-11-29. Calvin Pippin, b. ca 1815 N. C., to
Ala. from Ga. by 1846. Sarah ----- (wife), b. ca 1818 Ga..

Pitts, N. W.. 13,14&15-13-28(R). Nicholas W. Pitts, b. ca
1797 N. C., d. 1870 (OR 26, p. 312). He was an heir of
Noel Pitts, who was an heir of Martha Bustin of Halifax Co.,
N. C. - both died by Feb. 1845 (CR F, p. 321). Maria -----
(2nd wife?), b. ca 1817 Ga..

Pollard, Elias. 23&24-13-25(B). Elias Pollard, b. ca 1810/20 (1840 Census). In 1840, there was a female in his household, b. ca 1770/80. Isabella ----- (wife).

Pollard, J., John. 24-13-25(B). John Pollard was of Muscogee Co., Ga. in March 1845 when he bought this land from Leroy Pollard, also of Muscogee Co., Ga. (CR G, p. 32).

Pope, Joel. 1-12-29. There is nothing in the early records except his marriage to Piety Vick 23 Dec. 1849.

Post, J. E. C.. 25-9-24. No further record.

Post, W. D. C.. 25-9-24. No further record.

Posten, E.. 24-10-28. Emanuel Poston, b. ca 1803 S. C., d. by Aug. 1863 (OR 13, p. 111). Elizabeth ----- (wife?), b. ca 1818 Ga.. She may have been Elizabeth Taylor, dau. of John Taylor and Hannah Styron (m. 6 Feb. 1787 Craven Co., N. C.) who moved to Greene Co., Ga. ca 1800 (Mrs. Grady Fowler, LaGrange, Ga.).

Powell, Dan'l. 11-8-23. There is no Daniel Powell in the early records. There is a David Powell, b. ca 1801 S. C., d. by July 1854 (OR 6, p. 102). He married Mrs. Eady Lewis 7 Feb. 1847, b. ca 1806 Ga. - his second wife.

Powell, Geo. 10&15-10-26. George Powell, b. ca 1802 S. C.. In April 1840, the commissioners of Barbour Co. deeded the above land to George Powell by order of the court of Dale Co., Ala. - the land had been sold to George Powell in March 1836 by Abner Powell "in his lifetime" (CR B, p. 851). Bersheba ----- (wife), b. ca 1805 S. C..

Powell, J. S.. 11,12&13-13-28(R). Joseph S. Powell bought a lot in Glennville in Jan. 1853 (CR K, p. 284)- no further record. Antoinette A. C. Stovall (wife - m. 7 Dec. 1847, probably in Milledgeville, Ga.), daughter of Joseph Stovall of Milledgeville, Ga..("Southern Christian Advocate", 24 Dec. 1847).

Powell, Ransom. 11-8-23. Ransom Powell, b. ca 1825 S. C., heir of David Powell who died by July 1854, at which time Ransom Powell was of Dale Co., Ala. (OR 6, p. 232/3). Sarah C. ----- (wife?), b. ca 1822 S. C..

Powers, Thomas. 8-13-26(B). No further record.

Pratt, Wm.. 23&24-13-28(R). William Pratt owned a lot in Glennville (Russell Co.), Ala. (CR L, p. 191). No further record.

Price, B.. 1&2-9-25 & 10-10-26. Burrel Price, b. 16 Feb. 1810 N. C., d. 29 Nov. 1890. Rebecca ------ (wife), b. 30 Jan. 1811 N. C., d. 24 July 1888, both buried in the family cemetery.

Price, R. E.. 29&30-10-28. Robert E. Price, b. 1811 S. C., d. 27 April 1899. Celia Johnston (wife), b. 1 Aug. 1815 S. C., d. 22 Jan. 1872, both buried Mt. Aerial Cem.. She was a daughter of John Johnston and Molcie Hodges who came to Barbour Co., Ala. from Horry Co., S. C. (Vol. II, p. 69).

Price, Wm. E.. 10-12-29. William Edward Price, b. ca 1819 S. C., of Charleston, S. C. and Barbour Co., Ala., son of William E. and Eliza Ann Price, emigrants to S. C. (DAB, Vol. IV, p. 1390). Mary F. Colverd (1st wife - "Southern Christian Advocate", 26 June 1846 & 11 Jan. 1847), b. ca 1825 d. 7 Feb. 1848 ("Southern Christian Advocate", 17 March 1845), daughter of Thomas Colverd and Ann L. Winfrey (m. 25 June 1822 Columbia Co., Ga.). Emma E. (or M.) Hunt (2nd wife - m. 19 June 1849 Richmond Co., Ga.), widow of ----- Wood. She was born 1822 Ga., d. 1897, buried Fairview Cem., Eufaula, Ala.

Pruett, J. M., James M.. 30,31&32-13-26. James Madison Pruett, b. 1815 Ga., d. 17 Nov. 1878 Bullock Co., Ala., probably son of John Pruett (b. 3 Jan. 1785, d. 11 July 1842) and Mary ----- (b. ca 1790 Ga., d. 29 Oct. 1855). Louisa Feagin (wife - m. 17 May 1836), b. 28 March 1818 Ga., d. 8 Dec. 1895, all buried Fellowship Cem., Bullock Co., Ala.. She was a daughter of Samuel Feagin (Vol. I, p. 137).

Purswell, G., Gabriel. 16&21-9-27 & 21-10-27. Gabriel Purswell, b. ca 1810 S. C.. Elizabeth ----- (wife?), b. ca 1811 S. C.. She was an heir of William Condrey of Henry Co., Ala. (Henry Co., Ala., CR G, p. 478).

Purswell, Henry. 16-9-27. Henry Purswell, b. ca 1782 Pa., d. after June 1856 (CR N, p. 59). Catharine ----- (wife) b. ca 1796 S. C..

Pynes, Fair. 36-11-26 & 31-11-27. Fair Pynes, b. ca 1806 S. C., d. by Nov. 1854 (Original Papers, Box 256), son of (Daniel?) and Rutha Pynes (Vol. II, p. 150). Maryanna Creech (wife - m. 10 Jan. 1828 Henry Co., Ala.), b. ca 1810 Ga..

Quattlebaum, J.. 4-12-29 & 33-13-29(R). John Quattlebaum, b. ca 1802 S. C.. Mary ----- (1st wife - CR L, p. 196), b. ca 1823 S. C.. Margaret J. McDaniel (2nd wife- m. 5 March 1854).

Quick, M.. 17-12-29. Malichi Quick, b. ca 1830 Ga. (1860 Census), Louisa Hinson (2nd wife - m. 11 Feb. 1859), b. ca 1833 Ala. (1860 Census).

Rachels, George. 1-10-27. George Rachels, b. ca 1783
N. C., d. by Oct. 1858 (OR 9, p. 359/60). Pheriba -----
(wife), b. ca 1773 Ga. (1860 Census).

Raiford, J. M.. 27,34,35&36-13-28. Dr. John M. Raiford,
b. Feb. 1804 Abbeville Dist., S. C., d. 28 Nov. 1878.
Martha Jane ----- (wife), b. ca 1818 Ga., d. 20 Aug. 1857,
both buried Glennville Cem., Russell Co., Ala..

Rains, J. W.. 17,19,20&21-10-29. John W. Raines, b. ca
1807 Ga., d. by March 1858, at which time his next of kin
was R. H. Raines (OR 9, p. 124). He probably never married.

Rains, Wm.. 13&24-10-28. No further record.

Reeder, Matthew. 35-8-25. No further record.

Reese, Wm.. 8-11-26. William Reese (Rees), b. ca 1812
Ga.. Luraney Evans (wife - m. 16 Nov. 1830 Putnam Co., Ga.)
b. ca 1813 Ga..

Reeves, A.. 7&8-10-27. Asher Reeves, b. ca 1794 N. C.,
to Ala. from Ga. by 1838, d. by Jan. 1887 (OR 24, p. 423).
Ellender C. Parmer (2nd wife - m. 17 Dec. 1845), b. ca 1818
Ga., d. by Aug. 1887 (OR 24, p. 423), daughter of Jacob
Parmer and Martha Stripling (Vol. II, p. 135/6).

Reeves, H. D.. 29-13-25(B). Henry D. Reeves bought this
land 24 Dec. 1851 (CR J, p. 606). He and wife, Mary J.,
sold it ca Jan. 1854 (CR L, p. 112).

Reid, J., John. 21&22-11-27. John Reed, b. ca 1798 Ireland, to Ala. from S. C. by 1839, d. by Jan. 1852 (OR 4,
p. 154). Jane ----- (wife?), b. ca 1800 Ireland, d. July
1879 ("The Times & News", July 31, 1879). Also in this
household in 1850 was Margaret Reid, b. ca 1775 Ireland.

Reynolds, G.. 16-11-28. George Reynolds, b. ca 1827 Ala..
In 1850, he was enumerated next of James Reynolds, b. ca
1780 N. C.. Leta Ann ----- (wife - CR R, p. 593).

Reynolds, J. A.. 16,17,20&21-9-24. Dr. John A. Reynolds,
b. 6 Dec. 1819 Montgomery Co., N. C., d. 17 Sept. 1891.
Sarah Elizabeth Huey (wife), b. 6 Feb. 1828 N. C., d. 15
March 1906, both buried Bennett Cem.. Also buried in this
cemetery are Elliner L. J. Huey (b. 8 April 1795, d. 5 Aug.
1871), wife of Robert D. Huey, and Dr. James W. Huey (b. 7
March 1825, d. 20 Aug. 1855).

Richards, Jas.. 17-9-28. James Richards, b. ca 1811 S. C.,
d. ca Oct. 1893, son of William Richards of Coosa Co., Ala.
(Vol. II, p. 156). Elouisa Richards (wife), b. ca 1808

103

S. C., d. 2 April 1895, daughter of Robert Richards who died
18 July 1851. He and William Richards were half-brothers
(Vol. II, p. 156).

Richards, R.. 19-9-28. Robert Richards, b. ca 1776 Ireland,
d. 18 July 1851. Elleanor Black (?) (wife), b. ca 1770/80
S. C., d. 28 Sept. 1848 (Vol. II, p. 153).

Richards, T., Thos., Thomas. 36-9-27 & 18,29,30,31&32-10-28.
Thomas W. Richards, b. 14 Sept. 1798 Pendleton Dist., S. C.,
d. 23 June 1879, son of Robert Richards who died 18 July
1851. Lucy Carter (wife - m. 22 Aug. 1826 Henry Co., Ala.),
b. 10 May 1806 Ga., d. 14 Sept. 1890, daughter of Giles
Carter of Henry Co., Ala..

Richards, Wm.. 21,28&30-9-28. William Richards, b. ca 1802
S. C., d. by 1855, son of Robert Richards who died 18 July
1851. Matilda McVey (wife - m. 19 Jan. 1826 Henry Co., Ala.),
b. ca 1807 S. C., d. after 1870. (Vol. II, p. 153 & 155).

Richardson, W. N. & Mary. 6,7&8-13-29(R). Dr. William N.
Richardson, b. ca 1790 Ga., d. by Dec. 1853 (OR 5, p. 438),
son of Walker Richardson (Rev. Soldier) who died by Sept.
1822 Elbert Co., Ga. and Prudence Thompson (daughter of
William Thompson who migrated from Chesterfield Co., Va.
to Elbert Co., Ga. after the Rev. War, died there by Nov.
1813). She married (2) Benjamin Brown 3 April 1823 Elbert
Co., Ga.. Mary R. ----- (wife?), b. ca 1794 Va..

Riley, Joseph. 14-11-24. Joseph Riley, b. ca 1807 Ga..
Temperance ----- (wife?), b. ca 1813 Ga..

Rist, C.. 36-11-27. Calvin Rist, b. ca 1822 Mass., d. by
March 1852 (OR 4, p. 380). His heirs were brothers Ezborn
Rist. of Mass. and Amos Rist, residence unknown.

Rivers, J. F.. 3,14,21&22-13-27. John F. Rivers, b. ca
1818 Ga., d. by May 1875 (OR 20, p. 95), probably son of
Thomas Rivers and Mary Bonner. Sarah F. Upshaw (wife -
m. 17 June 1844), b. ca 1826 Ga., daughter of Leroy Upshaw,
Jr. (OR 25, p. 145).

Rivers, T. H. B.. 3&4-13-27, 1,11,12-13-29(R) & 7-13-30(R).
Thomas H. B. Rivers, b. 22 May 1811 Ga., d. 28 April 1885,
heir of Thomas Rivers and Mary Bonner (OR 16, p. 543). Ann
Dawson Persons (?) (wife - m. 13 Nov. 1835 Jasper Co., Ga.),
b. 13 Oct. 1815 Ga., d. 14 Dec. 1874, both buried Glennville
Cem., Russell Co., Ala..

Rivers, Thomas. 28-13-27. Thomas Rivers, b. 1775 Va., d.
1864. Mary Bonner (wife - m. 30 Nov. 1809 Hancock Co., Ga.),
b. 1792 Va., d. 1880, both buried Spring Hill Methodist Church
Cem..

Roach, N., Nathaniel. 33-10-26 & 4,27,33&34-13-29(R).
Nathaniel Roach, b. ca 1800 N. C.. Mrs. Nancy Scarbrough
(2nd wife - m. 24 Dec. 1843), b. ca 1808 Ga..

Robey, M., Matthew. 28-11-27 & 28-12-27. Matthew Robey,
b. ca 1801 Md., to Ala. from Ga. by 1845. Mary -----
(wife?), b. ca 1813 Ga.. She may have been Mary Jones
who married Matthew Robey 19 Dec. 1837 Putnam Co., Ga..

Robinson, A. J.. 12-11-28, 36-12-28 & 8-11-29. Alexander
J. Robinson was a partner in the Summerville Land Co. of
Barbour Co. about 1835. In Feb. 1834, he was of Houston
Co., Ga. (CR A, p. 140); in April 1836, he was of Stewart
Co., Ga. (CR A, p. 296) and in Dec. 1850, he was of Mus-
cogee Co., Ga. (CR J, p. 341). Amanda ----- (wife - CR J,
p. 341).

Robinson, T., Thos., Thomas. 24-11-25, 11-10-28 & 20-11-29.
Thomas Robinson, b. 15 Oct. 1812 N. C., d. 21 March 1888
Columbia, Ala. ("Eufaula Weekly Times & News", March 29,
1888). Sarah E. McDowell (1st wife), b. 10 May 1819 Ga.,
d. 5 June 1850, both buried Fairview Cem., Eufaula, Ala.
She was a daughter of Thomas C. and Eliza McDowell ("The
Eufaula Democrat", June 11, 1850). Martha M. ----- (2nd
wife), b. ca 1822, d. Jan. 1883 Henry Co., Ala., widow of
----- Standiford ("The Eufaula Weekly Bulletin, Jan. 10,
1883).

Rogers, B. A.. 27,28,29,33&35-12-29. Britton A. Rogers,
b. ca 1817 Ga.. Sarah ----- (wife - CR M. p. 535), b. ca
1824 Ga., probably Sarah Jamison who married Britton A.
Rogers 19 Dec. 1845 Bibb Co., Ga..

Rogers, G.. 9-12-29. No further record.

Rogers, O.. 10,14&15-11-29. Osborn T. Rogers, b. ca 1825
Ga.. Louisa ----- (wife?), b. ca 1826 Ga., probably Louisa
M. Neal who married Osborn T. Rogers 21 Oct. 1844 Newton
Co., Ga..

Rogers, P.. 30-13-26. Peter Rogers, b. ca 1800/10 (1840
Census), sold this land in Feb. 1847 (CR H, p. 40). Nelly
----- (wife - ibid), b. ca 1800/10 (1840 Census).

Rood, A. P.. 2&13-13-29(R). Asel P. Rood was of Stewart
Co., Ga. (CR K, p. 400/1).

Roquemore, T. J.. 24-12-28. Thomas Jackson Roquemore, b.
ca 1815 Ga., brother of Zachariah Roquemore. Eliza P. W.
Glenn (2nd? wife - m. by 1850), b. ca 1816 S. C.. She was
the widow of Dr. George Stovall who died by Dec. 1841 (OR
1, p. 270) - they married 7 June 1836 Franklin Co., Ga..

Roquemore, Z.. 17,19&20-12-29. Zachariah Roquemore, b.
20 Nov. 1809 Jones Co., Ga., d. 16 June 1868, buried in
the family cemetery, son of James Roquemore, Jr. (b. 2 Dec.
1780, d. 25 April 1865 Houston Co., Ga.) and Elizabeth A.
Tharpe (?)(b. 3 Feb. 1786, d. 31 Dec. 1825); grandson of
James (Pierre Jacques) Roquemore, Sr. (Rev. Soldier) (b.
ca 1745 France, d. 1803 Warren Co., Ga.) (DAR #270294).
Julia Ann Frances McGibboney (wife), b. ca 1819, d. 19 Jan.
1893 at the home of her sister at Salem, Ala., buried Salem,
Ala., daughter of James C. McGibonney (b. 3 Feb. 1796 Ga.,
d. 22 May 1847 Russell Co., Ala.) and Mary L. Adams
(d. 20 Aug. 1856, buried in the family cemetery) who married 21 Nov. 1816 Hancock Co., Ga.; granddaughter of William McGibboney who died by Sept. 1841 Greene Co., Ga. and
Nancy ----- who died April 1850 Greene Co., Ga..

Rouse, L., Lewis Sr.. 20&21-12-25(B) & 29-12-25. Lewis
Rouse, Sr., b. ca 1791 N. C., d.by Aug. 1865 (OR 14, p.
542/4). Mary R. ----- (2nd wife - m. by June 1835), b. ca
1801 S. C., widow of James Stafford (OR 1, p. 201).

Rushing, R.. 5-12-29. Richard R. Rushing, b. ca 1812
N. C.. Martha ----- (wife?), b. ca 1817 S. C..

Russell, G. W.. 34-12-26. George W. Russell, b. ca 1835
Ala.. In 1850, he was in the household of Joseph C. Russell.
He bought this land from Joseph C. Russell in March 1853
(CR K, p. 433).

Russell, J. C.. 10-11-26 & 2-12-26. Joseph C. Russell, b.
ca 1814 N. C., d. by Aug. 1866 (OR 15, p. 469). He owned
land jointly with Richard R. Russell who died by Jan. 1850
(OR 3, p. 408). In this estate, he was called Joseph Rus-
sell, Jr. (OR 4, p. 250). In Aug. 1841, he and Richard R.
Russell were of Russell Co., Ala.. In the 1850 Census,
there was a Joseph C. Russell, Sr. (b. ca 1783 Va.), wife(?)
Mary (b. ca 1795 N. C.). In 1860, she was living with Thomas
A. Hightower (b. 1804 Greene Co., Ga., d. 1896, buried Mt.
Nebo Cem.). Thomas A. Hightower married (1) Frances F.
Hudson (2) Emma Carter Russell, b. 1812 Anson Co., N. C.,
d. 1858, buried Mt. Nebo Cem.. (3) Rachel M. Russell 16
Dec. 1858. Emma C. and Rachel M. were daughters of Joseph
Carter Russell, Sr. (b. 1783/4 Halifax Co., Va.) and Mary
Ann Bentley (b. Anson Co., N. C.) (Mrs. J. B. Edwards, Mt.
Pleasant, Texas). Joseph Carter Russell, Sr. and Mary Ann
Bentley were probably the parents of Joseph C. Russell, Jr.
and Richard R. Russell, also.

Ryan, H., Hampton. 21,28&29-10-27. Hampton Ryan, b. 18
May 1797 Ga., d. 17 June 1869, buried in the family cemetery.
The first wife of Hampton Ryan may have been Sarah, daughter
of Littleton Beauchamp who died Henry Co., Ala. (Vol. I, p.
3). Rachel ----- (2nd wife?), b. ca 1796 Ga.. Susannah M.
Baker (3rd wife - m. 4 Feb. 1852), b. 3 July 1825 S. C., d.
9 Nov. 1881, buried in the family cemetery.

Ryan, R. B.. 29-10-27. Risdin B. Ryan, b. ca 1822 Ala.,
son of Hampton Ryan. In 1873, he was living in Fla. (OR
11, p.530). Malinda A. Mann (wife - m. 22 Dec. 1852), b.
ca 1833 S. C..

Salisbury, J. A.. 9-11-28. Joseph A. Saulsbury, b. ca
1815 Ga.. In July 1852, he borrowed money from Edwin
Saulsbury of Macon, Ga.. Sarah M. Wilson (wife - CR B, p.
152), b. ca 1815 S. C.. In 1838, she owned land in Randolph
Co., Ga. (CR B, p. 152).

Sanders, A.. 11-11-26. Andrew Sanders, b. ca 1825 S. C.,
son of Francis E. Sanders (CR J, p. 321). Nancy J. Winslett (wife - m. 13 April 1852), b. ca 1832 Ga. (1860 Census).

Sanders, F. E.. 15-9-25. Francis E. Sanders, b. ca 1777
N. C., to Ala. from S. C. by 1838. In May 1851, he was of
Pike Co., Ala. (CR J, p. 301). Barbara ----- (wife - ibid),
b. ca 1790 S. C..

Sanders, J. H. L.. 20-9-27. James H. L. Sanders m. Mary
Barry 5 June 1845. No further record.

Sanders, S. P.. 11-11-26. S. P. (Peter) Sanders, b. ca
1825 (1860 Census) Lexington, S. C. (1906 CSA Census). He
is buried in Mt. Nebo Cem. but no dates are given. In 1850,
he was in the household of Francis E. Sanders (b. ca 1777
N. C.). Margaret Ellen Flournoy (wife), b. ca 1820 N. C.
(1860 Census), d. 12 Sept. 1904, buried Mt. Nebo Cem..

Sanders, W.. 9-11-26. William B. Sanders, b. ca 1815 S. C..
Rachel M. ----- (wife?), b. ca 1827 S. C..

Sanders, Wm. P.. 36-9-26 & 20-9-27. William P. Sanders,
b. ca 1812 S. C.. In 1850, he was enumerated next to Andrew
Sanders. Margaret C. Farmer (wife - m. 9 June 1853), b. ca
1825 N. C..

Sanford, A. M.. 5,33&34-12-28, 4&24-13-28(R), 32,33&34-13-28
& 18-13-29(R). Adolphus M. Sandford, b. ca 1811 Ga., d. 11
April 1860 (OR 11, p. 948/9). Sophia ----- (wife - m. 7
Nov. 1835 - OR 11, p. 948/9).

Sanford, Wm.. 34-13-25(B). William Sanford, b. ca 1810 Ga.,
Sarah ----- (wife - CR H, p. 119), b. ca 1810 Ga..

Scott, D. C.. 10-11-28. Daniel Croly Scott, b. 1814 S. C.
d. 30 Aug. 1850, buried Fairview Cem., Eufaula, Ala.. He
owned land in Barbour, Chambers and Tallapoosa Cos., Ala.
(OR 3, p. 552). Mary H. F. Wellborn (wife - m. 19 Feb.
1846), b. ca 1828 Ga., d. Norcross, Ga. July 1886, daughter
of Mrs. Roxanna Wellborn ("Eufaula Daily Times", Aug. 11,

1886). She married (2) Adison D. Cleckley 5 July 1853.

Scott, J. N.. 8&9-9-28. James N. Scott, b. ca 1806 N. C.. Martha ----- (wife - CR L, p. 256), b. ca 1802 Va.. Also in this household in 1850 and 1860 was Mary Scott, b. ca 1838 Tenn. (a daughter?).

Screws, J., Jacob. 30&31-13-29(R). Jacob Screws, b. ca 1805 N. C., to Ga. by 1839, to Ala. by 1844. Nancy Denson (wife), b. ca 1813 N.C., daughter of Jethro Denson who died by 1851 (OR 4, p. 115/8).

Scroggins, G. R.. 30-10-25. George R. Scroggins, b. ca 1824 Ga.. Elizabeth ----- (wife - CR L, p. 47), b. ca 1820 Ga..

Scroggins, Jas.. 25-10-24. James Scroggins, b. ca 1790 Ga. (1860 Census). In Aug. 1842, Thomas Miller deeded this land to James and Juda Scroggins during their lives, to revert to Thomas Miller at their deaths (CR E, p. 391/2). Judy ----- (wife?), b. ca 1793 Ga. (1860 Census).

Seabrook, B. W.. 27-13-26. Benjamin W. Seabrook, b. ca 1818 S. C., to Ala. from Ga. by 1846. Harriet ----- (wife - CR L, p. 74), b. ca 1823 Ga., probably Harriet Bailey who married Benjamin Seabrook 24 Oct. 1839 Jones Co., Ga..

Seals, A.. 21-13-28. Archibald Seals, b. 1782 Va., d. 26 April 1851. Ann T. Burnley (wife - m. 11 March 1816 Warren Co., Ga.), b. 1794 Ga., d. 15 March 1877, both buried Enon Cem., Bullock Co., Ala., daughter of Henry Burnley (Rev. Soldier) and Lucy Barksdale Davenport (Early Georgia Marriages, p. 307, by Maddox & Carter).

Seals, D. M.. 19&30-13-28. Daniel Morgan Seals, b. 12 March 1818 Warren Co., Ga. ("Eufaula Times & News", July 7, 1883), d. 3 July 1883, buried Shorter Cem., Eufaula, Ala.. Eudoxia A. ----- (wife), b. ca 1830 Ga. (1860 Census), d. 1898 Headland, Ala., buried Headland, Ala. ("Eufaula Times & News", June 9, 1898). She may have been a sister to Moses Cox who died by Aug. 1860 (OR 11, p. 398).

Seals, J.. 19-9-24. John D. Seals, b. ca 1816 Ga.. Ellena Jane Faulk (wife), b. ca 1820 Ala., daughter of Henry Lawson Faulk, Sr. and Nancy Kelly (?) (Vol. I, p. 57/60)

Seals, J. W.. 4-10-28. James W. Seals, b. ca 1808 Ga.. Nancy W. Seals (wife - m. 20 Oct. 1831 Hancock Co., Ga.), b. 10 Sept. 1812 Ga., d. 12 Dec. 1881, buried Oakwood Cem., Troy (Pike Co.), Ala..

Searcy, G. W.. 35-9-27. George W. Searcy, b. ca 1816 Ga. (1850 Census Henry Co., Ala.), d. 26 April 1880 Henry Co.,

Ala.. Nancy Ann Wood (wife), b. 5 Jan. 1829 Wayne Co.,
N. C., d. 4 July 1905 Henry Co., Ala., both buried County
Line Cem., Henry Co., Ala.. She was a daughter of Young
Wood and Rosanna Byrd; granddaughter of Furnifold Wood and
Abigail ----- and of Richard Byrd: and Jean ----- (Vol.II,
p. 186).

Searcy, J., James. 36-9-27. James W. Searcy, b. ca 1832
N. C. (1860 Census), son of Lemuel Searcy and Annie Wood,
grandson of Furnifold Wood and Abigail ----- of Sampson
and Wayne Cos., N. C.. (Vol. II, p. 186 & 188). Mahala
----- (wife?), b. ca 1841 Ala. (1860 Census).

Searcy, John. 35-9-27. John G. Searcy, b. 17 April 1834
N. C., d. 16 Oct. 1908, son of Lemuel Searcy and Annie Wood
(Vol. II, p. 186 & 188). Catherine Pinkerton (wife), b. 6
April 1838 Ala., d. 22 March 1914, both buried Mt. Pleasant
Cem., probably daughter of Catherine Pinkerton (b. ca 1790).

Seay, J. W., John W.. 8&17-10-24, 15-11-24, 21-12-25(B),
26&27-13-25(B) & 8,10&18-12-26(B). John W. Seay, b. 18 Nov.
1796 S. C., d. 6 Feb. 1859. Barbara Leaphart (wife - m. 30
March 1830 - Seay Bible), b. 14 Dec. 1807 S. C., d. 30 Aug.
1854, both buried in the family cemetery. She was a daughter
of John and Elizabeth Leaphart (Seay Bible).

Seay, Wm. 22-13-25(B). No further record.

Sanks, J.. 13-9-25. Probably Jeremiah Shanks, b. ca 1827
S. C., d. by Aug. 1857 (OR 8, p. 285/6). In 1850, he was
living with James K. Turner, b. ca 1810 Ga.. Mary Ann
Eliza ----- (wife - OR 9, p. 697/700), b. ca 1833 Ga..

Shanks, George. 24-9-25. George Shanks, b. ca 1822 S. C.,
Mary ----- (wife?), b. ca 1827 Ala..

Shanks, Jas.. 24-9-25. No further record.

Shelby, John. 35-9-27. No further record.

Shelby, Moses. 27&34-12-25. Moses Shelby, b. ca 1795 N. C.,
in Washington Co., Ga. 1820, Coweta Co., Ga. 1827 and Barbour Co., Ala. 1840 - possibly son of John Shelby who served
in the Washington Co., Ga. Militia and grandson of Moses
Shelby who was born in Wales (Mrs. F. D. Switzer, McAllister,
Okla.). Harriet Hagler (wife - ibid), b. ca 1800 N. C..

Sheppard, J.. 8-11-29. John Sheppard, b. ca 1811 Ga.. He
sold this land in April 1852 (CR J, p. 636/7). Anna -----
(wife - ibid), b. ca 1808 Ga., possibly a sister of Samuel
Weathers who died by June 1854 (OR 6, p. 356/7).

Sheppard, Thos. 18-9-28. Thomas Sheppard, Sr., b. ca 1801

Ga.. He was household #707, P. O. Eufaula, Ala. in the
1860 Census. Emily ----- (2nd wife?), b. ca 1805 N. C..
                          OR
Thomas Sheppard, b. ca 1820 Ga., d. by 27 July 1876 (OR
21, p. 101/9). He was household #701, P. O. Eufaula, Ala.
in the 1860 Census. Margaret Cox (1st wife - m. 15 June
1843), b. ca 1825 S. C.. In 1850, John Cox (age 16, born
Ala.) was enumerated in this household. Charity Elizabeth
Johnson Flournoy (2nd wife - m. 7 July 1870), widow of
----- Flournoy. She was born ca 1827 Ala. (1880 Census),
daughter of Phillip Johnson (b. ca 1799 S. C. - 1880 Census).

Shipes, Cornelius. 34-8-26. Cornelius Shipes, b. ca 1827
S. C.. This land was patented by John Shipes in 1839 (Barbour Co., Ala. Tract Book). Mary A. M. Brewer (wife - m.
17 Oct. 1849), b. ca 1829 S. C..

Shipman, Jas.. 12,13,16,21,22&27-9-24 & 7&18-9-25. James
Shipman, b. ca 1789 N. C., d. by Aug. 1853 (Vol. I, p. 145).
Elizabeth ----- (wife), b. ca 1796 N. C..

Shorter, E. S., Eli S.. 36-11-28, 20&27-12-28 & 16,22&23-
11-29. Eli Sims Shorter, b. 15 March 1823 Monticello, Ga.,
d. 29 April 1879, son of Dr. Reubin C. Shorter and Mary
Butler Gill (DAB, Vol. IV, p. 1551/2). Marietta Fannin
(wife - m. 12 Jan. 1848 Troup Co., Ga.), b. 29 Nov. 1830
Troup Co., Ga.,d. 18 April 1898 Atlantic City, N. J., both
buried Fairview Cem., Eufaula, Ala..

Shorter, E. S. Estate. 8,18,21&27-11-28, 3&23-12-28, 2&22-
13-28(R), 6-11-29, 24,34&36-12-29 & 4,11&12-13-29(R). Eli S.
Shorter died before Dec. 1836, probably in Muscogee Co., Ga.
(CR A, p. 431). Sophia H. Watkins (wife - m. 18 June 1817
Elbert Co., Ga.), b. ca 1800 Elbert Co., Ga., d. 13 April
1856 Columbus, Ga. ("Southern Christian Advocate", 12 June
1856).

Shorter, J. H., Jas. H. Est.. 5,6,7,22,26,27&28-11-27 &
23-12-27. James H. Shorter was of Muscogee Co., Ga. in 1837
(CR A, p. 349) and probably died there. His wife may have
been Mary E. Hargroves, daughter of George Hargroves of
Columbus, Ga. - m. 17 March 1836 Columbus, Ga. ("Southern
Recorder").

Shorter, J. G., John Gill. 36-11-27, 5-11-28, 33-11-29 &
16&20-12-29. Gov. John Gill Shorter, b. 23 April 1818
Monticello, Ga., d. 29 May 1872, son of Dr. Reuben C.
Shorter (OR 5, p. 503/9). Mary Jane Battle (wife - m. 12
Jan. 1843 Stewart Co., Ga.), b. 20 Feb. 1825 Ga., d. 20
Jan. 1879, both buried Shorter Cem., Eufaula, Ala., dau.
of Dr. Cullen Battle and Jane Lamon (DAB, Vol. IV, p. 1552/3).

Shorter, R. C.. 2&11-10-28, 4-10-29 & 31-11-29. Dr. Reubin

Clark Shorter, b. 13 Feb. 1787 Culpepper Co., Va., d. 14
July 1853. He migrated to Twiggs Co., Ga., then Jasper
Co., Ga. then Barbour Co., Ala. by 1836 (DAB, Vol. IV, p.
1555). Mary Butler Gill (wife - m. 31 May 1812 Jasper Co.,
Ga.), b. ca 1797 Ga., d. ca 1868, both buried Shorter Cem.,
Eufaula, Ala..

Sikes, S.. 14&32-9-27. Solomon Sikes, b. ca 1793 Ga.,
a Baptist Minister (CR A, p. 324). Nancy Gibson (2nd wife -
m. 31 Dec. 1846), b. ca 1809 Ga..

Sims, H.. 21-12-26. Henry Sims, b. ca 1828 Ga., d. by
1870. Jane V. Crapps (wife - m. 9 Oct. 1851), b. 11 Nov.
1832 S. C. (1860 Census), d. 1 Jan. 1907, buried Mt. Zion
Cem.. She was a daughter of John J. Crapps who died by
Sept. 1835 Talbot Co., Ga. (OR 2, p. 201).

Sims, Joel. 17&18-10-27. Rev. Joel Sims, b. ca 1800 Ga.,
d. 18 Nov. 1879 ("The Times & News", Nov. 20, 1879). He
was a Baptist Minister (CR A, p. 324). Jane ----- (wife),
b. ca 1801 Ga., d. 6 May 1871 ("The Bluff City Times",
May 18, 1871).

Sims, W. W.. 2-10-26. William W. Sims, b. 29 Sept. 1826
Walton Co., Ga., d. 11 March 1898. Caroline McMurray
(wife - m. 27 Aug. 1846), b. 22 Jan. 1827 Ga., d. 24 May
1908, both buried Upper Prospect Baptist Church Cem..

Skiper, John. 16&17-10-25. John W. Skipper, b. ca 1809
N. C.. Demaris ----- (wife?), b. ca 1812 N. C..

Skipper, N. A.. 21-10-25. Nathaniel A. Skipper, b. ca
1792 N. C., to Ala. from Ga. by 1846. Elizabeth -----
(2nd wife?), b. ca 1812 Ga..

Slaughter, Jas. D.. 20-12-26. James D. Slaughter, b. ca
1812 Ga., d. by Aug. 1876 Orange Co., Fla. (Original Papers,
Boxes 322 & 361). He was probably a son of Daniel Slaughter
(b. ca 1780 Va.) who gave him some slaves in Jan. 1838 (CR
C, p. 316). He was a brother of George Slaughter (b. ca
1831 Ala) (ibid). Elizabeth ----- (wife?), b. ca 1829 Ga.
She may have been Elizabeth Sharp who married James D.
Slaughter 10 May 1843 Stewart Co., Ga..

Sloan, D., David. 21&22-12-27. David Sloan, b. ca 1809
N. C., to Ala. from Ga. by 1837. Margaret ----- (wife -
CR K, p. 370), b. ca 1814 Ga..

Sloan, John. 32&33-10-25. John Sloan, Sr., b. ca 1784
Ireland, died by 1856. Mary Grubbs (2nd wife - m. 22 July
1849), b. ca 1803 Ga.. She married (1) ----- McDowell (3)
Benjamin Parmer 1 Oct. 1856 (4) Matthew Laseter 24 Sept.
1857. She was a daughter of William Grubbs, Sr. (Vol. II,
p. 60).

Smiley, A. H.. 31-8-24. Austin H. Smiley, b. ca 1811 Ga.,
d. by Feb. 1866 (OR 15, p. 482/4). He sold this land in
June 1854 (CR N, p. 539). Adeline W. ----- (wife - ibid),
b. ca 1826 Ga..

Smith, G. W.. 6-11-25. George W. Smith mortgaged this
land in May 1853 (CR K, p. 445). He may have married
Sarah Mann 27 Sept. 1846 Muscogee Co., Ga..

Smith, H. S.. 33-12-25 & 33-13-25(B). Hampton S. Smith
was of Muscogee Co., Ga. in Aug. 1839 (CR B, p. 545). His
son, Charles V. Smith, was born 1827, died 1866 and is
buried in Enon Cem., Bullock Co., Ala... Sarah ----- (wife-
CR B, p. 720). She may have been Sarah H. Redd who married
Hampton S. Smith 19 Oct. 1825 Putnam Co., Ga..

Smith, I.. 1-10-26. Isaiah Smith, b. ca 1796 S. C., d. by
May 1857 (OR 8, p. 193/4). Elizabeth ----- (wife), b. ca
1803 N. C., possibly nee Grice.

Smith, J. B., Jas. B.. 28-12-25. James B. Smith, b. ca
1802 Ga.. Lucinda ----- (2nd wife?), b. ca 1822 Ga..

Smith, J. B. R.. 12&13-10-28. James B. R. Smith, b. ca
1808 (Wilkes Co., Ga.?), possibly a son of Nathan Smith
who died ca 1820 Wilkes Co., Ga.. He sold this land in
Nov. 1853 (CR K, p. 645). Barbara Nash (wife - m. 13 Dec.
1827 Wilkes Co., Ga.), b. 2 May 1809 Ga. (Nash Bible),
daughter of Acton Nash who died by Aug. 1854 (OR 6, p.
408/12).

Smith, J. H.. 34-12-26 & 34-10-28. James H. Smith, b. ca
1815 Ga.. Mary Johnson (2nd wife? - m. 14 Dec. 1843), b.
ca 1822 S. C..

Smith, J. R.. 8-9-29. John R. Smith is in the 1840 Census,
age 20/30. In Oct. 1846, he and Reddick Smith borrowed
money from Daniel C. Scott (CR G, p. 300).

Smith, L. S.. 1,2&12-12-27 & 35-13-27. Lovitt S. Smith,
b. ca 1818 Ga., d. by June 1858 (OR 9, p. 165). He was
a brother of Cincinnatus Smith (b. ca 1805 Ga., d. by June
1858 - OR 9, p. 385). Other brothers were William C.
Smith of Hancock Co., Ga., Robert M. Smith, deceased (heirs
lived in Upson and Talbot Cos., Ga.) and George Smith (1/2
brother) of Hancock Co., Ga.. He also had a sister, Lurena,
wife of Dr. S. N. Barney, of Monroe Co., Ga.. Sarah L. -----
(wife), b. ca 1824 Ga., d. by May 1860 (OR 10, p. 771/2).
She may have been Sarah Laura Cook who married Maj. Lovitt
S. Smith 28 Jan. 1841 Hancock Co., Ga..

Smith, Reddick. 24-12-25. Reddick Smith is in the 1840

Census age 40/50 with a family but is not in any later census In Dec. 1835, he sold land in 5-10-28 (CR A, p. 189).

Smith, S., Saml.. 3&4-11-27. Samuel J. Smith, b. ca 1806 Ga., in Ala. by 1829. He bought land in 3-11-27 in Aug. 1838 (CR B, p. 344) and may have been related to Sion Smith who bought adjoining land in Aug. 1839 (CR B, p. 574). Mary ----- (wife?), b. ca 1809 S. C..

Smith, Wm. R.. 35-10-27. William R. Smith, b. ca 1828 S. C., went to Texas ca 1870 (Vol. II, p. 143), son of Isaiah Smith (CR 8, p. 228/9). Eliza Parmer (wife - m. 29 Nov. 1849), b. ca 1832 Ga., daughter of George W. Parmer and Rightly Kent who married 6 June 1815 Jones Co., Ga. (Vol. II, p. 141 & 143).

Smith, Y.. 25-12-27 & 30-12-28. Young Smith, b. ca 1808 N. C., to Ala. from Ga. by 1843. In his household in 1850 were John G. Smith (b. ca 1836 Ga.), William J. Smith (b. ca 1835 Ga.) and Young H. Smith (b. ca 1842 Miss.), heirs of William T. Smith who died by Sept. 1846, probably in Miss. (OR 2, p. 274). In Feb. 1849, he and wife MARTHA sold land in 31-12-28 (CR H, p. 348/9); in the 1850 Census, SARAH (b. ca 1807) is listed directly after him and before the children; in June 1852, there is on record a marriage agreement between Young Smith and FRANCES Crow (CR L, p. 645/6).

Snipes, M. A., Maria A.. 6-10-28 & 6,18,19,20,29,30,31&32-11-28. William Henry Snipes, b. 22 Dec. 1798 S. C., d. 11 Sept. 1843. Maria A. ----- (wife), b. 25 Jan. 1802 Darlington Dist., S. C., d.18 Jan. 1859, both buried Fairview Cem., Eufaula, Ala..

Sparks, Saml. 16-11-28. Samuel Sparks, b. ca 1814 Ga. (1860 Census), d. 1874 (OR 28, p. 205/6). He was grandfather of Chauncey Sparks, Gov. of Ala. (DAB, Vol. IV, p. 1604). Mary Lawhon (1st wife), b. ca 1821 N. C. (1860 Census). They came to Barbour Co. from Muscogee Co., Ga. (DAB, Vol. IV, p. 1604). Martha A. Wills (2nd wife - m. 14 Dec. 1865), b. ca 1845 Ga. (1870 Census), d. after 1894 (OR 28, p. 205/6).

Spence, A. T.. 3-11-26. Aaron T. Spence, b. ca 1810 Ga. Feriby ----- (wife?), b. ca 1812 N. C..

Spruell, Jas. J.. 30-11-26. James J. Spruell, b. ca 1808 N. C.. Catharine Bush (wife - m. 18 Nov. 1845), b. ca 1826 Ga., daughter of Lewis Bush who died by Nov. 1836 (Vol. I, p. 27).

Spurlock, J. M.. 8-11-29. James M. Spurlock, b. 14 June

1822 Twiggs Co., Ga., d. 3 March 1884, son of Solomon Spurlock ("Eufaula Times & News", Dec. 20, 1900) who was born
ca 1798 Ga.. In the household of Solomon Spurlock in 1860
was John Spurlock (Rev. Soldier), b. ca 1756 N. C.. Tabitha
Lawhon (wife - m. 17 July 1851 - Spurlock Bible), b. 30 June
1832, d. 11 April 1912, both buried Fairview Cem., Eufaula,
Ala..

Stanley, Lewis. 5&8-13-26(B). Lewis Stanley, b. ca 1792
Ga., d.by Oct. 1858 (OR 6, p. 478/9). Elizabeth T. -----
(wife), b. ca 1805 Ga..

Starke, A. B.. 24-13-27 & 13,19&24-13-28(R). Abram B.
Starke, b. ca 1815 S. C.. In his household in 1850 was
Samuel Starke, b. 12 Aug. 1777 S. C., d. 29 March 1859,
buried Glennville Cem., Russell Co., Ala.. In March 1841,
he gave a slave to Abram B. Starke - the deed was written
in Elbert Co., Ga. and recorded in Barbour Co., Ala. in
June 1841 (CR C, p. 353). Frances H. Jackson (1st wife -
m. 8 Oct. 1844), b. ca 1823 Ga., d. 29 Sept. 1850, buried
Glennville Cem., daughter of Mark and H. T. Jackson ("Southern Christian Advocate", 15 Oct. 1850). Mary A. ----- (2nd
wife), b. ca 1834 Ala. (1860 Census).

Starke, John W. (or M.). 10&15-13-27. John W. Starke, b.
ca 1823 S. C.? Eliza M. Pope (wife), b. 12 March 1812, d.
20 Dec. 1858, daughter of Henry and Susan Pope - buried
Villula Cem., Russell Co., Ala..

Stephens, G., Green. 11&13-13-26. Green Stephens, b. ca
1804 Ga. (1860 Census), d. 6 Oct. 1883 (OR 23, p. 236/242).
His second wife may have been Margaret McRae - m. 19 Aug.
1849. F. Caroline ----- (3rd wife - m. after 1860), b. ca
1831 Ga. (1870 Census), d. after 1883 (OR 23, p. 236/242).

Stephens, W.. 36-9-26. William Stephens, b. ca 1822 S. C.
(1850 Census - 1860 Census says b. ca 1826 S. C.). Elizabeth ----- (wife?), b. ca 1822 S. C. (1850 Census - 1860
Census says b. ca 1825 S. C.).

Stephens, Wm. H.. 20-12-25(B). William H. Stephens, b. ca
1815 N. C.. Martha ----- (wife?), b. ca 1829 Ala..
OR
William H. Stephens, b. ca 1801 or 1810 N. C.,. Mary -----
(wife?), b. ca 1812 Ga..

Stephens, Wm. J.. 17-9-26. There is no further record of
him unless he was the William Stevens (wife Elizabeth) who
sold land in 25-9-26 in Dec. 1849 (CR J, p. 227).

Stephenson, C., Council. 3&4-12-29. Council Stephenson,
b. ca 1804 N. C., d. 29 Sept. 1871 (OR 17, p. 760/2). Jacky

114

Ann ----- (1st wife?), b. ca 1811 N. C.. Susan A. -----
(2nd wife), b. ca 1829 Ga. (1870 Census).

Stephenson, H., Hardy. 10&11-11-27. Hardy Stephenson, b.
ca 1823 N. C.. Sarah Reeves (wife - m. 7 Jan. 1842), b. ca
1826 Ga., daughter of Asher Reeves and Ellender C. Parmer
(Vol. II, p. 135/6).

Stewart, D. L., Danl., Daniel L.. 3,4,5&10-10-27 . Daniel
L. Stewart, b. ca 1815 N. C. (1860 Census), d. 20 Oct. 1882,
son of John Stewart who died by July 1852 (OR 4, p. 571).
Frances E. Smith (wife - m. 6 Feb. 1851), b. 1835 Ga. (1860
Census), d. 1923, both buried Mt. Serene Cem..

Stewart, J. G.. 34-11-27. John G. Stewart, b. ca 1770
Scotland, d. by July 1852 (OR 4, p. 571). Anna (Nancy) L.
----- (wife), b. ca 1777 N. C.. In 1860, she was living
with Daniel L. Stewart.

Stewart, J. L.. 3-10-27. John L. Stewart, Jr., b. ca 1800
N. C., son of John Stewart who died by July 1852 (OR 4, p.
571). Christian ----- (wife?), b. ca 1810 N. C..

Stewart, N.. 5,6&7-10-27. Norman Stewart, b. 1804, d. 26
May 1854, son of John Stewart who died by July 1852 (OR 4,
p. 571). John Stewart (Sr.) migrated from Scotland to
Newberry Dist., S. C. then to BarbourCo., Ala. in the 1820's
(MRA, Vol. I, p. 460/1). Jane Stewart (wife), b. 1824, d.
20 May 1893, both buried Mt. Serene Cem., daughter of Chas.
Stewart who was a brother of John L. Stewart (ibid).

Stewart, P.. 13&33-13-26(partly in Bullock Co.). Peter
Stewart, b. ca 1798 Scotland, died by Nov. 1856 (OR 7, p.
570). Peninna ----- (wife), b. ca 1808 S. C..

Stewart, Thomas. 30-11-24(Pike Co.). Thomas Stewart, b.
ca 1800 S. C. (1860 Census), d. by Jan. 1861 (OR 11, p.
481/4). Jane Sloan (wife - m. 29 Oct. 1822 Richmond Co.,
Ga.), b. ca 1802 Ga., d. by Nov. 1862 (OR 12, p. 570/1),
daughter of John Sloan, Sr. (CR H, p. 450).

Stinson, George. 8-8-28. George Stinson, b. ca 1796 Va.,
brother of Alexander Stinson who died by Aug. 1839 (CR B,
p. 561). Matilda ----- (wife?), b. ca 1800 Ga..

Stokes, H.. 32-9-25 & 32-10-25. Henry Stokes, b. ca 1811
S. C., d. 1 June 1885 (OR 23, p. 710/8). Martha A. Sloan
(wife), b. ca 1815 Ga., daughter of John Sloan, Sr. (CR H,
p. 453).

Stokes, Joel D.. 26-8-24. Joel D. Stokes, b. ca 1831 Ala.,
d. by Dec. 1862 (OR 12, p. 643), son of Irwin J. Stokes (b.
ca 1805 S. C.) with whom he was living in 1850 and 1860.

Elizabeth Ketchem (probably 1st wife - m. 8 April 1855).
Matilda J. Powell (2nd wife - m. 22 July 1860), b. ca 1843
Ala. (1860 Census). In 1860, she was in the household of
William Stokes, b. ca 1832 Ala.. In 1850, William Stokes
was in the household of Irwin J. Stokes and Matilda Powell
was in the household of David Powell (b. ca 1801 S. C.).

Streeter, M. H.. 15-12-27. Milton H. Streeter, b. ca 1818
N. C., d. by Oct. 1873, possibly never married, son of
Sheppard M. Streeter who died by March 1861 (OR 11, p.
807/12).

Streeter, R.. 10-12-26, 9-12-27 & 31&32-13-27. Reddick
Streeter, b. ca 1794 N. C., d. by June 1858 (OR 9, p.
245/7). Milton H. Streeter and S. M. Streeter were wit-
nesses to his will in Oct. 1850 (Original Papers, Box
304). Margaret ----- (wife), b. ca 1804 N. C..

Streeter, S. M.. 5&6-12-27 & 32-13-27. Sheppard M. Streeter,
b. ca 1787 Va., d. by March 1861 (OR 11, p. 600/2). Mary
----- (wife), b. ca 1805 N. C..

Stringer, J. A., Jas. A.. 27-11-26 & 22,23&27-12-26. James
A. Stringer, Jr., b. ca 1811 Ga., d. by Nov. 1854 (OR 6, p.
192), son of James A. Stringer, Sr. (OR 10, p. 285/9).
Sarah A. ----- (wife), b. ca 1823 Ga., d. by Aug. 1859 (OR
10, p. 285/9).

Stripling, A.. 30-13-25(B). Aaron Stripling, b. ca 1798
S. C., to Ala. by 1825, died in Pike Co., Ala. by Nov. 1859
(Pike Co., Ala. Will Book A, p. 193). Martha Parmer (1st
wife - source unknown). Susan Kelly (2nd wife - m. 12
Jan. 1821 Jones Co., Ga.).

Stripling, Jas. T.. 17-11-29. James Stripling, b. ca 1809
Ga.. Frances ----- (wife), b. ca 1806 Ga.. She may have
been the Frances Woods who married James Stripling 10 Dec.
1835 Monroe Co., Ga..

Stuckey, -----. 31-8-26. Starky Stuckey bought this land
in Feb. 1851 (CR J, p. 356).

Stuckey, Wm.. 5&17-11-29. William Stuckey, b. ca 1799
N. C.. Rosannah ----- (wife?), b. ca 1799 Ga.. In Jan.
1854, Rosannah Stuckey of Coffee Co., Ala. sold part of
the above land (CR Q, p. 823).

Sutton, C.. 25&36-11-27. Charles Sutton, b. ca 1787 S. C.,
Charity Bryan (wife - m. 28 Jan. 1819 Pulaski Co., Ga.).
Also in this household in 1850 was Mary Bryant, b. ca 1754
Va..

Sutton, J., Jesse. 6&7-8-24. Jesse Sutton, b. 12 Dec. 1793

S. C., d. 3 June 1860, buried family cemetery. Elizabeth
Bryant (wife), b. ca 1796 Ga., d. by Sept. 1874 (OR 20, p.
37).

Sutton, N. B.. 7-8-24. Needham B. Sutton, b. ca 1821 Ga.,
son of Jesse Sutton and Elizabeth Bryant. He was living
in Polk Co., Fla. by 1875 (Vol. I, p. 149). Amanda Caroline E. Campbell (1st wife - m. 12 March 1846), b. ca 1828
Ala., d. by 1859, heir of William D. and Mary (Elizabeth)
Campbell (OR 17, p. 203). Sarah Hall (2nd wife - m. 6 Nov.
1859), b. ca 1825 Ala. (1860 Census).

Swilly, Samuel. 16-10-26. Samuel Swilly, b. ca 1797 Ga.,
d. by Oct. 1864 Sumter Co., Ala.. He had a brother, Jaredo
Swilly, who died in Barbour Co. by Nov. 1834 (Vol. I, p.
154). Martha ----- (wife), b. ca 1800 Ga.(ibid).

Sylvester, M. A.. 13-11-28. Demarcus Sylvester, b. 27 Feb.
1797 Sumter Dist., S. C., d. 31 March 1870, son of Asbury
Sylvester and Martha Watkins (Locke-Sylvester Bible). Mary
Ann Rembert (wife - m. 18 Feb. 1818 Sumter Dist., S. C.), b.
29 Dec. 1798 Sumter Dist., S. C., d. 22 Jan. 1880, daughter
of Abijah Rembert and Elizabeth English (ibid). In 1838,
James E. Rembert of Sumter Dist., S. C., deeded slaves to
his sister, Mary Ann, wife of Demarcus Sylvester, of Houston
Co., Ga. (CR B, p. 528).

Sylvester, Thos. R.. 5-11-28. Thomas Rembert Sylvester,
b. 2 July 1820 Sumter Dist., S. C., d. 5 Dec. 1901, son
of Demarcus Sylvester and Mary Ann Rembert (Sylvester Bible).
Alethia Beckham (wife - m. 17 March 1842 Lancaster, S. C.)
daughter of Burrell and Rachel Beckham. Thomas R. and
Alethia Sylvester are buried in unmarked graves in White
Oak Methodist Church Cem.. (Sylvester Bible).

Talbot, P. E.. 31-10-29. James Talbot, b. ca 1810 Ga..
Phoebe Rains (wife - m. 2 July 1835 Talbot Co., Ga.), b.
ca 1814 Ga.. Also in this household in 1850 were John G.
Rains (b. ca 1809 Ga.) and Lucretia Rains (b. ca 1785 Ga.).

Tarver, James. 6-13-25(B). James Monroe Tarver, b. 25 Nov.
1821, d. 31 March 1894. Rachel Jones Banks (wife), b. 2
May 1826, d. 23 Oct. 1894, both buried Enon Cem., Bullock
Co., Ala.. Also buried in this cemetery is Mrs. Dicy Tarver,
b. 2 May 1785, d. 17 Nov. 1858.

Taylor, C., Chas., Charles. 15,21&22-12-29. Charles Taylor
was of Newark, N. J.. (CR J, p. 637).

Taylor, J. W.. 19-13-25(B). James W. Taylor was of Macon
Co., Ala. in Jan. 1851 (CR J, p. 474).

Taylor, Joshua. 26-10-25. Joshua Taylor, b. ca 1807 N. C.,
d. by June 1857 (OR 8, p. 286/7). Sarah Ann ----- (wife),
b. ca 1813 N. C..

Taylor, M. J.. 22-13-25(B). Meredith J. Taylor bought this
land in Nov. 1851 (CR J, p. 625).

Teal, A., Allen. 23&24-9-24. Allen Teal, b. ca 1800 N. C..
His firs wife was probably Margaret McRae, b. ca 1800/10
(1840 Census), heir of Christopher McRae who died by 1837
Anson Co., N. C.. (CR B, p. 561/2). Mary Mooneyham (2nd
wife - m. 12 Sept. 1850), b.ca 1831 S. C..

Teal, D. W.. 25-11-27. Daniel W. Teal, b. ca 1824 N. C.,
son of William Teal and Isabella McRae (OR 11, p. 609/16).
In 1861, he was preparing to move "out of the state (ibid).
Mary McLeod (wife - m. 17 Oct. 1852), b. ca 1826 N. C.
(1860 Census).

Teal, Wm.. 13,23&24-9-24 & 2&11-9-27. William Teal, b. ca
1799 N. C.. His first wife was Isabella McRae, who was an
heir of Christopher McRae who died by 1837 in Anson Co., N. C.
(CR B, p. 561/2). Charlotte Holland (2nd wife - m. 15 Feb.
1860), b. 16 April 1830, d. 1 Feb. 1913, buried Pine Level
Baptist Church Cem..

Temples, Mary. 3-10-27 & 26-11-27. Mary Temples, b. ca
1802 Ga.. She bought this land in Nov. 1848 (CR H, p. 303)
and sold part of it in Oct. 1853 (CR K, p. 654).

Terry, T. M., Thos., Thomas. 14&15-13-25(B) & 14-13-26.
In Jan. 1846, Francis J. Terry of Muscogee Co., Ga. bought
land in 14&15-13-25 (CR F, p. 464/5). There is no further
record of him or of Thomas Terry.

Tew, Jas., James. 23-8-26(Henry Co.) & 33-8-26. James Tew,
b. ca 1821 N. C.. Lavinia Wilkinson (wife - m. 5 Oct. 1845),
b. ca 1815 S. C. (1860 Census).

Tharpe, C. A.. 14,22&23-10-26. Charnick A. Tharpe patented
this land in 1836 (Barbour Co., Ala. Tract Book). He is not
in any early census of Barbour Co.. He may have been related
to the Tharpe family of Twiggs Co., Ga.. Mary J. E. Williamson (wife - m. 26 Jan. 1849).

Thigpen, J., Joseph. 15&16-12-25(B). Joseph Thigpen, b. ca
1800 N. C., d. by Nov. 1856 (OR 7, p. 560). Clara -----
(wife), b. ca 1795 N. C.. In Dec. 1858, she was living in
La. (OR 9, p. 145).

Thomas, Adam. 23-8-25. Adam J. Thomas, b. ca 1825 N. C..
In 1850, he was in the household of Moses Thomas, b. ca 1798
N. C..

Thomas, E., Elliott. 4-10-26 & 7,8&18-9-27. Elliott Thomas, b. ca 1789 Va., d. by Feb. 1852. Sarah Berry (1st wife), d. after 1833 (Vol. I, p. 156). Ann B. Grephill (2nd wife), d. by Dec. 1851 (OR 5, p. 532).

Thomas, J. E.. 14-8-25. James E. Thomas, b. ca 1821 Ga., son of Elliott Thomas and Sarah Berry (Vol. I, p. 156 & 158). He was deaf and dumb. Dorcas ----- (wife), b. ca 1818 N. C..

Thomas, Jonathan. 8-9-27. Jonathan Thomas, b. 3 May 1815 Ga., d. 3 April 1881, buried New Hope Cem., son of Elliott Thomas and Sarah Berry (Vol. I, p. 156). Maria J. Bush (wife - m. 12 Jan. 1834), b. 4 Aug. 1819 Ga., d. 25 Sept. 1904, buried Clayton Cem., daughter of Zachariah Bush (Vol. I, p. 156).

Thomas, Joseph. 27-11-26. Joseph Thomas, d. by 1857, son of Elliott Thomas and Sarah Berry (Vol. I, p. 156).

Thomas, M., Morton. 11&14-8-25. Morton Thomas, b. ca 1799 N. C.. He did not have a wife in his household in 1850 but he is named as a son-in-law in the will of Peter Hagler who died by May 1852 (OR 4, p. 471/3).

Thomas, Wm. B.. 12-9-27 & 7-9-28. William Berry Thomas, b. ca 1816 Ga., son of Elliott Thomas and Sarah Berry (Vol. I, p. 156 & 158). Catharine McInnis (wife), b. ca 1815 N. C., daughter of Angus McInnis (ibid).

Thompson, A.. 12-8-23. Alladin Thompson, b. ca 1818 S. C., d. 24 June 1874 (Vol. II, p. 53), son of Robert Thompson and Rhoda Grubbs (Vol. I, p. 149/50). Susan N. Sutton (wife), b. ca 1825 Ga., daughter of Jesse Sutton and Elizabeth Bryant (ibid).

Thompson, Alfred. 1&12-10-28. Alfred Thompson bought this land in April 1850 (CR O, p. 232). He and wife, Lucindy, sold part of it in Dec. 1859 (CR P, p. 607). In Feb. 1857, John Thompson gave a slave to his son, Alfred Thompson of Russell Co., Ala. (CR N, p. 239).

Thompson, S., Shadrack. 1-11-28 & 36-12-28. Shadrack Thompson, b. 26 March 1815 N. C., d. 25 Jan. 1907 Quitman Co., Ga. ("Eufaula Times & News", Jan 31, 1907. Martha ----- (wife), b. ca 1827 Ga., d. 1915, both buried Fairview Cem., Eufaula, Ala.. Also in this household in 1850 was Elva Thompson, b. ca 1787 N. C..

Thompson, Wm. O.. 12-10-27. William O. Thompson, b. ca 1811 N. C., to Ala. from Ga. by 1848. He bought this land from Shadrack Thompson 8 May 1849 (CR H, p. 417) and sold it on 1 Dec. 1850 (CR J, p. 137). Eliza ----- (wife?), b.

ca 1812 Ga.. She may have been Eliza C. Leonard who married William O. Thompson 4 Jan. 1832 Baldwin Co., Ga..

Thorn, Joseph W.. 6-8-24. Joseph W. Thorn, b. ca 1820 Ga. (1850 Census - 1860 Census says b. ca 1821 S. C.). Martha Davis (wife - m. 28 July 1853), b. ca 1836 Ala. (1860 Census). In 1850, she was in the household of John Davis, b. ca 1801 N. C..

Thorn, N.. 11&12-8-23. Nicholas Thorn, b. ca 1790 S. C., to Ga. by 1836, in Ala. by 1850. Martha ----- (wife - CR L. p. 296), b. ca 1802 S. C.. In 1870, she was living with her daughter, Matilda, who had married Joseph Powell 2 Jan. 1853.

Thornton, Wm. H.. 11-12-25(B) & 8,16&17-10-29. Dr. William Horatio Thornton, b. 8 May 1816 Wilkes Co., Ga., d. 27 Jan. 1881, son of Dr. John Thornton of Culpepper Co., Va. and Rebecca Carter of Ga.; great-grandson of Matthew Thornton of New Hampshire, a signer of the Declaration of Independence (DAB, Vol. IV, p. 1671). Mary Butler Shorter (wife - m. 10 April 1845), b. 1828 Ga., d. 1914, both buried Fairview Cem., Eufaula, Ala.. She was a daughter of Reuben Clark Shorter (ibid).

Tigh, J. J.. 7&8-10-27 & 18-9-29. In Aug. 1843, John P. Tigh of Montgomery Co., Ala. bought the above land (CR E, p. 414/5).

Tillman, S.. 24&34-10-24. Stephen Tillman, b. ca 1827 Ga.. No further record.

Tindal, John. 5-10-27 & 28&29-10-28. John Alexander Tindal, b. 1796 S. C., d. 16 April 1864 Henderson Co., Texas (Mrs. D. Louise Cumbie, Rockdale, Texas). Mary Ledbetter (wife), b. 1807 Jones Co., Ga., d. 10 April 1875 Henderson Co., Texas (ibid).

Tinsley, C. C.. 5-11-26. Dr. Charles C. Tinsley, b. 26 Jan. 1814 Ga., d. 13 April 1852, buried Clayton Cem.. Albena A. ----- (wife), b. 9 May 1814 Ga., d. 22 Feb. 1887, buried Perote Cem., Bullock Co., Ala..

Tison, J. G., Jas. J. 10,11,14&15-11-27. James G. Tison, b. ca 1820 S. C., may have been living in Orange Co., Fla. in 1888 ("Eufaula Weekly News", 12 April 1888). He had a brother, Henry C. Tison, who died by July 1862 in Henry Co., Ala. (Henry Co., Ala. OR M, p. 420). Adrianna C. Ott (wife- m. 12 Sept. 1841), b. ca 1824 S. C., sister of Edward S. Ott and Mary M. Ott Treadwell (OR 15, p. 155/8).

Tomlin, C., Carson. 3&9-9-24. Carson Tomberlin, b. 1813

Anson Co., N. C. (MRA, Vol. II, p. 465), d. by Feb. 1868
(OR 16, p. 657). Mary Bain (wife), b. ca 1813 N. C., m.
ca 1834 N. C., d. 1880 (MRA, Vol. II, p. 465).

Torrence, J. E.. 34-12-29. John E. Torrence, b. ca 1831
Ga., minor heir of Ebenezer Torrence (OR 4, p. 594) who was
born 8 May 1784 Warren Co., Ga., d. 16 July 1837, buried
Fairview Cem., Eufaula, Ala.. Ebenezer Torrence married
Louisa Beard 19 Jan. 1830 Greene Co., Ga.. In 1840, Louise
S.(?) Torrence was the guardian of John E. Torrence; in
1841, his guardian was Rev. Green Malone. Mrs. Louise S.
Torrence married Green Malone 4 Aug. 1840 ("Southern
Christian Advocate", 21 Aug. 1840).

Towns, Wm.. 8&17-12-25(B). William Towns was of Tallapoosa Co., Ala. in Dec. 1849 (CR H, p. 603).

Trammell, P. N.. 1&2-12-26, 36-13-26 & 31-13-27. James J.
Trammell died by Aug. 1843 (OR 2, p. 2). Penelope N. Maddox
(wife - m. 6 Jan. 1825 Laurens Co., Ga.), b. ca 1804 Ga..
She married (2) Simeon R. Cannon.

Trawick, Jas.. 25&36-13-25(B). James Trawick, b. ca 1804
Ga.. Nancy ----- (wife?), b. ca 1811 Ga..

Treadwell, B. F.. 1,11&12-11-27 & 6-11-28. Benjamin F.
Treadwell, b. ca 1808 S. C.. Mary M. Ott (wife), b. 12 Dec.
1817 Orangeburg Dist., S. C., d. 6 Oct. 1865, buried Fairview Cem., Eufaula, Ala.. She was a sister of Edward S.
Ott (OR 15, p. 155/8).

Tucker, Jas.. 16&21-11-27. James Tucker, b. ca 1800 Ga.
(1860 Census), d. 17 Dec. 1887 (Original Papers, Box 482).
Eliza ----- (wife), b. 12 Sept. 1810 Ga. (1860 Census), d.
25 Dec. 1890, buried in the family cemetery.

Turner, Jas. R.. 18-9-26. There is no James R. Turner in
the early Barbour Co. records. There is a James K. Turner,
b. ca 1810 Ga., d. by Sept. 1865 (OR 15, p. 43/4). Sarah
----- (wife?), b. ca 1806 Ga..

Turner, N. W.. 22,23,26&27-10-26. Noel W. Turner, b. ca
1802 S. C., d. by Nov. 1865 (OR 14, p. 612). He may have
been a son or grandson of Noel Turner,(Rev. Soldier), b.
11 May 1764, d. 21 Jan. 1837 (DAR Patriot Index, p. 691),
wife Sarah. In 1850, Sarah Turner, b. ca 1766 S. C., was
in the household of Noel W. Turner. Melinda ----- (1st
wife - CR C, p. 145). Margaret McDonald Stewart (2nd wife -
m. 12 Dec. 1849), b. ca 1805 N. C., daughter of John Stewart
who died by July 1852 (OR 4, p. 571).

Tyler, J. J.. 2-11-26. Rev. Joshua Tyler, b. 18 Nov. 1818
S. C. (1860 Census), d. 28 Oct. 1880, buried Mt. Pleasant

Cem.. Ann J. ----- (wife - m. 9 Sept. 1838, probably in
S. C.,)b. 6 April 1819 S. C. (Tyler Bible).

Upshaw, J. R.. 6-13-27 & 6&7-13-28. James R. Upshaw, b.
ca 1818 Ga., d. 16 May 1852, buried in the family cemetery,
son of Leroy Upshaw, Sr. (b. 1785, d. 22 Sept. 1841) - his
widow, Catharine (OR 1, p. 228), b. ca 1802 Ga., m. Robert
O. Dale 31 July 1843. She was Mrs. Catharine Ellington and
married Leroy Upshaw 18 Nov. 1830 Elbert Co., Ga.. His first
wife was Prudence T. Richardson (m. 14 May 1814 Elbert Co.,
Ga.), daughter of Walker Richardson (Rev. Soldier) who
died by Sept. 1822 Elbert Co., Ga.,whose wife was Prudence
Thompson. Leroy Upshaw was a son of John Upshaw (Rev. Soldier)
(b. 22 Feb. 1755 Essex Co., Va., d. 1834 Elbert Co., Ga.) and
Amy Gatewood -(m. 5 May 1776 Amherst Co., Va.), daughter of
Larkin Gatewood and Catherine Penn (T. O. Brook, Marietta,
Ga.). Maria G. Brown (wife - m. 24 Dec.1844), b. ca 1826
Ga.. She married (2) George D. Conner 17 Jan. 1856.

Upshaw, L.. 2-13-27. Leroy Upshaw, Jr., b. ca 1823 Ga., d.
ca 1 Oct. 1888 (OR 25, p. 145), son of Leroy Upshaw, Sr. (see
J. R. Upshaw). Ann S. ----- (wife?), b. ca 1835 Ga. (1860
Census). Also in this household in 1860 and 1870 was Jane
Richardson, b. ca 1801 Ga..

Upshaw, Wm. T.. 2-13-27. William T. Upshaw, b. ca 1821 Ga.,
d. by May 1855 (OR 7, p. 138), son of Leroy Upshaw, Sr. (see
J. R. Upshaw). Mary E. ----- (wife), b. ca 1824 Ga..

Upshaw, W. & L.. 11,12,13&14-13-27. William T. and Leroy
Upshaw, Jr., sons of Leroy Upshaw, Sr..

Urquahart, H. M.. 3-12-27. Henry M. Urquahart, b. ca 1820
Ga.. Adeline Williamson (wife - m. 11 Feb. 1844), b. ca
1825 Ga., daughter of Green Williamson and Elizabeth Head;
granddaughter of William Head who died by 1857 (OR 9, p.
135). There was another Henry Urquahart in Barbour Co. as
follows: Rev. Henry Urquahart, b. 18 Feb. 1833 Montgomery
Co., Ala., d. 6 July 1902 Tate Springs, Tenn, buried Fairview Cem., Eufaula, Ala.. ("History of Methodism" by Lazenby). He married Missouri Ann Phillips, b. 11 Nov. 1838, d.
7 Nov. 1884, buried Fairview Cem., Eufaula, Ala., daughter
of Elam Phillips and Mary Ann Ethridge of Mobile, Ala. (DAB
Vol. IV, p. 1702).

Utsey, J., Jacob. 25-9-24 & 24&30-9-25. Jacob Utsey, b. ca
1790 S. C.. Mary ----- (wife), b. ca 1800 S. C..

Utsey, John. 30-9-25 & 30-9-27. John J. Utsey, b.ca 1826
Ala., probably son of Jacob Utsey. Martha ----- (wife?),
b. ca 1829 Ala..

Vann (Vaun?), Edw. W.. 32-12-28. Edward W. Vann (Vaun), b. ca 1816 S. C.. In his household in 1850 was Sarah Vann (Vaun), b. ca 1790 S. C. and Joseph Vann (Vaun).

Vann (Vaun?), J. S.. 7-13-29. Joseph Vann (Vaun), b. ca 1834 S. C.. He was a minor heir of Isaac Vann (Vaun) who died by Nov. 1848. From 1848 to Jan. 1853, his guardian was Edward W. Vann (Vaun). In 1853 & 1854, his guardian was Sarah Vann (Vaun), b. ca 1790 S. C.. Her securities were Joseph M. Vann (Vaun) and Henry M. Vann (Vaun) (Original Papers, Box 340).

Varner, Wm.. 1&2-11-25 & 14,23,24,25,26,27,35&36-12-25. William Varner bought part of the above land in Nov. 1838 and Aug. 1839, at which time he was of Monroe Co., Ga. (CR A, p. 160 and CR B, p. 834).

Ventress, Thos. 15-10-26. Thomas Ventress, b. 8 Sept. 1813 Jones Co., Ga., d. 17 Oct. 1866, buried Clayton Cem., probably son of Stephen Ventress who married Nancy Wilkerson 8 Nov. 1808 Putnam Co., Ga. (Vol. II, p. 161). Mary A. Loveless (?) (1st wife), b. ca 1818 Ga.. Mary A. Norton (2nd wife - m. 21 March 1854), b. 15 June 1826, d. 26 Sept. 1906, buried Clayton Cem., daughter of John Johnston Norton and Nancy J. Floyd; granddaughter of William Norton, Jr. and Lucretia Harrelson; great-granddaughter of William Norton (Rev. Soldier) (Vol. II, p. 120/1).

Vickers, J. R.. 15-10-26. John R. Vickers, Sr., d. by 1838 in Fla. leaving minor heirs John R., Jr., Michael P., Joseph W., Sidney Dean, Solomon W., Mary B. & James M. Vickers - Thomas Vickers was their guardian (Original Papers, Box 340). In the 1850 Census, John R. Vickers, Jr. had in his household Nancy Vickers (b. ca 1783 Va.),

Vickers, M. P.. 22-10-26. Michael P. Vickers, b. 8 April 1816 Ga., d. 10 April 1868, buried Faulk Cem.. He was an heir of John R. Vickers who died by 1838 in Fla. (Original Papers, Box 340). Sarah Ann Wall (wife - m. 18 Sept. 1845), b. ca 1826 Ga..

Vickers, T. T. B.. 3&4-9-24 & 11,14&16-10-26. Thomas T. B. Vickers, b. ca 1807 Ga.. He was guardian of the minor heirs of John R. Vickers who died by 1838 in Fla. (Original Papers, Box 340). Mary ----- (wife?), b. ca 1816 Ga..

Vining, J. A.. 1-11-28. Jefferson A. Vining, b. ca 1821 Ga. (1860 Census). Elizabeth Fry (wife - m. 9 May 1847), b. 20 July 1831 Ga., d. 20 Aug. 1904, buried Fairview Cem., Eufaula, Ala..

Vinson, W., Wesley. 2,11&12-12-29. Wesley Vinson, b. ca
1796 Ga.. Sarah Ann Eubanks (wife - m. 9 May 1826 Hancock Co., Ga.), b. ca 1810 N. C..

Vinson, Wiley. 1-12-29. Wiley Vinson died by Sept. 1843
(OR2, p. 9). In June 1832, he bought land in Jones Co.,
Ga. from Henry Vinson, John Vinson, Jarret Williams, John
Morgan and Jesse K. King, legatees of John Vinson (Judge
Ezell Fox, Dumas, Texas).

Volentine, M.. 7&8-11-26. Matthew Volentine, b. ca 1798
N. C., d. by June 1869 (OR 17, p. 380/1). Catherine -----
(wife), b. ca 1805 N. C.

Walker, G.. 23-12-26. George Walker, b. ca1822 S. C.. In
1850, he was enumerated next to George Walker, Sr., (b. ca
1787 S. C.) and wife (?), Sarah (b. ca 1785 N. C.). in 1860,
George Walker, Sr. was gone and Sarah Walker was living with
the above George Walker. Mrs. Mary Ann Amanda Arnold (wife -
m. 15 April 1849), b. ca 1826 Ga..

Walker, L. W., Lewis. 26-13-25(B), 32-12-26 & 4&5-9-27.
Lewis Walker, b. 6 Jan. 1791 N. C., d. 23 Nov. 1877, son
of Solomon Walker (Rev. Soldier) (b. 1 Aug. 1757, d. 11
Aug. 1837 Barbour Co., Ala.) and Gooden Cox (b. 15 Nov.
1762 N. C., d. 5 Nov. 1838). Nancy McInnis (wife), b. 10
March 1810 N. C., d. 29 March 1893, all buried in the family
cemetery. She was a daughter of Angus and Catherine Mc-
Innis (Vol. I, p. 113 & Vol. II, p. 166). Note: the
Lewis Walker who owned land in 26-13-25(B) could have been
a different Lewis Walker.

Walker, N. H.. 6-11-26 & 31-12-26. Nathan Walker, b. ca
1810 S. C.. Elizabeth Dykes (2nd? wife - m. 14 April 1842),
b. ca 1812 N. C.. He may have married twice more - to Jane
----- (b. ca 1818 S. C.) and to Joyce ----- (b. ca 1810 S. C.)

Wall, J.. 35-8-23. Josiah Wall, b. ca 1817 Ga. (1860 Census). In 1853, he received a military land grant in 26-8-23.
(#58501). In June 1855, he was given a power-of attorney
from Asa Whitehurst of Hillsborough Co., Fla. to receive
his share of the estate of Levi Whitehurst (CR M, p. 221).
Lavica ----- (wife?), b. ca 1815 Ga. (1860 Census).

Warlick, Wm.. 5-12-29. William Warlick, b. ca 1826 S. C..
In this household in 1850 were A. H. Warlick (b. ca 1798
S. C.) and Ruth Warlick (b. ca 1808 S. C.). Martha Ann K.
McLendon (wife - m. 23 Dec. 1851), b. ca 1835 Ala. (1860
Census). She was an heir of Matthew Averett who died by
July 1857, possibly a child of John McLendon and Mary Ave-
rett who was a daughter of Matthew Averett (Russell Co., Ala.
Settlement Record, 14 Sept. 1858).

Warr, John. 4-9-26. John Warr, b. ca 1797 S. C.. Nancy
----- (wife?), b. ca 1796 S. C..

Warren, B.. 1-10-25, 5,6,7&8-10-26 & 28&33-11-26. The
1854 Tax List gives both Bates and Burris Warren (Lucinda
Warren, guardian). Both were sons of Burris Warren and
Lucinda Efurd (Vol. I. p 166/8). James Burris Warren, b.
1 Jan. 1839 Ala., d. 28 Jan. 1912. Mary Jane Dickert, b.
27 Oct. 1853, d. 17 May 1920 (wife), both buried in the
Warren family cemetery. She was a daughter of James W.
and Jane M. Dickert (Vol. I, p. 168). Bates Warren,b. 19
June 1842 Ala., d. 21 Aug. 1860, buried in the family cem..

Warren, B. & Lucinda. 1-10-25, 5,6,7&8-10-26, 6,28&33-11-26.
Burris Warren, b. 21 July 1788, d. 21 Nov. 1845, son of
Thomas Warren who died by 1821 Edgefield Dist., S. C. (Vol.
I, p. 166) and Elizabeth Eidson (Mrs. J. L. Eidson, Weather-
ford, Texas). Lucinda Efurd (wife), b. 28 Feb. 1811 S. C.,
d. 10 March 1888, both buried in the family cemetery. She
was a daughter of Adam Efurd and Lucy ----- (Vol. I,p. 166/7).

Warren, E.. 12-10-25. Edward Warren, b. ca 1780/90 (1840
Census), d. by Dec. 1850, son of Thomas Warren who died by
Jan. 1821 Edgefield Dist., S. C.. (Vol. I, p. 166 & 168).
Nancy ----- (wife), b. ca 1808 S. C.. She married (2)
William Loveless 9 June 1850.

Warren, G .. 35-11-27. Georgianna Warren, b. 13 Oct. 1840
Ala., d. 17 Nov. 1919, buried in the Warren family cemetery.
She was a daughter of Burris Warren and Lucinda Efurd (Vol.
I, p. 166 & 168). She married Wilson S. Smart 29 Dec. 1857.

Warren, Jas., Jas. E.. 11,12,13&14-10-25 & 7-10-26. James
E. Warren, b. ca 1827 Ala., living in Texas in 1855, son of
Thomas Warren, Sr. and Rebecca ----- (Vol. I, p. 166/7).

Warren, J. D., Joel D.. 14,15,16,22&23-10-25. Joel D.
Warren, b. ca 1826 Ala., son of Thomas Warren, Sr. & Rebecca
----- (Vol. I, p. 166/7). Hannah M. Lampley (wife - m. 4
March 1851), possibly daughter of Jacob Lampley (1850 Cen-
sus).

Warren, J., J. J., Jeremiah. 1&2-9-24 & 26&32-10-25. Jeremiah Warren, b. ca 1810 Ga.. Mary ----- (wife), b. ca 1812
Ga..

Warren, Thos. Jr. heirs. 13,14&15-10-25. Thomas J. Warren,
Jr. died by July 1850, son of Thomas Warren, Sr. and Rebecca
-----. Sarah Lightner (wife), b. ca 1820 Ga.. She married
(2) Thomas C. Helms by 1856 (Vol. I, p. 167).

Elizabeth - dau. of Michael Lightner

Warren, Thos., Sr.. 9&23-10-25. Thomas Warren, Sr. died by

Feb. 1849, son of Thomas Warren who died by 1821 Edgefield
Dist., S. C.. Rebecca ----- (wife), b. 1790 N. C., d. 26
May 1854 (Vol. I, p. 166/7).

Waterman, N. M.(?). 32-9-28. By 1853, Nathaniel Waterman
owned much land in Barbour Co. but he is not in any early
census.

Watkins, W.. 31-13-25(B). In Nov. 1838, William Watkins
bought land in 36-12-25 (CR B, p. 358). In March 1839, he
sold this land to Samuel E. Watkins (CR B, p. 471) - he
and wife, Rhoda, sold it in Aug. 1839 (CR B, p. 553). In
Dec. 1846, William Watkins was of Macon Co., Ala. (CR G, p.
377).

                           30-9-24.
Watson, D., agent. / William C. Watson entered land in this
area in 1827 (Barbour Co., Ala. Tract Book). He died by
March 1833 - his executor was James C. Watson of Muscogee
Co., Ga. (Vol. I, p. 170). He may have been related to
David Watson, b. ca 1800 Ga., m. Jincey Grubbs, daughter of
William Grubbs, Sr. (b. 6 Oct. 1776 Chesterfield Dist., S.C.,
d. 26 Feb. 1849, buried Bennett-Lee Cem.). She was born 26
Aug. 1808 N. C. (?).

Watson, Elizabeth. 7-13-25(B). Peter Watson, b. 2 April
1793 (Watson Bible), d. by 1836 (OR 1, p. 71), son of Thomas
Watson (b. 18 Oct. 1764, d. 9 June 1834, buried Watson Cem.,
Monroe Co., Ala.) and Susan Zachary (b. 26 May 1770, d. 9
May 1815 - Watson Bible). Thomas Watson married (2) Ann Dun-
ham, (b. ca 1768, d. 17 Oct. 1830) and (3) Martha Ellis 6
Oct. 1831 (Watson Bible). Elizabeth ----- (wife), b. ca
1798 Ga..

Watson, G., George. 13,23&26-10-27 & 7&18-10-28. George
Watson, b. ca 1798 Pa., to Ala. from Ga. by 1827. Sarah
----- (wife - CR N, p. 545), b. ca 1795 Va.. She may have
been Sarah Boyd who married George Watson 10 March 1824
Richmond Co., Ga..

Weaver, A.. 28-13-26(B). Absolom A. Weaver, b. 15 June
1805 Ga., d. 27 July 1889. Mary H. ----- (1st wife), b.
30 March 1808 Ga., d. 12 Dec. 1877, both buried Ramah Baptist
Church Cem.. She may have been Mary H. Perry, m. 6 Jan. 1829
Early Co., Ga.. (Mrs.?) Elizabeth Britt (2nd wife - m. 16
Dec. 1880), d. after 1889 (OR 25, p. 319/20).

Weber, John. 25-11-27. No further record.

Weldon, W. A.. 21&30-13-25(B). William A. Weldon, b. ca
1824 Ga.. Rebecca Taylor (wife - CR H, p. 393), b. ca 1825
Ga., daughter of Joseph Taylor of Macon Co., Ala. (CR H,
p. 393).

Wellborn, A.. 21-12-29. Alfred Wellborn of Meriweather Co.,
Ga. (CR J, p. 383/4), b. 29 Nov. 1793, d. 9 Dec. 1857 Meriweather Co., Ga. ("Southern Christian Advocate", 18 March
1858). Elizabeth T. Martin (wife), b. 2 Dec. 1801, d. 9
Sept. (?) 1848, daughter of Marshall and June M. C. Martin,
all of Meriweather Co., Ga. ("Southern Christian Advocate"
6 Oct. 1848).

Wellborn, Johnson. 29-12-28 & 31-12-29. Johnson Wellborn,
b. ca 1796 Ga., d. by Sept. 1857 (OR 8, p. 328/9). Elizabeth
----- (wife - CR L, p. 36), b. ca 1820 Ga..

Wellborn, Roxanna. 6-12-28. Dr. Levi Thomas Wellborn, b.
27 Sept. 1790, d. 3 Oct. 1841, probably son of Thomas Wellborn who died by Sept. 1826 Putnam Co., Ga. (Putnam Co.,
Ga. Will Book B, p. 57/60). The Wellborn family came from
England to Jamestown, Va. in 1609, later migrated to Acco-
mack Co., Va., N. C. and Wilkes Co., Ga. (DAB Vol. IV, p.
1744/5). Roxanna Bethune (wife), b. 21 Oct. 1801 Ga., d.
25 Feb. 1890, both buried Fairview Cem., Eufaula, Ala.. She
came to Barbour Co. in 1837 from Taliaferro Co., Ga. ("Eufaula Daily Times", Feb. 26, 1890).

West, Joseph. 8&16-12-26(B). Joseph West, b. ca 1806 N.C.,
probably son of Joseph West of Lenoir Co., N. C. and Baldwin
Co., Ga. ("The Eufaula Weekly Bulletin", Dec. 3, 1881). Mary
Humphries (2nd ? wife - m. 25 Oct. 1832 Baldwin Co., Ga.),
d. by Dec. 1856. Elizabeth ----- (3rd wife?), b. ca 1828.

Westbrook, F. S.. 8-10-24. Furney Westbrook, b. ca 1813
N. C., patented the above land in 1848 (Barbour Co., Ala.
Tract Book) and sold it in Sept. 1852 (CR K, p. 153).
Zilpha ----- (wife?), b. ca 1817 N. C..

Westbrook, Z.. 4&9-9-24. John Westbrook patented part of
this land in 1836 (Barbour Co., Ala. Tract Book), died by
April 1840 (OR 1, p. 32). Zilpha ----- (wife - Original
Papers, Box 353), b. ca 1792 N. C..

Wethers, S., S. W.. 4-12-29 & 31-13-29(R). Samuel Weathers,
b. ca 1810 Ga., d. by June 1854 (OR 6, p. 39). He may have
been a son of William Weathers, b. ca 1790 Ga.. He enlisted
in the War of 1812 from Lincoln Co., Ga.. Jane Helms (wife),
b. ca 1815 N. C., daughter of Uriah Helms who died Muscogee
Co., Ga. in 1847 (Original Papers, Box 365). She married
(2) Wilson H. Stearn by Dec. 1854 (OR 6, p. 200).

Wheeler, N., Noah. 3,5,9&10-10-26. Noah Wheeler, b. ca
1783 N. C., d. by Sept. 1857 (OR 8, p. 344/52). Mrs. Luraney Oliver (2nd wife), b. ca 1800 S. C..

Whigham, J.. 8-11-27. Joseph Whigham, b. ca 1799 Ga., to

Ala. after 1841. In Nov. 1848, he and Thomas Whigham bought the above land (CR K, p. 47). Thomas Whigham, b. ca 1795 Ga., was enumerated next to him in the 1850 Census. Elizabeth ----- (wife - CR K, p. 304), b. ca 1799 Ga.. She may have been Elizabeth Hannah who married Joseph Whigham 4 Feb. 1819 Jefferson Co., Ga..

Whigham, Joseph. 16-11-27. Joseph Whigham, Jr., b. 1824 Ga., d. 15 Sept. 1880, buried Bethel Hardshwll Baptist Church Cem.. Jane ----- (wife?), b. ca 1831 Ga..

Whigham, T. 3-10-28. Thomas Whigham, b. 11 Feb. 1794 Jefferson Co., Ga., d. 22 Sept. 1859. Margaret ----- (wife), b. 24 Jan. 1799 Jefferson Co., Ga., d. 22 Aug. 1857, both buried Pea River Presbyterian Church Cem..

Whigham, W.. 15-11-27. William Whigham, b. ca 1822 Ga. (1860 Census). He sold this land in Jan. 1859 (CR P, p. 210). Sarah J. ----- (wife - CR N, p. 157), b. ca 1829 Ga. (1860 Census).

White, John. 30-12-25. John C. White, b. 1818 Ga., (1860 Census), d. 1920 (?). Susan A. Lewis (wife - m. 17 Jan. 1861), b. 6 Jan. 1844 Ala. (1870 Census), d. 9 March 1905, both buried Clayton Cem.. ("The Clayton Record", March 17, 1905). She may have been a daughter of Neecy Lewis.

White, John H.. 11-9-24. John H. White, b. 15 Feb. 1789 N. C., d. 14 July 1861 Macon Co., Ala.. Rebecca ----- (wife), b. 24 June 1783 Bladen Co., N. C., d. March 1866 Macon Co., Ala., both buried Fairview Cem., Eufaula, Ala..

White, R. T.. 33-11-26. Robert T. White, b. 26 April 1806 near Warrenton, Ga. (White Bible), d. by Sept. 1862 (OR 12, p. 453). Mary E. Seals (wife - m. 23 Jan. 1830 Sparta, Ga. - White Bible), b. 4 March 1810 Ga., d. 1903, buried Clayton Cem., daughter of Spencer Seals (CR Q, p. 414).

White, Willis. 21-11-28. Willis White, b. ca 1802 S. C.. Louisa L. ----- (wife - CR B, p. 751), b. ca 1809 S. C., probably his second wife.

Whitehurst, L. 23&24-8-23. Levi Whitehurst died by Oct. 1853 (OR 5, p. 358/9). He patented land in Henry Co., Ala. in 1836 (Henry Co., Ala. Tract Book). (Mrs.?) Mary B. Smith (wife - m. 31 Jan. 1849), b. ca 1815 Ga. (1860 Census)

Whitsett, Thos. 6-10-27. Thomas Whitsett, b. ca 1824 N. C.. He bought this land in April 1851 (CR J, p. 252/3) and sold it in Feb. 1855 (CR L, p. 604). In 1850, he was living with Samuel Whitsett (b. ca 1798 N. C.) and Elizabeth (Lowe?) Whitsett (b. ca 1799 N. C.). Elvira Mehetabel Daniel (wife - m. 3 Oct. 1850).

128

Whittle, M., Maston. 16-11-27. Maston Whittle, b. ca 1816
S. C.. In Dec. 1851, he received a military land grant in
30-11-27(#5541). Elizabeth ----- (wife - CR J, p. 535), b.
ca 1814 S. C..

Wiley, J. Mc.. 5-11-25, 2-10-27 & 6-11-30. James McCaleb
Wiley, b. 12 March 1806 Cabarrus Co., N. C., d. 1877 Pike
Co., Ala., buried Oakwood Cem., Troy, Ala.. He was a
physician and moved from Lawrence Co., Ala. to Miss., then
to Mexico, then to Barbour Co., Ala., then to Pike Co., Ala.,
son of Evan Shelby Wiley and Mary McCaleb who migrated to
Lawrence Co., Ala. ca 1818 ("History of Pike Co., Ala." by
Farmer, p. 67); grandson of James McCaleb (Rev. Soldier), a
signer of the Mecklenburg Convention (DAB Vol. IV, p. 1764).
Elizabeth T. Duckworth (1st wife - m. 19 April 1827 Dallas
(?) Co., Ala.), daughter of Randolph Duckworth of N. C. and
Dallas Co., Ala.(ibid). She was born ca 1811, d. 20 Sept.
1842, buried Clayton Cem.. Cornelia Appling (2nd wife -
m. 15 Nov. 1843 where?-ibid). She was born 3 Nov. 1816 Ga.,
d. 8 May 1872, buried Oakwood Cem., Troy, Ala.. Rebecca
Covington Wales (3rd wife - m. 3 Jan. 1875 where? - ibid).

Wiley, L. H. & J. B.. 14,15,22,25,26&27-12-28. Laird H.
Wiley, d. by 1851 Houston Co., Ga.. James McCaleb Wiley
was his administrator (CR M, p. 8/10).
AND
John B. Wiley, brother of Laird H. Wiley, of Macon, Ga. in
1853 (OR 5, p. 393). He married Ann G. Clopton 18 Feb. 1836
Bibb Co., Ga..

Wiley, L. M.. 1&2-11-29 & 26,35&36-12-29. Leroy M. Wiley
of New York, probably brother of James McCaleb Wiley, and
brother of Laird H. Wiley (OR 5, p. 393).

Wilkes, T. U., Thos. U.. 15,22&27-10-24. There is no
record to show that Thomas U. Wilkes ever lived in Barbour
Co.. In Jan. 1837, Thomas U., William U. and Elisha U.
Wilkes bought the above land (CR A, p. 311). In Jan. 1847,
William U. and Elisha U. Wilkes sold their interest to
Thomas U. Wilkes (CR G, p. 478). In the 1850 Census, there
is an Elias Wilkes (b. ca 1782 S. C.), wife Hannah (b. ca
1780 S. C.). A descendant believes her maiden name was Usher.
This middle initial ("U") was used by Thomas U. Wilkes,
William U. Wilkes (b. ca 1818 S. C.), Elisha U. Wilkes (b.
ca 1811 S. C.) and Jesse U. Wilkes (b. ca 1823 S. C.) (1860
Census).

Wilkinson, Asa. 27-8-26. Asa Wilkinson was ordained a
Baptist Minister 21 Aug. 1847 (Mar. 4, p. 13). Elizabeth
----- (wife - CR L. p. 189/90).

Wilkinson, S.. 33-8-26. Samuel Wilkinson, b. 11 Sept. 1816
N. C., d. 5 Nov. 1912. In the will of Wallace Tew, he was

called "brother" (Original Papers, Box 316). Elmira -----
(wife), b. 1 May 1814 Ga., d. 3 March 1886, both buried in
Shiloh Cem..

Wilkinson, W. D.. 2&11-13-26, 10&11-12-27 & 17-13-27. No
further record.

Williams, A.. 32-11-26. Ann M. Williams, b. ca 1833 Ala.,
d. after 1880, m. Augustus L. Oliver 16 Jan. 1850. She was
a daughter of Osborn J. Williams who died by July 1854 (Vol.
II, p. 174). Augustus L. Oliver was a son of Mrs. Lurena
Oliver who married (2) Noah Wheeler.

Williams, Alexr. 16,17&21-10-27. Alexander D. Williams,
b. ca 1813 Ga., in Ala. by 1836. Lucinda ----- (wife -
CR E, p. 348), b. ca 1813 Ga..

Williams, B.. 32-11-26. Buckner Williams, b. ca 1795 Ga.,
son of William Williams who died ca 1805 Hancock Co., Ga.
(Vol. II, p. 173/4). Rhoda ----- (wife), b. ca 1811 S. C.,
d. after 1895 (ibid).

Williams, B. C.. 28-11-27. Barley (Bartlett) C. Williams,
b. ca 1781 Ga.. In 1841, he was administrator of Robert
Williams (OR 1, p. 37). Mary ----- (wife?), b. ca 1782 Va..

Williams, G. D.. 25,26,35&36-13-29(R), 6-12-30 & 30&31-
13-30(R). Gazaway Davis Williams, b. 1 May 1804 Ga., d.
2 Oct. 1884, son of Zachariah Williams (b. 10 March 1778,
d. 15 Sept. 1840) who married (1) Martha Walton 5 Oct.
1800 (b. 11 April 1780, d. 9 Oct. 1807 (?) (2) Sarah Davis
23 June 1807 Richmond Co., Ga. (b. 16 March 1774, d. 24 Dec.
1849). She was the widow of John E. Anderson (m. 4 Feb.
1792 Columbia Co., Ga. (Vol. II, p. 176/7). Sarah Edwin
Abercrombie (1st wife), b. 21 April 1824, d. 17 May 1865,
daughter of James Abercrombie and Evalina Ross (DAB, Vol.
IV, p. 1771). Belle Puryear (2nd wife), b. 15 Sept. 1840,
d. 30 Sept. 1896. All are buried in the family cemetery
near Twin Springs, Russell Co., Ala.. Also in this household in 1850 was "Cousin" Matt Harris, b. 28 Aug. 1798 Ga.,
d. 3 April 1858, daughter of Ezekiel Harris.

Williams, G. W., Geo. W.. 8,17&21-10-27. George Walker
Williams, b. 3 April 1816 or 1818 Ga., d. 10 July 1900
(Vol. II, p. 171). Sarah A. Ryan (wife - m. 15 Dec. 1841),
b. ca 1825 Ga., daughter of Hampton Ryan (ibid).

Williams, J. S.. 25&36-10-24 & 36-10-25. Judge Stith
Williams, b. 17 Feb. 1804 Hancock Co., Ga., d. 29 May 1878,
son of William Williams who died ca 1805 Hancock Co., Ga..
Euphemia McNeill (wife), b. 19 Jan. 1808 N. C., d. 4 Apr.
1889, both buried Clayton Cem.. She was a daughter of
John McNeill and Nancy Mastin (or Martin) (DAB, Vol. IV,
p. 1772).

Williams, J,, John... 17-9-24. John G. Williams, b. ca
1821 Ala., d. 1 Jan. 1857, son of Jarrett Williams who d.
by Jan. 1842; grandson of William Williams who died by
Nov. 1846 (Vol. II, p. 168/9). Christian Margaret Ann
McLean (wife - m. 23 March 1845), b. ca 1829 Ala.. She
married (2) William J. Martin 12 Nov. 1857.

Williams, J. A.. 16-9-27. John A. Williams died by May
1859 (OR 9, p. 937). No heirs were named.

Williams, John L.. 27-11-27. John L. Williams, b. ca 1804
Ga., d. by Sept. 1873 (OR 19, p. 469/72), son of William
Williams who died by Nov. 1846 (Vol. II, p. 168/9). Sarah
------ (wife), b. ca 1813 Ga.. Also in this household in
1850 was Lively Leverett (female), b. ca 1795 Ga..

Williams, O. J.. 21-13-25(B), 3-11-26 & 15&16-10-27.
Osborn J. Williams, b. ca 1799 Ga.,d. by July 1854, son
of William Williams who died by 1805 Hancock Co., Ga.
(Vol. II, p. 173/4). Sophia Ventress (wife - m. Oct.
1830), b. ca 1810 Ga., d. 5 July 1892 ("The Clayton Courier", July 9, 1892); probably a daughter of Stephen Ventress and Nancy Wilkerson who married 8 Nov. 1808 Putnam
Co., Ga. (ibid).

Williams, R. W.. 1,3,10,12,14,15,16,22&23-12-29 & 6-12-30.
Dr. Robert Walton Williams, b. 30 Sept. 1803 Ga., d. 8 Jan.
1859, buried in the family cemetery, son of Zachariah
Williams and Martha Walton (Vol. II, p. 176). Geraldine
E. Carter (wife - m. 18 May 1853), b. ca 1828 Ga. (1860
Census), daughter of Judge William Carter of Stewart Co.,
Ga.. She married (2) Dr. Henry M. Hunter 26 May 1862(Ibid)

Williams, S. E.. 26-11-26. Sarah Elizabeth Williams, b.
ca 1843 Ala., daughter of Wesley Williams (CR K, p. 97).

Williams, Tempe. 4-9-27. Jarret Williams, b. ca 1790/
1800 (1840 Census), d. by Jan. 1842 (OR 1, p. 223), son of
William Williams who died by Nov. 1846 (Vol. II, p. 168).
Tempe Vinson (wife - maybe married 21 Sept. 1811 Jones Co.,
Ga.), b. ca 1790/1800 (1840 Census), d. by 1849 (ibid).

Williams, Wesley. 26-11-26. Wesley Williams, b. ca 1301
Ga., son of William Williams who died by Nov. 1846 (Vol. II,
p. 168/9). Charity ------ (2nd wife?), b. ca 1817 Ga..

Williams, W.. 33-10-27. William Williams, Jr., b. ca 1817
Ga., son of William Williams who died by Nov. 1846 (Vol. II,
p. 168 &171). Arincy Bush (wife), b. ca 1825 Ala., d. by
1852, daughter of Zachariah Bush who died by March 1851
(Vol. I, p. 24/5).

Williamson, Chas.. 16-10-27. Charles Williamson, b. ca

1799 N. C., d. 1867 (OR 26, p. 276). Sarah ----- (wife?) b. ca 1802 N. C..

Williamson, Mary. 28&33-11-25. Mary Williamson, b. ca 1798 S. C., d. 25 June 1884 (OR 23, p. 586/91).

Williamson, N.. 21-12-25(B). Nathan Williamson, b. ca 1811 S. C.. He sold this land to William Williamson in Feb. 1853 (CR K, p. 514). Also in this household in 1850 was Eva A. Williamson, b. ca 1766 S. C..

Williamson, Shadrack. 16-10-27. Shadrack Williamson, b. ca 1823 N. C.. Matilda Catherine McIntosh (2nd? wife - m. 1 Aug. 1844), b. ca 1827 Ala..

Williamson, W., Wm.. 15&21-12-25(B). William Williamson, b. 17 Dec. 1802 Lexington, S. C., d. 1 Dec. 1889. Naomi ----- (wife), b. 4 Aug. 1810 S. C., d. 20 March 1881, both buried in the family cemetery. Also buried in this ceme- tery is Eva Williamson, b. 1 Feb. 1766 S. C., d. 17 April 1854. In 1850, she was in the household of Nathan Wil- liamson, who was enumerated just after William Williamson.

Willis, E. G.. 28-12-25. Edmond G. Willis, b. 17 April 1820 Ga., d. 11 June 1888 Texas, son of Joel Willis (b. 12 Feb. 1789 N. C., d. 24 Oct. 1874 Dale Co., Ala.) and Elizabeth R. Head (b. 29 April 1794, d. 29 Aug. 1876 Dale Co., Ala., daughter of Richard Head) (Vol. I, p. 174/5). Missouri Ann Baker (1st wife - m. 2 Aug. 1846), b. 5 Feb. 1828, d. 27 May 1880, daughter of Jeremiah Baker. Lucinda Pickett (2nd wife) (Vol. I, p. 174/5).

Wilson, A. J.. 22&27-12-27. Andrew J. Wilson, b. ca 1815 S. C.. In Aug. 1852, he was trustee for Ann S., wife of Lycourgus S. Wellborn (CR K, p. 111). Hephzibah E. ----- (wife - CR K, p. 58/9), b. ca 1820 S. C..

Wilson, David. 1-9-27. David Wilson, b. ca 1805 N. C., d. by May 1863 (OR 12, p. 924). Nancy ----- (wife), b. ca 1813 S. C., heir of James Baker who died ca 1847 (Or- phans Court Minutes 1847-1852, p. 125/7).

Wilson, J., Joseph. 22-9-28. Joseph Wilson, b. ca 1795 Va., d. by May 1851 (OR 3, p. 605). Piety Alden (wife - m. 28 May 1844 Bibb Co., Ga.).

Wilson, W.. 17-12-29. No further record.

Windham, A.. 5-10-27. Anthony Windham, b. ca 1808 S. C., d. after 1860. Hepsey Flowers (1st wife), b. ca 1817 Ga., daughter of Abner Flowers (Vol. I, p. 180). Martha A. McMurray (2nd wife - m. 29 April 1860), b. ca 1836 Ala., (1860 Census), probably daughter of Samuel F. McMurray.

Also in this household in 1850 was Charlotte Hope, b. ca
1787 S. C..

Windham,, W.. 7,16,17&18-10-25. William Windham, b. ca
1789 S. C.. He acquired this land by patent and deed in
1849 (CR H, p. 639). Abagail ----- (wife?), b. ca 1799
S. C..

Winslett, Joel. 32-12-27. Joel Winslett, b. 19 Dec. 1802
Ga., d. 8 April 1860, son of John Carson Winslett (Vol. II,
p. 179). Mary McLeod (wife), b. 14 Oct. 1814 S. C., d. 8
Feb. 1902, both buried Little Oak Methodist Cem., Pike Co.,
Ala..

Wise, Ezekiel. 16-10-27. Ezekiel Wise, b. ca 1797 N. C.,
d. 1874. In 1835, Ezekiel Wise and wife, Wineford, and
Allen Williams and wife, Sarah, heirs of Burwell Bullock,
deceased, of Bibb Co., Ga., sold land in Randolph (formerly Lee) Co., Ga. (CR A, p. 113). Wineford ----- (wife),
b. ca 1805 Ga..

Wise, E.. 10,11,14&15-10-27. Ephriam Wise, b. ca 1800
S. C., d. 21 Nov. 1882 (Vol. II, p. 183). Martha Ann
(Milligan?) (wife), b. ca 1815 N. C..

Wood, M. K.. 23-9-28. McKinney Wood, b. 17 Jan. 1811 N.C.,
d. 12 Aug. 1884, son of Furnifold Wood and Abigail -----
of Wayne and Sampson Cos., N. C. (Vol. II, p. 186 & 189).
Frances Landrum (wife - m. 30 Aug. 1837), b. 28 Dec. 1820
Ga., d. 25 Jan. 1905, both buried Mt. Pleasant Cem.. She
was a daughter of George Landrum (ibid).

Wood, O. M. P.. 32&33-9-28. Ollin M. P. Wood, b. ca 1803
N. C., d. July 1871, son of Furnifold Wood and Abigail
-----. He never married (Vol. II, p. 186 & 188).

Wood, W. R., Wm.. 32&35-9-27. William R. Wood, b. ca 1812
N. C.. Hannah E. Wood (wife - m. 3 Sept. 1840 Henry Co.,
Ala.), b. ca 1825 N. C..

Wood, Young. 35&36-9-27. Young Wood, b. 22 Sept. 1794
Sampson Co., N. C., d. by April 1862, son of Furnifold
Wood and Abigail ----- (Vol. II, p. 186). Rosanna Byrd
(wife - m. 22 Dec. 1825 Wayne Co., N. C.), b. 27 Sept.
1802 Lenoir Co., N. C., d. by Dec. 1884 Henry Co., Ala.,
daughter of Richard Byrd and Jean ----- (ibid).

Wood, W., Wm.. 1&15-12-29. William Wood, b. ca 1820 Ga.,
in Ala. by 1848. Sarah Ann ----- (wife - CR L, p. 273),
b. ca 1825 Ga.. Also in this household in 1850 was John
Wood, b. ca 1794 Ga..

Worrell, E.. 28-10-28 & 1-11-28. Elisha Worrell, b. ca

1800 N. C., d. by Jan. 1857 (when his widow remarried).
Mary McMillan (1st? wife - m. 21 Jan. 1841). Lincy A.
Coats (2nd? wife - lic. issued 1 May 1843),b. ca 1825 Ga..
She married (2) John L. Parsons 11 Jan. 1857.

Worsley, M.. 6-10-28. Mary Worsley, b. ca 1827 Ga.. She
bought this land in Oct. 1851 (CR K, p. 138). In 1850 &
1860, she was living in the household of Dr. Sampson Worsley (b. ca 1782 N. C.). Also in this household was Albina
Worsley (b. ca 1810 N. C.). In 1870, Mary Worsley was in
the household of Albina Worsley, "living with sister".

Worthington, R.. 12&13-12-26 & 18,19&20-12-28. Robert
Worthington (Witherington), b. 23 Feb. 1801 N. C., d. 26
May 1858, buried Batesville Baptist Church Cem.; son of
William Witherington and Sylvia Little, probably from
Pitt Co., N. C.. Sylvia Little was a sister of Crisey,
wife of Phillip Causey - in 1850, she was living with
Robert Witherington. Holland ----- (wife?), b. ca 1802
N. C..

Wright, Chas.. 35-13-25(B). No further record.

Wright, M.. 2,11,14&24-13-27 & 19-13-28. Meredith Wright,
b. ca 1800/10 (1840 Census), probably left Barbour Co. by
1842 (CR G, p. 19). In Dec. 1837, he was of Lincoln Co.,
Ga. (CR B, p. 553). Jane ----- (wife - CR G, p. 19), b.
ca 1800/10 (1840 Census).

Wright, R. S.. 7-13-27. Richard S. Wright, b. ca 1817 Ga..
He sold this land in Nov. 1855 (CR M. p. 326). Nancy J.
----- (wife - ibid), b. ca 1822 S. C..

Young, E. B.. 11-11-27. Edward Brown Young, b. 24 Aug.
1802 New York City, d. 22 May 1879, son of James Young and
Christina Ridaback of New York City (DAB, Vol. IV, p. 1826/7).
Ann Fendall Beall (wife - m. 11 June 1832 Warren Co., Ga.),
b. 9 Oct. 1810 Ga., d. 5 June1876, both buried Fairview Cem.,
Eufaula, Ala..

Young, James B.. 20&29-10-24. James Bunberry Young, b. ca
1816 N. C., d. 8 Sept. 1861 (Mrs. Paul Lancaster, Forson,
Texas). Cynthia Ann Sutton (1st wife - m. 26 Dec. 1843
where?), b. ca 1820 Ga., d. 29 Dec. 1856 (ibid). Emily
Jones (2nd wife - m. 9 Dec. 1857), b. ca 1833 Ga..

Young, Wm.. 19-9-26. William C. Young, b. 21 Oct. 1811 S.C.,
d. 17 Oct. 1851, son of Joseph and Nancy Young, buried in
Clayton Cem.. He probably never married.

Zales, Z.. 2-11-25. No further record.

Ziterow, N.. 20-9-25. Nathaniel Ziterow, b. ca 1791 Ga..
Sarah ----- (wife?), b, ca 1795 Ga.. In Nov. 1854, Mrs.
Sarah Ziterow asked for her letter from Pea River Presby-
terian Church as she planned to join a church in Chickasaw
Co., Ala. (Pea River Presbyterian Church records).

Zorn, N., Nicholas. 25-9-26 & 19-9-27. Nicholas Zorn,
b. ca 1808 S. C.. In 1852, he was granted land for military
service in 9-9-27 (#9321). Sarah (Condry?) (wife), b. ca
1808 S. C..

The following entries were illegible:
Floyd, S. or Loyd, S. F.   35-10-25.
Ganby (?), Z.. 16-12-29 & 16-13-29.
Kemp or King, Albert. 34-10-24.
McLeod, ----- 5-9-25.
Marsh, ----- 22-11-27.
Marsteman(?), J. S.. 30-12-30
Martain, ----- 8-11-28.
Price or Pierce, Jesse. 7-9-26.
Rains (?), Hamilton. 7-10-29.
Rob-----. 33-10-28.
Thew (?), Bryan. 32-13-29(R).

The following are business firms:
Beauchamp & Moore. 20-11-27.
Bedingford & Vinson. 10-12-29. This land was patented by
     Bryan Bedingfield in 1837 (Barbour Co., Ala. Tract Book).
Bethune, Jas., J. N. & Co.. 24-13-26 & 29,30,31&32-13-27.
     James N. Bethune was of Columbus, Ga. in 1838 (CR B,
     p. 443).
Bogart & Kneeland. 4,5,9,15&34-13-26, 6,18&20-12-26, 34-13-
     26 & 12-12-27. Henry K. Bogart & Charles Kneeland,both
     of New York.
Crawford, J. T. & Co.. 10&11-13-25(B). Joel T. Crawford, b.
     9 Oct. 1812, d. 18 Dec. 1875. Sarah Ann ----- (wife),
     b. 7 Sept. 1815 Greene Co., Ga., d. 24 Nov. 1890 Birming-
     ham, Ala., both buried Enon Cem., Bullock Co., Ala..
Fontaine & Hardaway. 11-12-27. John Fontaine (wife Mary)
     and Robert S. Hardaway (wife Martha B.) were of Musco-
     gee Co., Ga. in 1842 (CR E, p. 171/2).
Hardwick & Fontaine. 12,25&35-12-27. John Fontaine of Mus-
     cogee Co., Ga. and George W. Hardaway (Barbour Co., Ala.
     Tract Book).
Hodges & Pugh. 16-13-26(B). Elias G. Hodges & James L. Pugh.
Jernigan & Daniels. 19-13-26(B). Patented by Henry W. Jer-
     nigan in 1847 (Barbour Co., Ala. Tract Book).
Kiels & Sylvester. 1-11-28. William D. Kiels & Thomas R. ·
     Sylvester.
Lampley, I. & J.. 5-9-25. Ira & John M. Lampley.
Robinson, Templeton & King. 16-12-29.

Shorter & CAto. 21-8-26, 18-13-26(B), 14-10-27, 4&12-12-27,
    10&15-13-27, 6-10-28, 7-9-29 & 34-13-29(R). Eli S.
    Shorter and Lewis L. Cato.
Shorter, CAto & Sayre. 5-13-28(R).
Shorter & Gow. 23&24-11-27. John Gill Shorter & John Gow.
Smith, T. W. & Co.. 11-12-27. Foster Reynolds and Morris
    Reynolds, merchants operating under the firm name of
    T. W. Smith & Co. of Liverpool, England.
Stewart & Fontaine. 33&36-12-27 & 24&34-11-28.
Thomas & Powers. 12,22&27-13-26(B), 19-22-27-29,30&35-
    13-26(partly in Bullock Co.). Grigsby E. Thomas (wife
    Elizabeth A. S.) and Edward E. Powers of Muscogee Co.,
    Ga..   4-10-26.
Tompkins & Cowen./ Henry M. Tompkins & William R. Cowan.
Wellborn & Comer. 20-13-27.

Selected items from " Abstracts of Deaths Reported in the
Columbus (Georgia) Enquirer" 1832 - 1852 and "Abstracts of
Marriages Reported in the Columbus (Georgia) Enquirer" 1832-
1852, both by Buster W. Wright.

Henry Benton m. Luraney Wilkins 18 Feb. 1846, both of
    Georgetown (Randolph Co.), Ga.
James Bryant of Barbour Co., Ala. m. Margaret McDaniel,
    daughter of Rev. Arch'd McDaniel, 25 Jan. 1844 in
    Pulaski Co., Ga.
Dr. R. L. Butt of Columbus, Ga. m. Elizabeth Leonard, d/o
    Van Leonard of Wynnton, 29 July 1846 Muscogee Co., Ga.
Col. William H. Betts, graduate of West Point, aide to Gen.
    Scott, d. 16 July 1841 Irwinton (Barbour Co.), Ala.
Elizabeth Burt, age 72, wife of Zacheus Burt, d. 16 June
    1851 Talbot Co., Ga.
Elizabeth W. Kennon, age 23, died at the residence of G.
    Beauchamp 17 March 1845 Eufaula (Barbour Co.), Ala.
Philip A. Sapp of Sycamore Grove, Burke Co, Ga. m. Julia
    Baker, d/o Alpheus Baker of Lumpkin (Stewart Co.),
    Ga. 23 April 1850.
Col. John Cochran of Barbour Co., Ala., m. Mary Jane Well-
    born, d/o Col. Alfred Wellborn 8 Oct. 1845 Meriwether
    Co., Ga..
Howard Chandler Clapp, age 1½, s/o Julius R. & Eleanor M.
    Clapp, d. 23 March 1843 Columbus, Ga..
Caroline E. Cochran, wife of John Cochran, d/o William
    Wellborn, d. 20 Nov. 1843 Eufaula (Barbour Co.), Ala..
Eliza Ann Crawford, age 22, w/o William M. Crawford, d. 13
    May 1852 Enon, Ala.
Dr. Thomas H. Dawson m. Martha A. Hardwick 27 July 1843
    Columbia Co., Ga..
Dr. Thomas H. Dawson of Marietta (Ga.) m. Anna Maria Snider
    of Savannah (Ga.) 25 Sept. 1849.
Ann S. L. Dawson, d/o Dr. Thomas H. Dawson, d. 24 July 1842.
    Her mother died a month before.
James A. Everett, age 61, d. 23 June 1848 Houston Co., Ga.
James N. Feagin of Midway (Barbour Co.) and Almira Cox
    (should be Cole), d/o N. B. Cole, m. 3 Dec. 1840 in
    Marion Co., Ga..
George S. Hawkins of Apalachicola, Fla. m. Mrs. J. Sullivan
    20 Dec. 1842 Columbus, Ga.
Joseph B. Hill of Columbus (Ga.) m. Henrietta W. Dawson,
    d/o Hon. Wm. C. Dawson, 11 July 1849 Greensboro, Ga.
Asa Holt m. Melissa Glenn, d/o Rev. John B. Glenn, 7 Jan.
    1847 Glennville, Ala.
James W. Hodges, age 4, s/o George C. & Martha Hodges, d.
    16 July 1842 Barbour Co., Ala.
Mary Frances Howell (should be Harwell), age 11, d/o Samuel
    & Birchett Howell (Harwell), d. 17 Oct. 1841 Macon Co.,
    Ala..

Harriet Eliza Jordan, age 1, d/o Junius and Frances H.
    Jordan, d. 12 Oct. 1839 Stewart Co., Ga.
Catherine Long, age 36, w/o Col. N. W. Long of Russell Co.
    (Ala.), formerly of Twiggs Co. (Ga.) ,d. 20 Aug. 1840.
James F. Marshall m. Virginia A. Leonard, d/o James C.
    Leonard, 11 Nov. 1845 Talbot Co., Ga. (Note: was she
    his first wife?).
Dr. David C. Miller or Barbour Co., Ala. m. Mildred R.
    Alston, d/o William H. Alston, 13 Aug. 1844 Columbus,
    Ga.
Asel P. Rood m. Blanche Evelina Gipson, d/o late Felix G.
    Gipson, 28 July 1842 Florence, Ga.
James H. Shorter m. Mary F. Hargraves, d/o George Har-
    graves, Sr., 17 March 1836 Columbus, Ga.
Col. James M. Tarver m. Rachel J. Banks, d/o James Banks,
    9 Oct. 1845 Enon, Macon Co., Ala.
William A. Whigham m. Sarah Jane Bigham, d/o James Bigham,
    14 Dec. 1843 Marion Co., Ga.

Brooks, E. 14; Esau B. 14
Broughton, Elizabeth Mary 26
Browder, Elizabeth 14; I.C. 14;
Isham C. 14; M.A. 14; Milton
A. 14
Brown, Benjamin 103; C.L. 14;
Charles L. 14; D. 14;
Dorothy 14; Eliza 15; Eliza-
beth 14; J. 15; J.W. 14;
Jesse 14(3); John 14; John P.
14(2); John W. 14/15; Jonathan
15(2); Josephine 82; Julia 14;
Lorenzo D. 43; Mariah G. 25,
121; Mary 43; Mary M. 14;
Reuben E. 14; Susan 67; Thos.
15; Thomas 15
Browning, Jane 15; Jesse 15(2)
Brunson, C.J. 15; Charles J.
15(2); Joel 15; M.A. 15;
Marion A. 15; Mary Jane 15;
Bryan, Annis 15(2); Charity 115;
H.L. 15(2); Harriet 16; J.C.
15; Jas. 15; James 15(2); John
C. 15(3), 16(4); Mary 15(2);
N. 15; Needham 15(2); Robert
16(2); Susan 16(2); T. 16;
Tabitha 16; Theophilus 16(2);
W.M. 16; Wm. 16(2); William 16
Bryant, Anice 57; Anna 20;
Elizabeth 1,19,116(2),118;
James 136; Lucinda, Mrs. 57;
Mary 99,115
Buford, Caroline A.A. 55; J. 16;
Jeff 16; Jefferson 16; John
R. 55; John Ragsdale 16
Bullard, H. 16; Henry 16(2)
Bullock, Burwell 132; Ruthy
Jane 93
Burch, Amanda 80; Jesse 80
Burgess, D. 16; Dempsey 16;
Roxanna 16
Burke, S.G. 17; Solomon G. 17
Burleson, Aaron 17; Eliza Jane
64; Molsey 17; S.J. 17;
S.W. 17; Seaborn J. 17;
Simeon W. 17
Burnet, Al. 16; Alexander 16;
Martha 16
Burnham, James 17; Sarah 17;
W. 17; William 17
Burnley, Ann T. 107; Henry 107;
J.B. 17; Jeremiah B. 17
Burt, Elizabeth 136; H.Z. 17;
Hilliard Z. 17; Zacheus 136
Bush, Arincy 130; C. 17;
Catharine 112; Council 17(2);
Council Vernon 17; D. 17; D.A.
17; David Allen 17; E. & N.
17; Elizabeth C. 18; G. 17;
G.T. (?) 17; Greenberry 17;
J. 18; Jane 94; John Council
17; Joseph A. 18; Julia Ann
42; L.R. 18; Levi R. 18; Lewis
112; M.A. 17; Maria J. 118;
Mary A. 18; Moses E. 17(2),
42,94; Moses Eason 17,18; N.
18; N.J. 17; Nancy 17; Nancy
J. 17; Nathan 18(3); R. 18;
Rebecca 17; Richard 18; Sarah
18; Susannah Whitfield 1;

Bush contd. W.G. 18; William 17;
William, Sr. 18; William Green
18; Z. 18; Zachariah 18(2),118,
130
Bustin, Martha 99
Butler, Cassandra A., Mrs. 27;
Elizabeth 18; Thomas W. 27
Butt, Ann W., Mrs. 18; R.L., Dr. 136
Butts, Ann, Mrs. 48; Catharine 18;
Charles 18(2); Eliza C. 31; F.C.
18; Francis C. 18; Jeremiah 18(2),
48; Jeremiah, Dr. 18; Louisa 18;
Moses 18(2),19; Priscilla 18; R.
19; Richard Lemuel, Dr. 19; Sarah
19; Solomon 19(2)
Byley, Anna 21
Byram, S.L. 19
Byrd, ----- B. 19; Burtis 19; Edw.
19; Edward 19; Jean 108,132;
Reddin 19; Richard 108,132; Ros-
anna 108,132

Cabaniss, Amanda M. 26; J. 19; Jesse
M. 19; Patty 70; Sarah 19
Cade, Jas. 19; James 19; James J.
19; Susan B. 19
Cadenhead, Francis M. 39; John 84
Caldwell, G. 19; Graves, Dr. 19;
John 19; Joshua 19
Calhoun, J.A. 19; John A. 19(2);
Julia Ann 17(3),42,94; Sarah M. 19
Calloway, D. 19; Daniel 19; Eliza-
beth 19; H. 20; Henry 20; Joshua
S. 20; Mary Ann 86; P.M. 20; Pitt
Milner, Rev. 20; Priscilla 20
Calvin, Mary Russell 40
Cameron, A. 20; A.M. 20; Archibald
M. 20; Catherine 79; Christian 20,
81; Eliza 99; John 81; L. 20;
Lauchlin 99; Locklin 29(3); Louisa
20; Margaret G. 8; Mary 29(2);
Mary Ann E. 85; N. 20; Nancy 29(2)
Campbell, Amanda Caroline E. 116;
Cornelia M. 20; D. 20; Daniel 20;
Elizabeth 20; Malinda 22; Mary
(Elizabeth) 116; Nancy A. 85; R.
20; Robert 20; Wm. D. 20; William
D. 20(2),22,116
Canady, Felix 20
Cannady, Catherine 20; Joseph 20(2);
Silva 20
Cannon, Caroline Elizabeth 26; P.N.
20,26; Simeon R. 20,26,120
Capel, Jas. 21; James 21; Mary 21
Capers, ----- 47
Cargill, John 66
Cariker, G.W. 21; George W. 21;
Mary M. 21
Carlisle, Sophia 76
Carmichael, A. 21; Archibald, Dr.
21; Elizabeth 21; H.W. 21; Malcolm
21
Carol, Henry 21
Carpenter, Dwight 21; Gillum 21;
Jemima Ellen 21; R.E. (A.) 21;
Richard A. 21(2)
Carr, Mary 21; Thos. 21; Thomas 21
Carrol, John 21
Carroll, Elizabeth 21; Henry 21;
John 21; Selety 6

Carter, Geraldine E. 130; Giles
103; J.D. 22; John D. 22;
Lucy 103; Rebecca 119;
William, Judge 130
Casey, Jas., Jr. 21; James, Jr.
21; James, Sr. 21,22; L. 22;
Lemuel 22(2); Nancy 22
Castello, Bertha 1; James 1
Cato, Lewis L. 135
Causey, Creasey 22; Crisey 133;
Cullen 22(2); Dorothy 22; P.B.
22; Philip 133; Phillip B. 22(2)
Cawthon, Josiah Dabney 22; W.W.
22; Wm. 22; William Dabney 22;
William W. 22
Chambers, I.H. 22; Isaac H. 22;
L.D. 22; Lorenzo D. 22; Wm.
H., Rev. 29
Chancey, John 22(2); Milbrey 22
Chaney, Hally 54; John 54;
Milbry 54
Chany, Sarah Adeline 67
Chapman, Jas. 22; James A. 22;
Eliza Ann 4; Elmira B. 22
Chappell, Sarah Ann 40
Cheesbro, Anna 23; James 22(2)
Chesnut, M. 23; Mitchell 23;
Sarah 23
Childs, E.C. 23; Elijah C. 23;
Eliza 23; J. 23; John 23(2)
Nancy 23
Chisholm, Janet 79; Roderick C. 79
Christian, Lewis 23(2)
Clapp, Eleanor M. 136; Howard
Chandler 136; Julius R. 23(2),136
Clark, Eleanor 61; Elizabeth C.
27; James 23(2),27(2); Narcissa
98; Whitfield 23
Cleckley, Adison D. 107
Clements, Benjamin 23; James 23;
J. 23; Nancy 23
Cliatt, William 23
Clopton, Ann G. 128
Cloud, Alice Hardin 13
Clyatt, Lucy 29; Wm. 23
Coaker, Elizabeth 23; I.N. 23;
Isaac N. 23
Coats, Lincy A. 133
Cobb, J. 24; J.A. 23; Jacob 23,24;
James A. 23; Jos. 24; Joseph 24;
M. 24; McCuin 24
Cochran, Caroline E. 136; J. 24;
John 24,136; John, Col. 136
Cody, James 24; Mary 24(3)
Coker, John M. 29; Nancy 29
Cole, Almira 136; Almira C. 40;
Daniel 24; N.B. 24,136; Noah B.
24,40(2); Sarah C. 3
Coleman, B.F. 24; Benjamin F. 24;
Keziah 24; W. & K. 24; William
24(2)
Collins, C.B. 24; Elizabeth 64;
W. 24; Wilson 24(2)
Colverd, Mary F. 101; Thomas 101
Comer, Hugh Moss 24/25; J.F. 24;
John Fletcher 24
Comm, Anna 6; George 6
Commander, Martha 59
Condiff, Peggy 41
Condrey, John 25; William 101

Condry, Elizabeth 25; G.M. 25;
George M. 25; John D. 25; Sarah
134
Connelly, Jas. Z. 25; James Zacha-
riah, Rev. 25; William Pearce
Harmon 25
Conner, ----- 46; Adele 6; Belinda
W. 77; F., Dr. 77; Geo. D. 25;
George 25; George D. 121; George
D., Dr. 25; Louisa M. 25
Cook, A. 25; Amanda Cynthia 71;
Archibald 25; Elizabeth 24; Ellen
89; G.P. 25; George P. 25; Henry
S. 71; J. 25; James M. 60; John
25; John, Sr. 25,48; John C. 25;
Mary Jane 48; Sarah 52; Sarah
Laura 111
Cooley, Sarah 50
Cooper, A.D. 25; Archibald 4; Arch-
iblad D. 25,26,70; Elizabeth 25,
26(2); Emeline 70; Mary 4; Thos.
26; Thomas 26; Wiley L. 26(2)
Cope, Mary 36; Sarah 3
Copeland, John N. 26; John Nelson
26
Costello, ----- 26; Daniel Edmond
26; Pierre Darcy 26
Coston, Susannah 9
Cotton, A.W. 26; Avent W. 26(2);
Dorinda 26; Mary T. 73; R. 26;
Richard 26; W.W. 26; William W.
26
Cowan, E.B. 26; Ebenezer B. 26;
F. 26; Franklin 26; J.G. 26;
John 26; John G. 26; Mary 26;
Sara P. 76; W.L. 26; W.R. 27;
Wm. R. 27; William L., Dr. 26;
William R. 27,135
Cowart, Wm. 27; William 27
Cowles, G.W. 27
Cox, E. 27; Edward W. 27; Emanual
27(2); Gooden 28,123; Jane 27(2);
John 109; Margaret 109; Moses
107; Nancy 27(2); Wm. 27; William
27(2)
Cox (Cole), Almira 136
Crapp, L.C. 27; Louisa C. 27
Crapps, Jane V. 66,110; John J.
66,110
Crawford, A.P. 27; Alexr. 27; Alex-
ander P., Dr. 27; Arthur 28;
Eliza Ann 136; J. T. & Co. 134;
Joel T. 134; N. 27; Nicholas 27;
Nicholas W. 27; Sarah Ann 134;
Wm. M. 28; William M. 136
Creech, Aaron 28(2); Charity 28;
David 33,74; Elizabeth, Mrs. 46;
J.C. 28; Jane 28; Joshua C. 28,
46; Laura 33; Lydia Ann 73; Mary-
anna 101; U.L. 63; Wm. C. 28;
William Carter 28
Creel, Jackson 28; John 28(2); John
28(2); Levi 28(3); Lewis (Levi)
28; Louisa 28(3); Mahaley 28;
Sarah 28; Sinia 28; Solomon 28;
Thomas 28(2); Wm. 28; William 28
Crews, A. 28; Arthur 11,28,29;
Arthur A. 28; Cynthia 11; John
29; John E., Dr. 29; W.B. 29;
William B. 29

Crocker, J.M. 29; M. 29; Monroe 29
Crossley, A. Estate 29; Andrew 29
Crow, Frances 112
Cumbie, A. 29; Andrew 29(2);
  Celia 29; Daniel 29; J.J. 29;
  Jas. 29; James 29; James C.
  29; James O. 29(2); John J. 29
Cunning, Elizabeth Ann 29; J. 29;
  John 29
Cunningham, D. 29; Dovey E. 30;
  Duncan 29,82; Elizabeth 34;
  Elizabeth R. 33,34; Flora 84;
  Jane 82; P. 30; Peter 30
Curenton, H. 30(2); W. 30(2)
Cureton, Reason 30; William 30
Curington, J. 30
Currie, Alexander H. 45; Angus, Sr
  8,30; Catharine 30; D. 30; Danl.
  30; Daniel 30(2); Lauchlin 82;
  Sarah 8
- Curry, Angus 81; Catherine 81;
  Jane A. 39(2),61; Margaret 81;
  Sarah j. 61(2); Wm. 30;
  William 30(2),61

Danford, Abraham 30(2); Danl. 30;
  Daniel 30; E. 30; Edmund (Edward)
  30; J. 30; J.M. 71; Joseph 30;
  Malinda Jane 30; Sarah 30;
  Thomas 31(2)
Danforth, Joshua H. 31; S.A. 31
Daniel, Benjamin 31; Catherine
  90; Elvira Mehetabel 127; J.L.
  31; J.L. Estate 31; James L. 2,
  31(2); John 31; John William 31;
  L.L. 31; Levi L. 31; Margaret 9;
  Martha 2; Martha P. 31; Robert
  31(2)
Daniels, Amanda Elizabeth 28; ·
  James L. 18
Danner, Abraham 31; Mary A. 31;
  T.M. 31; Thomas M. 31
Dansby, I. 31; Isham 31; Isham M.
  31; Mary 90; Winza 90
Dantzler, Jacob 94
Davenport, Elva 74; Lucy Barksdale
  107
Davis, Alcey 44,60(2); Ben 32;
  Catherine 32,75; E. 31; Elisha
  31,83; G. 31; Gardner 31;
  Gardner Harwell 31; J. 32; J.F.
  32; Jacob 32; John 32(5); 119;
  John C. 27; John F. 32(2);
  Malachi 60(2); Margaret 32(2);
  Martha 119; Martha Harwell 31;
  Mary 60(2); Mildred 32; Sarah 32,
  129; Sina 83; W.E. 32; W.K. 32;
  Western K. 32; William E. 32
Dawson, Ann S.L. 136; Annie 32;
  Henrietta W. 136; J. 32; John 32;
  Joseph 32; Keziah 32; Thos. H.
  32; Thos. H. 32; Thomas H., Dr.
  136(3); Thomas H., Rev. 32;
  Thursey 12; Wm. C., Hon. 136
Dawson (or Davidson), Edeline 1
Dean, Mary 13
Dellafield, N. 32; Nicholas 32
Dendy (or Denby), Samantha A. 61
Dennard, America A. 32; Emily E.
  94; Jared 94; John E. 32(2),37;

Dendy conts. Mariah Louise 37
Dennis, Mary 18(2)
Denson, Bethia 33; Jethro 33(3),90,
  107; M. 33; Martha 90; Matthew
  33; Nancy 107; Rebecca 33
Dent, J.H. 33; John Herbert, Com-
  modore 33; John Horry 33(2)
Deshazo, B.F. 33; Benjamin Frank-
  lin 33(2); Gracy 33(3); H.P.(or
  P.H.) 33; John E. 33; Martha 63;
  Paul Hamilton 33; Robert, Sr. 33;
  Thomas J. 33; William R. 33;
  Wilson 33,63
DeVane, Ann 12
Dewitt, A. 33; Ann 33(2); Eliza-
  beth 30; Elizabeth R. 33,34;
  John 33; Saml. 33; Samuel B. 33;
  Sarah 33; W.T. 34; William T. 34
Dickert, James W. 124; Jane M. 124;
  Mary Jane 124
Digby, Rebecca 54
Dike, Sarah 61
Dismukes, George 97; Harriet Maira
  97; William 97
Dixon, Ambrose 8; J.J. 34; Luna
  34; Sarah 8
Dixon (or Dickson), John J. 34
Dobbins, J.S. 34; John S. 34
Dodson, Wm. 34
Dorman, Penelope 57; Wm. 34;
  William 34,57
Doster, W. (?) B. 34
Doughtie, Catherine 1
Douglass, Mary Catharine 82
Dowd, Elizabeth Ann 33
Dowling, E. 34; E.G., Jr. 34; Elias
  34(3); Elias G. 34; H. 34; Hans-
  ford 34(2); Mary 34(2); Seny
  Lena 34
Drewry, Catharine Lucinda 25; J.
  34; John 25,34(2); W. 34
Dubose, A. 35; Asa 35(2); Caroline
  Sophronia 35(2); D. 35; Deshabo
  35(2); Deshabo D. 35; E.E. 35;
  Edwin E. 35(2); Frances W. 35;
  J. 35; James 35(2); Jeptha 35
  (2); Joel 35(3); John 35; Mali-
  kiah 35; Margaret E. 29; Martha
  E.J. 93; Mary 24,35; Peter 35;
  R. 35; R.E. 35; Robert E. 35;
  S.J. 35; Sarah Scisscon 35; Sea-
  born J. 35; Zilpha 35
Duckworth, Elizabeth T. 128; Joseph
  12,45(2); Mary 45; Randolph 128
Duke, D. 35; David 35(2); Margaret
  36; Wm. 36; William 36
Dunford, Sarah 36; Thomas J. 36(2)
Dunham, Ann 125
Dunn, J.M. 36; John M. 36
Dykes, Abigail 36; Eliza 36; Eliza-
  beth 123; Hiram 36; s. 36; Shad.
  36; Shadrack 36; Susan 16

Early, Elizabeth 24; Jesse 24
Earp, Margaret 64
Eaves, Esther 16
Echols, C. 36; Clark 36(2); Eliza-
  beth 15; Hester 36; M.E. 36;
  S.C. 36; Sanders C. 36
Edge, Cassia 36; Jane 73; Wm. 36;

Edge conts. William 36
Efurd, Adam 36(2),68,72,124; J.A.
  36; John 88; John Adam 36;
  Lucinda 77,124(3); Lucy 36(2),
  68,88,124; Lucy Ann 72; Mary
  88; Mary Ann Louisa 68; Thos.
  C. 36; Thomas C. 36,68,72
Eidson, Elizabeth 124; F.W.
  (Francis) 14; Francis 14; James
  14(3); Nancy 14; Rhoda 14(3);
  W. 36; Wiley 36(2)
Eiland, A. 37; Allen 37; Elizabeth
  37
Elder, Winnie 65
Eikins, J.B. 37; John B. 37;
  Julia 37
Ellington, Catharine, Mrs. 121
Elliott, J. 37; James 37; Jane 37
Ellis, Fielding 32; Martha 125
Elmer, Luke 37; M. 37; Matthew 37;
  Sarah 37
Elmer (Elmore), Mark 37(2)
Ely, Elizabeth 95
Emerson, B.H. 37; Benjamin H. 37
English, Elizabeth 116
Engram, O.C. 37; Oliver C. 37
Ethridge, Mary Ann 121; R.C. 37;
  Richard C. 37
Eubanks, Chas. 37; Charles 37(2);
  Edward 37(2); Edward Thomas 37;
  Mary 37; N. 37; Nancy 37;
  Nancy C. 37; Sarah Ann 123; T.
  37; Thomas 37(2)
Evans, Drucilla, (Mrs.?) 47; Eman-
  uel 38; H. 75; J.L.C. 38; Jas.
  38; James 38; John L.C. 38;
  Luraney 102; Martha 38; Mary 75;
  Melinda 38; S. 75; W. 38;
  William 38
Everett, J.A. 38; James A. 38,
  136(2); Martha 1; Mary 76; Mary
  T. 76; Turner 76

Faison, Louisa Caroline 21; N. 38;
  Nancy 38(2); Thomas J. 21,38
Fannin, Marietta 109
Farmer, Abel 38(2); Margaret C.
  106; Molsey 38
Farrior, Bryant 38; Sarah A. 38;
  Wm. 38; William M. 38
Faulk, A.W. 38; Alfred Wright 38;
  Andrew S. 39; Ellena Jane 107;
  H., Jr. 38; H., Sr. 38; Henry
  L., Sr. 38(2); Henry Lawson 38;
  Henry Lawson, Jr. 38,75; Henry
  Lawson, Sr. 39,107; J. 39; Jas.
  39; James, "Black" 39; James,
  "Red" 39(5); Jesse 39; John 38;
  Levi 39(2); Lorenzo 39(2);
  Lucretia 39; N. 39; Nancy 63,75;
  Nancy L. 39; W.J. 39; Wm. L.
  (K.) 39; William J. 39; William
  Kendrick 39
Favors, W.R. 39(2); William R. 39;
  Winneford 39
Fulton, J. 44; John 44
Futch, Nancy A., Mrs. 65
Feagin, J.M. 40; James M. 40(2);
  James Madison 40; James N. 136;
  Louisa 101; Richard 40; S. 40;

Feagin contd. Samuel 40,101; Samuel
  Estate 40; Samuel T. 40
Fenn, Lucinda 44; M. 40; Matthew
  40,44
Ferguson, Sarah Bradwell 59
Field, Amanda 40; B.B. 40; Bennet
  B. 40; H.H. 40; Henry 40; Henry
  Hill 40
Fields, Bartholemew 92
Finley, Elizabeth 40; Jas. 40;
  James 40
Flake, Sarah J. 3; S. 30; Seaborn
  J. 40; Wm. 40; William, Dr. 3,40
Fleming, Theresa Ann Elizabeth 21
Flewellen, E.R. 40; Enos R. 40;
  Sarah A. 57; Susan 41
Florence, John 41; Mary A. 43;
  Thos. J. 41; Thomas 41(2); Tho-
  mas, Sr. 41; Thomas J. 41; Wm.
  41; William 41
Flournoy, ----- 108; Charity Eliza-
  beth Johnson 109; H. 41; Harriet
  G. 42; J.E.P. 41; James 41;
  Joseph E.P. 41; Josiah 41; Josiah
  Jr. 41(2); Josiah, Sr. 41;
  Lucilla S., Mrs. 34; Margaret
  Ellen 106; Martha V. 91; Mary
  41; Mary Ann 19; Nelson 41,42;
  R.W. 41; Robert W. 41; Sarah A.M.
  18; T. 41; Thos. 41; Thomas 41
  (2),91; W.A. 42; William 42
Flowers, Abner 17,42(4); Celia F.
  42; H. 42; Harrell 42; Hepsey
  131; Julia Ann 17; Penelope 59;
  Rebecca 17,42; W. 42; Wright 42
Floyd, Francis, Sr. 42; Harriet L.
  67; Isabella 93; Nancy J. 122;
  Page 42(2); Sarah S. 35; Theo-
  philus 42,93
Fontaine & Hardaway 134
Fontaine, John 134; Mary 134
Ford, E.N. 42; Eli N. 42(2); Eliz-
  abeth 43; G. 42; Gardner 42(3);
  Jane E. 42
Forehand, Martha 43; Stephen 43(2)
Fort, D.M.B. 43; Duncan M.B. 43;
  Isaac 43
Forte, Jane A. 46
Foster, B. 43; Beaufort 43; E. 43;
  Pheba 84; Sarah 43
Fowler, Catharine 47; Nathan 47
Franklin, E. 43; Edwin 43
Frasier, A. 43; Addison 43; M. 43
Frazier, Addison 43; Arthur 43;
  Malcom 43; Mary Sewell 41
Freeman, Lucy 43; W. 43; Wm. 43;
  William 43(2)
French, J.P. 43; Joseph 43; Josey
  P. 43; Mary 43
Fry, Elizabeth 122
Fryer, G.H. (W.) 43; George W. 43;
  Matilda 43; R.H. 44; Richard H.,
  Dr. 44

Gachet, Dr. 44; Ann 44(2),62;
  Caroline Sarah Mildred 62;
  Charles, Dr. 44; Charles Nicho-
  las 44; Charles Nicholas Deleigh
  44; J.E. 44; James E. 44(2),62;
  Jane M. 44; Jas. E.44; Levinia 44
  N. 44

Galloway, Jas. 44; James 44
Gammon, Sarah E. 45
Ganby, Z. 44
Garland, E. 44; Edward 44
Garner, J. 44; Jane 44; Jesse
  44; John 44(2); Joseph 44;
  Vicey 44
Garrett, David 44; Elizabeth 44;
  Wm. D. 44; William D. 44
Garris, J.G. 45; John 45
Gatewood, Amy 121; Larkin 121
Garvin, ----- 26
Gary, Jas. 45; James 45(2);
  Wm. Lee 45; William 45
Gerkey, C.F. 45; Charles F. 45;
  Sina 45
Gibbons, S. 45; Stephen 45(2)
Gibson, B. 45; G.T. 45; George M.
  T. 45; Nancy 45,110; W.H.C. 45;
  William C. 45; William H.C.
  45(2)
Giddens, Eliza 45; J. 45; Jacob 45
Gilchrist, D. 45; Daniel 45(2),46;
  Gilbert 45(2); John 45(2); M.
  46; Malcolm 46
Gill, Mary Butler 109,110
Gillinwater, A. 46; James A. 46;
  Nancy H. 46; T. 46; Thomas 46
Gillis, A. 46; Alexr. 46; Alexr.
  Estate 46; Alexander C. 46;
  Catherine 46; Christian 46,79;
  D. 46; Daniel M. 46; Hugh 79,80;
  J. 46; John 46; Margaret 79;
  Mary 86; N. 46; Neill 46; Sarah
  79,80
Gilmore, Elizabeth 46; W. 46; Wm.
  46; William 46
Ginwright, Sarah 33
Gipson, Blanche Evelina 137; Felix
  G. 137
Glass, Levi 46(3); Mary Ann 95;
  Sarah 46
Glenn, Cornelia Susanna 77; Eliza
  P.W. 104; James E., Rev. 46,47;
  John B., Rev. 136; M.M. 46;
  Massillom McKendry 46; Melissa
  136; Melissa H. 58; T.S. 47;
  Thompson S., Rev. 47
Glover, H.G. 19; Hilliard 47(2);
  J.P. 47; John P. 47; Louvinia
  19; T.J. 47; Thomas J. 47; W.E.
  47; William E. 47
Goodrum, Mary 43
Gow, John 135
Graham, Jane 84; Nancy Jane 64
Granead, Sarah G. 97
Grant, Elizabeth 47; J.H. 47;
  John H. 47; Larkin W. 47; Little-
  berry 47; Mariane E. 9; Martha
  47; T.M. 47; Thos. M. 47; Thomas
  M. 47(2)
Grantham, Edw. 47; Edward 47; Eliz-
  abeth 47; Stephen 47
Graves, H. 48; Hardy 48(2)
Green, A. 48; Amos 48(2); Emeline
  48; Marvin 73; Sarah 48; Thos.
  C. 48; Thomas C. 48; Wm. E. 48;
  William E. 48
Greenwood, E.S. 18,48(2); Jane E.
  18,48; S. 48; Samuel 48

Gregory, Mahala 48; W.B. 48; Wilson
  B. 48
Grephill, Ann B. 118
Grice, Elizabeth 111
Griffin, Ida 72; Margaret 32; Mary,
  Mrs. 39; Rachael 32
Griffith, Sallie 32
Grimsley, Celia 47
Grissett, D.M. 48; Daniel M. 48(2)
Grubbs, Adam 48,90; Demaris 48;
  Elizabeth 49; Friendly 49; James
  Jefferson 84; Jincey 125; John
  Tillman 49,84; Mary 70,96,110;
  Mary A.S. 49; Mary Ann Cadenhead
  84; Rhoda 118; Rhoda Ann 48; Wm.
  Sr. 48; William, Jr. 49; William,
  Sr. 48,49(5),70,110,125; Wineford
  84(2); Worthy Jordan 49
Grubs, A. 48; F. 49; J.T. 49; W.J.
  49; Wm. 49; Wm. Estate 49
Guerry, Legrand 47
Guice, S. 49
Guice (or Grice), Samuel 49
Gunn, Matilda A. 61

Hagler, Chas. 49; Charles W. 49;
  Elizabeth 49,74; Harriet 108;
  Henry 49(2); Jackson 49(2); John
  49(2); Lydia 50; Margaret 50;
  Nancy 49; Peter 49(2),50(3),74,
  118; Thos. 50; Thomas 50
Hagood, A. 50; Appleton 50; Eliza-
  beth C. 50; John 50; Polly 50
Hailey, Jas. 50; James 50; Eliza-
  beth 50
Hall, Daniel 50; Elisha 50; Euge-
  nia A. 50; G. 50; Goodwin 50;
  H. 50; Henry 50; Henry, Sr. 50
  (2); J.B., Rev. 50; J.W. 50;
  Jas. B. 50; James B. 50; John W.
  50; M. 50; M.C. 50; Mary C. 50;
  Matthew 50(2); R.G. 51; Robert
  51; Robert G. 51; Sarah 116;
  Sarah R. 51; W. 51; William 50,
  51
Ham, Jesse 51(2); Mary 51
Hameter, Elizabeth 51; J. 51; Joel
  51(2)
Hamilton, Jas. 51; James 51
Hammock, Caroline Jane 51; Simion
  J. (or G. or T.) 51; Thomas 51
Hammonds, Elizabeth 51; H. 51;
  Henry M. 51; Mary 51
Hamock, S.J. 51; T. 51
Hancock, Angelina 35
Hanley (Henley), ----- 53
Hannah, Elizabeth 127
Hanrick, Edw. 51; Edward 51
Hardaway, George W. 134; Martha B.
  134; R.S. 51; Robert 51; Robert
  S. 51,134; Robert Stanfield 51
Hardwick & Fontaine 134
Hardwick, C.A. 51; Charles A. 51;
  J. 51; Jos. 51; Martha A. 136
Hardy, Elizabeth, Mrs. 78
Hare, Eliza Ann 95; Edmund 95
Hardgraves, George 137; Mary F.
  137
Hargrove, Elizabeth 52; H. 52;
  Henry 52(2); John W. 52; Lemuel
  52

143

Hargroves, George 109; Mary E. 109
Harmon, Rachel 25
Harper, Benjamin 52; Elizabeth G.
  68; H. 52; Margaret 52; Sarah
  Ellen 45; W.F. 52; W.H. 52;
  Wm. 52; William 52,68; William
  F. 52
Harrel, J. 52
Harrell, Isaac H. 68; Jesse 52;
  Nancy 56
Harrelson, H. 52; Josiah 10,93;
  Lucretia 93,122; Moses 10; Nancy
  10(2); Susannah 9/10
Harris, D.W. 52; Ezekiel 129; Henry
  52(3); John M. 52(2); Matt.
  "Cousin" 129; Wiley 52; Wiley
  J. 52
Harrison, ----- 78; Charles 78;
  L.C. 52; L. (Leonard?) C. 52;
  L.L. 78; Mary A.R. 78
Harrod, Jas. 52; James 52; Martha
  53; Nancy 34; S. 53; Sarah 42,
  53; Sarah Elizabeth 42; Thos.
  53; Thomas 53
Hart, Major 55; J. 53; John 53(2)
Hartzog, Betha Ann 53; David 53(2);
  F. 53; Francis 53(2); George
  53; Jas. Estate 53; Rebecca 53;
  Sarah 53
Harveston, ----- 48,90
Harwell, Birchett 136; Burket 53;
  Mary Frances 136; Mourning 86;
  Saml. 53; Samuel 53(2),57,136
Hawkins, G.S. 53; George S. 53,136;
  Hiram 13; Josephine Olivia 53;
  Mary B. 53; Thomas 13
Hayes, Calvin 28; Lincey D. 28
Haynie, Polly 13
Hays, C. 53; C.D.L. 53; Calvin S.
  53; Clarissa 53; Comfort 53;
  J.L. 53(2); J.L. & Co. 53;
  Jane 53; Jesse L. 53; John 53(2);
  Mahala 53; R.T. 53; Wm. B. 53;
  William B. (or R.) 53
Head, Eliza J. 46; Elizabeth 39,
  121; Elizabeth R. 131; Epsey
  16; Nancy 39; Richard 46,54,131;
  Richard, Sr. 16; William 15,16,
  45,46,54(2),121
Heath, Britton 54; I. 54; Isaac
  54(2); R. (B.) 54
Helms, Aaron 54; Aaron, Rev. 54;
  Abraham 54(2); Abram 54; H. 54;
  Hilliard 54; Jane 126; John 54;
  John, Rev. 54; Mahala 54; Malinda
  49; Nancy 54; Thomas C. 124;
  Uriah 126
Henderson, Eliza 54; J. 54; John
  54(2); Joseph 36,54(3)
Hendrick, ----- 38
Hendricks, Elizabeth G. 37;
  Mary M. 37(2); Micajah 37
Hendrix, Jane A. 54; John 54;
  Lucinda 54; W., Sr. 54; Whit-
  field B. 54
Henley, A. 54; Adam 54; Priscilla
  55
Herndon, Barbara Wesley 46;
  Stephen 46
Heron, E.M. 55(2); Edward M. Dr. 55

Herring, Charity 55; Chloe A. 68;
  G. 55; Geo. 55; George 55(2); J.
  55; John 55; Mary Jane 55; Nancy
  46; Sarah 55; Tabitha 39; W. 55;
  West 55(2); William 55(4)
Hickman, John 55; M. 55; Mary 15
  (3),55; Polly 15; W. (?) R. 55
Hicks, Sarah 51
Highnote, B. 55; Benjamin F. 55;
  Elizabeth 55
Hight, Cathy 32
Hightower, A.W. 55(2); Sarah 55;
  T.A. 55; Thos. A. 55; Thomas A.
  55,105(2)
Hill, A.S. 56; Abraham 56; Abraham
  S., Dr. 56(2); Ann 56; B.M. 56;
  Blanton M. 56; E.P. 56; Edney
  56; Elizabeth A. 56; Elizabeth
  A., Mrs. 56; Ephriam 56; F.W.
  56; Felix 56(2); Frances 40;
  Francis W. 56; H.W. 56; Henry
  40; J.B. 56; J.T. 56(2); Joseph
  B. 56,136; Mariah H. 92; Martin
  M. 92; Miles 56(2); Tabitha 56
Hinson, Louisa 101
Hobdy, Edmond 56; H. 56; Harrell
  56
Hodges & Pugh 134
Hodges, E.G. 56; Elias G. 56,134;
  G.C. 57; Geo. C. 57; George C.
  56,57,136; James W. 136; Martha
  136; Martha R.W. 57; Mary Cathe-
  rine 47; Mary (Molsie) 47,64;
  Molcie 93,101; Richard 57; Sarah
  J. 56
Hogan, Mary 65
Holder, A. 57; Abraham 57; John
  57(2); Mary 57; Mary A. 63
Holland, Arpy 57; Charlotte 117;
  J.A. 57; Jesse 57(2); Joseph 57;
  Joseph A., Dr. 57; Lucinda 15;
  Wm. 57; William 15,57
Holleman, Aeson B. 57; E.C. 57;
  Eli C. 57; Polly 6
Holliday, Drucilla 57
Holly, Martha 73
Holmes, Jerusha 57; N.G. 57;
  Nathaniel G. 57; Sarah 57; Wm.
  57; William 57
Holoman, A.B. 57
Holston, J.W. 57; James W. 57;
  Nancy 58
Holt, A. 58; A.A. 58; Abden A. 58;
  Asa 58(2),136; W. 58; Wm. 58;
  William 58(3)
Hood, Bold Robin 58; Elizabeth 58;
  J.T. 58; Joshua T. 58
Hooks, Charles M. 58; Marshall H.
  58; T.J. 58; Thos. J. 58; Thomas
  J. 58
Hoole, Bertram J. 58; E.S. 58;
  Eugene S., Dr. 58
Hooten, H.T. 58; Henry 58; Henry
  T. 58
Hope, Charlotte 132
Hopkins, Andrew Jackson 58; J. 58
Horn, Elizabeth 96; J.F. 58; Joseph
  58; Judy 96; Louisianna W. 59;
  Margaret 58; Nancy 59; Nathan
  58(2); Wm. D. 58; William D. 58(2)

Lowe, Bird 75; John W.S. 75; Mary
H. 75; Robert 75; Robert N. 75
Lowman, Elizabeth 12; G.W. 75;
George W. 75; H. 75; J. 75;
J.J. 75; J.L. 76; James L. 76;
John J. 8,12; John Jacob 75(2),
76(2); Joseph 75; Martha E. 76;
Mary 8; Mary H. 75; Sarah A. 8;
Wm. H. 76; William H. 76

McAlpin, A.S. 76; Alexander S. 76;
Frances 76
McAskill, Daniel 76; John 76;
Mary 76(2)
McBride, J. 76; Jane 76; John 76
(4); John, Jr. 76; Rachael 76;
Mary 76(2); Mary Ann 76; S. 76;
Saml. 76; Samuel 76
McCaleb, James 128; Mary 128
McCall, A. 76; Alexander, Judge
76; C. 76; Charles 76; D. 77;
Daniel 76,77(2); Daniel A. 77;
G. 77; Gilbert 77; H. 77;
Hartwell 77; Mary 77; Paul 77(2)
McCarty, Martha 73; Wm. 77;
William Allen 77
McClure, Abigail J. 31
McCoy, David 14; Frances 59;
Martha P. 14
McCraney, Arabella 77; Malcolm
77(2)
McCrary, Ann 77; Jas. 77; James
77(2); Rebecca 77; Thomas 77
McDaniel, Arch'd., Rev. 136; Ellen
5; Margaret 136; Margaret J. 101
McDonald, Alexander 78; Angus R.
77; Arch'd. 77; Archibald 77(2);
C. 78; Colin 78; Colon, Mrs. 85;
D.B. 78(2); Daniel 78; Daniel B.
78; Elizabeth 65; H.W. 78; Hugh
78; James 78; James Gabriel 77;
John 78(2); John Crofford 77;
Joshua 77; M. 78; M.P. 78; Mal-
colm 78(3); Margaret 54; Mary
78(3); N. 78; Neil 78; R. 77;
Sarah A. 80
McDougald, Ann Eliza 78; D. 78;
Daniel 78; J. 78
McDowell, ----- 70,110; Eliza 104;
Sarah E. 104; Thomas C. 104
McEachern, D.C. 79; Daniel C. 79;
Gilbert 79
McGaines, Bidsey 75
McGehee, A. 79; Abner 79(2); Al-
fred 79(2); Caroline 79; E.M.
79; Edward M. 79; Mary 79
McGibboney, James C. 105; Julia
Ann Frances 105; Nancy 105;
William 105
McGilvray, Daniel 79; Duncan 79(2);
Jas. 79; James 79(2); Janet 79;
Janet, Mrs. 79; John 79(4); M.
80; Malcolm 79; Martin 79,80(2);
Mary 79
McGreggor, N. 80(2)
McInnis, Angus 118,123; Catharine
118,123; Christian 80; Duncan
80(3); H. 80; Hector 80(2);
Janet 80; John 80(2); John B.
30; Miles 80(2); Nancy 28,123;

McInnis cont.   Sarah 80
McIntosh, Catherine 26,82; D. 80;
Daniel 26,80; Elizabeth 30;
J.G. 80; John G., Jr. 80;
Margaret 80; Matilda Catherine
131; Sarah 80
McKay, Donald 80(2)
McKenney, Benjamin 92
McKenzie, Catherine 46; D. 80;
Danl. 80; Daniel 80(2); J.K. or
H. 81; John H. 81; Kenneth 80;
Martha 81; Sarah 78; W.A. 81;
William A. 81
McKinnon, Isabella 30
McLaney, Mary V., Mrs. 20
McLean, Alexr. 81; Alexander 81;
Catharine 8,81(2); Christian 81;
Christian Margaret Ann 130; Colon
81(2); D. 81; Danl. 81; Daniel
81(3); Hugh 81(3); J. 81; James
81(3); John 81(3); John W. 81;
Mary Ann 8; Sarah 81; Sibby 81
McLendon, Francis 81; Frank 81;
J.G. 81; John 4,81(2),123; John
G. 81(2); M.M. 82; Martha Ann K.
123; Martin M. 82; Mary 81; Sarah
4
McLeod, Alex. 82; Alexander 82(2);
Angus 82(7); Christian 85(2),93;
D. 82; Daniel 82(2); Daniel D.
82; Daniel S., Sr. 82; Elizabeth
82; Janet 15,86; John 82(4);
Katie 81; Margaret 82; Margarite
82; Mary 82,86,117,132; Nancy
70,81; Norman 82,86; Sarah 46,83
McLure, John 83; Mary 83; R. 83;
Richard Rankin 83(2); Thos. C.
83; Thomas C. 83
McMillan, A. 83; Alexander 83(2);
Danl. 83; Daniel 83(3); Finley
83; John 83(2); Mary 83(2),133
McMurray, Caroline 110; Martha A.
131; Mary 83; Nancy 83; Robert
83; S.F. 83; Samuel F. 83(3),
131; W. 83; William M. 83
McNab, A.C. 83; Archibald C. 83;
D. 83; D. & J. 83; Duncan 83(2),
84(2); Isabella 83; Jno. 84;
John 83,84
McNair, Ann C. 84; Elizabeth 44,
71,79; Gilbert 71; J.P. 84; John
84(2); John P. 84(2); Louisa M.
21
McNamara, Mary 26
McNeal, Hector 84(2); Mary 84
McNeil, Abigail 84; Daniel 84(3);
John 84; Nancy 84; R. 84; Rode-
rick 84
McNeill, Abigail 79; Anna 79;
Daniel 79; Elizabeth H., Mrs. 16;
Euphemia 129; Jennie 56; John
27,55,56,129; Mary 55; Sarah 27
McPhail, Alexander 84; Daniel 85;
Davis 85; E. 84; E.C. 84; Edward
C. 78,84; Elizabeth 78; Michael
84
McRae, A.D. 85; A.K. 85; Abigail
85; Alexr. 85; Alexr. K. 85;
Alexander 80,86; Alexander D. 85;
Alexander Keane 85; Amm 96,97

McRae cont. C. 85; C.C. 85; C.G.
85; Catherine 86; Christopher
21,82,85,117(2); Christopher C.
85; Christopher M. 85; Daniel
78; Duncan 86; Elizabeth 85;
F. 85; F.A. 85; F.C. 85; Farquhar
A. 85; Farquhar C. 85; G.W. 85;
George Washington 85; Isabella
117(2); J. 85; J.C. 86; John 85
(2); John A. 86(4); John C. 86;
John R. 85(2); Margaret 88,113,
117; Martha 78; Mary 21,82,85;
Phillip 80,85; Virginia 85;
William 85; Winney 80
McSwean, Angus 86; Catherine 29,
86; Daniel 86(3); Daniel, Jr.
86; Malcolm 86; Mary 86; R.
86; R.C. 86; Roderick 29,86;
Roderick C. 86
McSwean (McSwain), D. 86; Danl.
86; Daniel 86(2)
McTyere, Caroline J. 60; Eliza-
beth 60; John 60
McVey, Matilda 103

Mabry, Allen 86(2); Elizabeth J.
Caroline 49; J.W. 48; Jas. W.
86; James Walton 86; Joshua 86
(2); Nancy 48,49(2),90; Nancy
Ann 90; Nancy J. 48; S. 86;
Seth 86(2)
Maddox, Amanda 74; Eliza Ann 87;
J.P. 74; John P. 86; Lovey 3;
Penelope N. 120
Madox, J.P. 86
Mallard, P.C. 87; Peter C. 87
Malloy, Duncan 87; Mary 87
Malone, G. 87; Green 87,120;
Green, Rev. 120
Maloy, D. 87
Man, G. 87; R. 87
Manley, John 41; Martha 41
Mann, Gilbert 87(2); Robert 87(2);
Malinda A. 106; Sarah 111
Marcus, Daniel 65; Mary Elizabeth
65
Marley, Dianna 87; H.J. 87;
Horatio J. 87
Marshall, James F. 72,87,137
Martial, J.F. 87
Martin, Charlotte 88; D. 88;
Delia 88; E. 87; Elizabeth 87;
Elizabeth T. 126; Ezekiel 87;
F. 87; Felix 87; Frederick 72;
J.L. 87; J.T. 88; James L. 87;
John T. 88; June M.C. 126;
Lucitta 49; Lydia Ann E. 10;
M.D. 88; Marshall 126; Martin D.
88; Mary A. 6; Nancy 84,87,129;
Robert 88(2); S. 88; Sally 46;
Sylvester 88; Wm. 88; William
88; William J. 130
Massey, Nathaniel D. 88; Ruthy 88
Massy, N. 88
Mastin (Martin), Nancy 129
Mathews, A. 88
Mathis, Jincey 88
Mathis (Matthews), Abel (or
Abraham) 88
Matthews, Abraham 50; Mary Ann 50

Mayo, John 88(2); Olive 88
Meadle, Eldridge 88
Meadley, H. 88; Roderick 89; Wm.
89
Medley, Eldridge 88; Hansel 88;
Jemima 88(2); Judith 88(2); Mary
88; Milly 88(2); William 89
Mellard, Catharine C. 15; James
H., Rev. 15
Miles, A.B. 89; Abram Baldwin 89
Miller, A.T. 89; Ann 60; Asa T.
89; Caroline Matilda 45; D.C.
89; David C., Dr. 89,137; Dorot-
hea Jane 30; G.S. 89; George W.
S. 89; I.L. 89; George W.S. 89;
I.L. 89; Irwin L. 89; J.C. 89;
J.H. 89; James 4; Jane 89; John
H. 89; Keziah 4(3); Lewis 89(2);
M. 89; Margaret 6; Martha A. 89;
Martin 89; Mildred 89; Temperance
89; Thomas 107(2)
Milligan, Martha Ann 132
Mims, Benjamin 16; C.C. 89; Eliza
16
Minshew, Ava 56; Harriet 90; J.
90; Jacob 89(2); Jacob, Sr. 68,
90(2); John 90; John M. 90; N.
90; Nathan 56,90; Wineford (Winey)
68
Mitchell, Americus C. 90(2); Avey
52,90; Benjamin 90; Benjamin J.
J., Dr. 90; C. 90; Elizabeth M.
90; James 90(3); Julius C.B. 90;
Julius Caesar Bonaparte 90; Mary
Ann E. 52; Randolph 52,90(2);
Sarah G. 90
Moats, J. 90; Jonathan 48,90;
Sarah 90; Wm. 90; William 90
Mobley, Mary 54
Moffett, H. 90; Henry 90; Lorinda
90
Moody, J. 91; John 91
Mooney, Mary A. 32; William 32
Mooneyham, Mary 117
Moore, J.C. 91; James 91; James C.
91; John C. 91; Martha 91;
Melissa 92; W. 91; William M. 91
Moreland, Elizabeth 90
Morgan, J.C. 91; James C. 91; John
123; Simon S. 91; Thomas 57
Morris, ----- 76; Daniel 5; Gatsey
A. 91; Jas. 91; James, Sr. 5,91;
Laura 5; Mary 5
Morrison, Catharine 91; D. 91; Danl
91; Daniel 91(2); Mary A., Mrs.
33; Mary Elizabeth 33; Neill 18
Morton, Eliza B. 91; Julia Ann 91;
Lucy 91(2); W. 91; Wm. 91;
William 91
Moseley, F.M. 91; Francis Marion
91; John A. 33; Sally 6; Wm. 91
Mosher, Wm. 91; William H.G. 91
Mosser (or Mosses), Epsey 54
Mothershead, Levi 92(2); Lucy 92
Muldrough, Elizabeth 70,71(2),72
Murphy, Sarah 70
Murray, W. M. 83
Murry, Nancy Ann 92
Myers, Elizabeth 92; Elizabeth
Jane 43; Jas. 92; James 92

Nance, Catherine 92; Martha 92; S.
92; Sylvester 92
Nash, Acton 36,47,92(2),111;
Barbara 111; M.B. 92; Milton B.
92; Sarah Damascus 47
Neal, Louisa M. 104
Neece, David 92; Elizabeth 92
Newman, Saml. 92; Samuel 92(2)
Newsome, Olive 7
Niece, J. 92; Jacob 92; John 92
(2); H. 92; Henry 92; Mary 92
Nobles, A. 92; Archibald 92; Eliza
Jane 92
Nolin, Avery 92(3); D. 93; Danl.
93; Daniel 92,93; Dennis 93;
Elizabeth 93; J. 93; J.B. 93;
James 93; James B. 92,93;
Mary 93(2); Melinda 92; Simp-
son W. 93; W.S. (S.W.) 93
Norton, D.A. 93; Daniel Asbury
93(4); Georgiann Dickinson 97;
J.K. 93; J.R. 93; J.W. 93;
James Russell 93; John Johnston
122; John K. 93; John Kennedy 93;
John W., Rev. 93,97; Lewis
Fletcher 93; Lucretia 64; Mary
A. 122; Patience Elizabeth 64;
W.V. 93; William 64,93(2),97,
122; William, Jr. 93,122;
William Vick 93
Noyes, Daniel 61; Eleanor Clark
61; Ephriam 61
Nuchols, Louisa Anna 13

Odom, Clarissa 94; H.S. 93; Hub-
bard S. 93; Jas. 94; James 94;
Marinda Ann 94
O'Flarity, Mr. 26
Oliver, Augustus L. 129(2);
Elizabeth 94; J. 94; John L. 94;
Lurena, Mrs. 129; Luraney, Mrs.
126; M. 94; McDonald 94(2);
Milbrey 94(2); W. 94; Wiley 94(3)
Orr, Jas. 94; James 94
Ott, Adrianna C. 119; Ann C. 89;
Catharine 94; E.S. 94; Edward S.
94,119,120; Mary M. 120; Wm.
94; William 94(3)
Owens, Elizabeth A. 95; Nancy A.
95; T.C. 94(2); Thaddeus C. 94;
W.J. 95; Whitman H. 94; Whitman
Hill 94; William 95; William J.
95

Padget, E. 95; Elijah 95; Henry 95
(2); Josiah 95(2); Luke 95(2);
Penelope 95
Page, Delilah 42,93
Palmer, Benjamin 96; Dan'l. 95;
M.G. 95; Matthew G. 95(2);
Susan Ann 95(2)
Parish, Spivey 95(2)
Parker, C.A. 95; Cader A., Sr. 95;
E.M. 95; Edward M. 95; Louisa C.
95; M.B. 95; Martha 95; Milo B.
95; Sherrod 95; Stephen 95; W.
96; Walter L.B. 96
Parmer, B. 96; Benj. 96; Benjamin
49,70,89,96(2),110; Benjamin, Sr.
96(3); Eliza 112; Ellender C.

Parmer contd. Ellender C. 102,
114; George W. 96(2),112; Hattie
89; Jacob 72,96(2),102; Jacob,
Sr. 96; Jefferson 96(2); L.B.J.
96; Littleberry B.J. 96; Martha
115; Mary Pary 72; Nancy 49,96;
Z.W. 96; Zachariah Wesley 96
Parramore, William 96
Parremore, W.E. 96
Parsons, Jeremiah 96; John 96;
John L. 96,133
Passmore, J.R.A. 97; John 97(3);
John Robert Allen 97; L. 97;
Lemuel 97(2); M. 97; Mary 97(2)
Pate, Elizabeth 97; Isaac 62; Le-
nora 97; Sarah 62; Wm. 97;
William 97
Patisals, Joshua 97
Patrick, H.R. 97
Patterson, Ann 97; M.A. 97; M.A.,
Rev. 97
Paullin, Clementine 97; Lewis 97(2)
Payne, Ellender 65,85
Pearson, B.F. 97,98; Benjamin
Franklin 97; C.R. 98; Clinton R.
98(3); Herbert 97; Hubbard
(Herbert) 98; Robert H. 98
Peck, Ira 98(2); Penelope 98; W.A.
98
Penn, Catherine 121
Perkins, Nancy 8
Perry, Mary C. 56; Mary H. 125;
Sarah Ann, Mrs. 95
Persons, Ann Dawson 103
Peterson, Batte 98(3); Batte, Dr.
98; Martha Ann 98; Mary Jane 3;
Sarah 3; Sarah Eugenia 98
Pettus, Harriet 65
Petty, B.F. 98; Benjamin Franklin
98; C. 98; Chas. 98; Charles 98
Phillips, Arrington H.H. 99(2);
Burrell 98(2); C.S. 99; Caroline
S. 99; Charity 93; Council 99(2);
Elam 121; H. 99(2); H.H. 99;
Henry H. 99(2); Hester 99; Isham
98; J., Maj. 52; Kinchen W. 99;
Lewis D. 93; Missouri Ann 121;
Nancy A. 93,97; Virginia 52
Picket, Thos. C. 99
Pickett, Elizabeth Ward, Mrs. 97;
Joseph 97; Lazarus N. 99; Lucin-
da 131; Mary 99; Thomas C. 99;
Thomas J.H. 99
Pierce, Ann Jane 99; Elizabeth 14;
L.L. 99; Lovard L. 99
Pinckard, Sarah 98
Pinkerton, C. 99; Catherine 99,
108(2); David 99
Pipkin, H. 99; Haywood 99
Pippin, C. 99; Calvin 99; Sarah 99
Pitts, Maria 99; N.W. 99; Nancy
11(4),17,70; Nicholas W. 99;
Noel 99
Polk, Sarah Jane 71
Pollard, Elias 100(2); Isabella
100; J. 100; John 100(2); Leroy
100
Pope, Burwell, Col. 56; Eliza M.
113; Henry 113; Joel 100; Susan
113; Tabitha 56(2)

151

Urquahart cont. Henry, Rev. 121;
Henry M. 121
Utsey, J. 121; Jacob 121(3); John
121; John J. 121; Martha 121;
Mary 121

Vann (Vaun?), Edw. W. 122(2);
Edward W. 122; Henry M. 122;
Isaac 122; J.S. 122; Joseph 122
(2); Joseph M. 122; Sarah 122
(2)
Varner, Wm. 122; William 122
Vaun - see Vann
Veasey, Sarah 51
Ventress, Sophia 130; Stephen 122,
130; Thos. 122; Thomas 122
Vick, Mary 93; Piety 100
Vickers, J.R. 122; James M. 122;
John R. 122(2); John R., Jr.
122(2); John R., Sr. 122;
Joseph W. 122; M.P. 122; Mary
122; Mary B. 122; Michael P.
122(2); Nancy 122; Sidney Dean
122; Solomon W. 122; T.T.B.
122; Thomas 122; Thomas T.B. 122
Vining, J.A. 122; Jefferson A.
122; Rachael 47; Samuel 76
Vinson, Henry 123; John 123(2);
Tempe 130; W. 123; Wesley
123(2); Wiley 123(2)
Volentine, Catherine 123; M. 123;
Matthew 123

Wadsworth, James 40; Nancy 40(2)
Wales, Rebecca Covington 128;
Samuel A. 41
Walker, G. 123; George 123(2);
George, Sr. 123(2); Jane 123;
John 62; Joyce 123; L.W. 123;
Lewis 28,123(4); Lucinda 62;
Maisy C. 28; Martha 62; Memor-
able 51; N.H. 123; Nathan 123;
Sarah 123(2); Solomon 28,123;
William 62
Wall, J. 123; Josiah 123; Lavica
123; Sarah Ann 122
Wallace, Elizabeth 25,34
Walls, Nancy Jane 17
Walton, Martha 129,130
Warburton, Margaret 42
Ward, Mary 57
Warlick, A.H. 123; Ruth 123; Wm.
123; William 123
Warr, John 124(2); Nancy 124
Warren, Adeline 77; B. 124(2);
Bates 124; Burris 77,124(4); E.
124; Edward 124; G. 124; Georgi-
anna 124; J. 124; J.D. 124; J.J.
124; Jas. 124; Jas. E. 124;
James Burris 124; James E. 124;
Jeremiah 124(2); Jno. 27; Joel
D. 124(2); Lucinda 124(2);
Mary 124; Milly P. 69; Nancy 3,
124; Rebecca 3(2),124(3),125;
Thomas 3(2),69,77,124(2),125;
Thos., Jr. 124; Thos., Sr. 124;
Thomas, Jr. 124; Thomas, Sr. 69,
124(4)
Waterman, N.M. (?) 125; Nathaniel
125

Watkins, Martha 116; Rhoda 125;
Samuel E. 125; Sophia H. 109;
W. 125; William 125(2)
Watson, D. 125; David 125; Douglas
98; Elizabeth 125(2); James C.
125; L.J. 98; Louisa Jane 98;
Mary Ann 91; Peter 91,125; Sarah
125; Susan 45; Thomas 125(2);
William 125(2)
Weathers, Levina 16; Samuel 108,
126; William 126
Weaver, A. 125; Absolem 23,87;
Absolom A. 125; Elizabeth Jane
23; Ella Clifford 87; J.C. 8;
John C., Rev. 34; Louisa M.M. 11;
Martha 34; Mary H. 125
Weber, John 125
Welder, Malinda 17
Weldon, W.A. 125; William A. 125
Wellborn & Comer 135
Wellborn, A. 126; Alfred 126,136;
Alford W. 24; Ann S. 131; Eliza-
beth 126; Johnson 126(2); Levi
Thomas, Dr. 126; Lycourgus S.
131; Mary 24; Mary H.F. 106;
Mary Jane 136; Roxanna 126; Rox-
anna, Mrs. 106; Thomas 126;
William 136
Wethers, S. 126; S.W. 126
West, Elizabeth 126; Joseph 126(3)
Westbrook, F.S. 126; Furney 126;
John 65,126; Rebecca 65; Z. 126;
Zilpha 126(2)
Weston (or Watson), Martha Cordelia
40
Weyman, Edward 65; Eliza 65;
Francis Harriet 65
Sheeler, N. 126; Noah 126(2),129
Whiddon, ----- 69
Whigham, Elizabeth 127; J. 126;
Jane 127; Joseph 126,127(3);
Margaret 127; Mary Magdaline 54;
Sarah J. 127; T. 127; Thomas
127(3); W. 127; William 127;
William A. 137
Whipple, Fanny A. 33
White, John 127; John C. 127;
John H. 16,127(2); Louisa L. 127;
Mary Ann Rebecca 16; R.T. 127;
Rebecca 16,127; Robert T. 127;
Willis 127(2)
Whitehurst, Asa 123; L. 127; Levi
123,127; Mattie 84
Whitsett, Elizabeth (Lowe?) 127;
Samuel 127; Thos. 127; Thomas 127
Whittle, Elizabeth 128; M. 128;
Maston 128(2)
Wiley, Evan Shelby 128; J.B. 128;
J. Mc. 128; James McCaleb 128(3);
John B. 128; L.H. 128; L.M. 128;
Laird H. 128(3); Leroy M. 128
Wilkerson, Nancy 122,130
Wilkes, Elias 128; Elisha U. 128
(3); Hannah 128; Jesse U. 128;
T.U. 128; Thos. U. 128; Thomas
U. 128(4); William U. 128(3)
Wilkins, Luraney 136
Wilkinson, Asa 128(2); Elmira 129;
Elizabeth 128; Lavinia 117; S.
128; Samuel 128; W.D. 129

Willaford, Mary 4
Williams, A. 129; Alexr. 129;
  Alexander D. 129; Allen 132;
  Amanda 30; Ann M. 129; B. 129;
  B.C. 129; Barley (Bartlett) C.
  129; Buckner 129; Charity 130;
  Effie, Mrs. 85; Eliza J. 75;
  Evelina 34; G.D. 129; G.W. 129;
  Gazaway Davis 129; Geo. W. 129;
  George Walker 129; J. 130; J.A.
  130; J.S. 129; Jarret 123,130;
  Jarrett 130; Jeremiah, Capt. 64;
  John 130; John A. 130; John G.
  130; John L. 30,130(2); Judge
  Stith 129; Leta 54/55; Lucinda
  129; Matilda 40; O.J. 130; Osborn
  J. 129,130; R.W. 130; Rhoda 129;
  Robert 129; Robert Walton, Dr.
  130; Rosanna 64(2),93; S.E. 130;
  Sarah 1,130,132; Sarah Elizabeth
  130; Tempe 130; Turner 76; W.
  130; Wesley 130(3); William 30,
  40(2),129(2),130(5); William, Jr.
  130; Zachariah 34,129,130
Williamson, Adeline 121; Chas. 88,
  130; Elizabeth 45; Eva A. 131(2)
Wright, Chas. 133; Elizabeth 41;
  Jane 133; M. 133; Meredith 133;
  Nancy J. 133; R.S. 133; Richard
  S. 133
Wyatt, John 59; Mary Lingard 59

Young, E.B. 133; Edward Brown 133;
  James 133; James B. 133; James
  Bunberry 133; Joseph 133; Martha
  Ann 69; Mary 83; Nancy 133;
  Wm. 133; William 69; William C.
  133

Zachary, Susan 125
Zales, Z. 133
Ziterow, N. 134; Nathaniel 134;
  Sarah 134; Mary L. 68
Zorn, N. 134; Nicholas 134(2)